The Poetry of Nizami Ganjavi

The Poetry of Nizami Ganjavi: Knowledge, Love, and Rhetoric

Edited by Kamran Talattof and Jerome W. Clinton

palgrave

First published 2000 by
PALGRAVE™
175 Fifth Avenue, New York, N.Y. 10010 and
Houndmills, Basingstoke, Hampshire, England RG21 6XS.
Companies and representatives throughout the world.

PALGRAVE™ is the new global publishing imprint of
St. Martin's Press LLC Scholarly and Reference Division and
Palgrave Publishers Ltd (formerly Macmillan Press Ltd).

ISBN 0-312-22810-4

A catalogue record for this book is available from the British Library.

Library of Congress Cataloging-in-Publication Data

The poetry of Nizami Ganjavi: knowledge, love, and rhetoric / edited by
Kamran Talattof and Jerome W. Clinton.
    p. cm.
  Consists of the majority of the papers presented at a
commemoration symposium for K. Allin Luther at
Princeton University on February 21–22, 1998.
  Includes bibliographical references and index.
  ISBN 0-312-22810-4 (cloth)
    1. Niòåmå Ganjavå, 1140 or 41-1202 or 3—Criticism and
interpretation—Congresses. I. Talattof, Kamran. II. Clinton, Jerome W.
III. Luther, K. Allin, d. 1997.

PK6501 .Z928 2000
891'.5511—dc21   99-056710
                                                                       CIP

First edition: December 2000

10 9 8 7 6 5 4 3 2 1

Printed in the United States of America.
Design by Newgen Imaging Systems (P) Ltd., Chennai, India

In Memory of K. Allin Luther

Contents

Preface

The work of Nizami Ganjavi, one of the great Persian poets, has achieved enduring significance. A year does not go by without the publication of new books and articles about his poetry, and although he belongs to the classical period of Persian poetry, the interpretation of his work has fueled a cultural debate in Iran in recent years. A reexamination of Nizami's work will not only shed light on the complex aspects of his poetry, but will also contribute to the ongoing cultural debate and the question of interpretation.

For the editors and some contributors, however, Nizami has additional personal significance. Our esteemed professor, K. Allin Luther, taught the poetry of Nizami for more than a decade at the University of Michigan, finding in it a source of strength and fortitude as he struggled with terminal illness. He died in 1997. To commemorate the life and work of K. Allin Luther, we organized a symposium on the poetry of Nizami Ganjavi on February 21-22, 1998, at Princeton University. This volume includes the majority of papers presented at that symposium, as well as two added later.

A well-known scholar of Iranian history and Persian studies, Luther received a B.A. from the University of Florida in 1955, a master's degree from Princeton University in 1959, and a Ph. D. from Princeton University in 1964. He studied at Hamburg University with Professor Berthold Spuler and, as part of his graduate studies, conducted research in Iran and Turkey. He taught at Portland State University and then joined the faculty at the University of Michigan, where he taught until 1995. He wrote about the history of the Saljuqs, Ilkhanids, and Atabaks of Azerbayjan.

Serious academicians often develop great respect over time for the subjects of their studies. They become closely associated with their topics and their lives become enmeshed in their research. Luther was no exception. He devoted himself to Iranian history, Persian literature, and his students in Iranian studies. He went beyond his official teaching responsibilities to organize the Nizami reading group in Ann Arbor and continued to lead it long after his retirement. For those who knew Allin Luther, this volume will have particular significance. Moreover, we hope that this book encourages more study of the works of Nizami Ganjavi.

A Note on Transliteration

The contributors to this volume have employed different systems of transliteration. In an attempt to be consistent, we have generally adjusted these to conform to the transliteration system of the Library of Congress. We have not, however, employed this system with complete fidelity, so the reader will find both *Iskandar Nama* and *Iskandernameh*. We have also left unchanged the transliteration of original poetry and excerpts in order to respect the authors' choices.

Introduction:
Nizami Ganjavi and His Poetry

The poet Nizami Ganjavi (1140-1202) is one of the giants of the Persian literary tradition. As a narrative poet, he stands between Abolqasem Firdawsi (ca. 940-ca. 1020), the poet of Iran's heroic tradition and the author of the *Shahnamah* (*Book of Kings*), and Jalaluddin Rumi (1207-1273), whose *Divan-i kabir* (*Great Divan*) and *Kitab-i Masnavi Ma'navi* (*Spiritual Couplets*) virtually define the forms of mystical lyric and mystical narrative poetry, respectively. Nizami's narrative poetry is more comprehensive than that of either Firdawsi or Rumi, in that it includes the romantic dimensions of human relations as well the heroic, and plumbs the human psyche with an unprecedented depth and understanding. To be sure, a profound spiritual consciousness pervades his poetry, and to suggest otherwise would be to do him a disservice, but he does not, as does Rumi, make the whole focus of his work the evocation and articulation of the transcendent dimension of existence.

Nizami brought about a comparable expansion of the language of poetry, as well. He was among the first poets in Iran to wed the lyric style of court poetry, with its rhetorical intricacy and metaphoric density, to narrative form, and his language is as much a presence on the narrative stage as are the characters and events it depicts. For him, discourse or eloquent speech (*sokhan*), or more particularly, the precise, beautiful, and signifying language of the poet, is his main or principal concern. For Nizami, poets have a nearly divine status. He repeatedly draws attention to the shaping and educative function of *sokhan* in his books, and goes so far as to liken his poetry to the *Qur'an* itself as a source of clear moral guidance, a bold assertion for his time.[1] In Makhzan al-asrar (*The Treasure House of Mysteries*), he writes, "The first manifestation of existence was speech. ... Without speech the world has no voice."

The five long poems, known collectively as the *Khamsa* (Quintet) or *Panj Ganj* (Five Treasures), composed by Nizami in the late twelfth century, set new standards in their own time for elegance of expression, richness of characterization, and narrative sophistication. They were widely imitated for centuries by poets writing in Persian, as well as in languages deeply influenced by Persian, like Urdu and Ottoman Turkish.[2]

Nizami's unparalleled genius was mirrored in equally exceptional personal qualities. As E. G. Browne expressed it, "He was genuinely pious, yet singularly devoid of fanaticism and intolerance ... he may justly be described as combining lofty genius and blameless character in a degree unequaled by any other Persian poet. ..."[3]

Despite Nizami's great importance, we know little about the events of his life. As is so often true of Iran's premodern poets, there are virtually no contemporary sources about his life, and the occasional biographical notices that appeared in subsequent centuries are all too often charming fictions. Only his poems contain reliable biographical information.[4] From these, we learn that he was born some time during the year 535 of the Islamic calendar (1140 A.D.) in the trans-caucasian city of Ganja (Elizavetpol, Kirovabad), a prosperous orthodox (Sunni) Muslim community on the border of Byzantium. He appears to have spent his entire life in the same region, dying there approximately seventy-five years later. He was married and widowed three times but recorded only the name of his first wife, Afaq, whose family was Kurdish. He had one son, Mohammed. His father, Yusuf, and mother, Ra'iseh, died while he was still relatively young, but his maternal uncle, Umar, assumed responsibility for him.

Nizami lived at a time when Iran or, more accurately, the Islamic world from the Mediterranean to Central Asia, was enjoying a period of great cultural efflorescence. The Saljūqid state, which included Ganja and the surrounding area, extended from the Mediterranean to Central Asia. A Turkish tribal confederation, the Saljūqids had conquered this vast region in the middle of the eleventh century and established a state over which they would continue to rule until shortly before Nizami's death. In the initial phase of its rule, the Saljūqid state was dominated by single individuals—Toghril I (1038-1063), Alp Arsalān (1063-1072), Malishāh (1072-1092), and Sanjar (1097-1157)—who ruled in the tradition of Iranian monarchy. Authority was more equally shared within the family during most of the period of Nizami's life, and provincial rulers exerted a large degree of autonomy and maintained separate, substantial courts. Happily, the Saljūqid rulers proved to be exemplary patrons of learning and the arts. If the eighth through tenth centuries witnessed the remarkable growth of Arabic literature and the Islamic sciences, Persian became the second great literary language of Islam in the eleventh and twelfth centuries. Among Nizami's illustrious contemporaries were the poets Khaqani Sharvani (1121-1199), panegyrist to the Sharvanshahs and also a native of the Caucasus region; Awhad ad-Din Anvari, premier poet of the court of Sultan Sanjar; and Farid ad-Din Attar (1142-1220), author of a famous and widely admired poetic anthology of mystical tales, the "Conference of the Birds" (*manteq at-tayr*), and of a biographical dictionary of Sufi saints (*tazkirat al-awlia*).

Nizami found patrons for his poetry among the local princes of the Saljūqid dynasty, but he seems not to have been a fixture at any of their courts. Although he left behind a small collection of lyric poems, these are of various natures and do not include the panegyrics and occasional odes that were the stock in trade of court poets. While Ganja was not a major metropolis, it lay astride important trade routes that linked the cities of what are now Iran, Iraq, and Turkey with their neighbors to the north on the one hand and the Caspian and Black seas on the other. Nizami must have had contact with merchants and travelers from many regions and different faiths, and it is tempting to think that this may account in part for his remarkable liberality and freedom from bias.

He displays in his poetry an impressive familiarity with all the branches of learning of his day—philosophy, poetry, geometry, astronomy, geography, history, music, architecture, jurisprudence, and logic—which suggests that his family was urban and of sufficient means to provide him with a good education.[5] As with his life, so with his work; only Nizami's third poem, *Layli and Majnun,* composed in Rajab 584/September 1188, is dated unambiguously. The dates of his other four poems can be determined only indirectly from allusions to historical names and events in the manuscripts themselves, and there are significant variations among such details, even in the earliest of these works.[6]

Nizami's first major work, the *Makhzan al-asrar (The Treasure House of Mysteries)*, written some time around 1165, is also the shortest and least characteristic. It contains not a single, continuous narrative but a collection of tales for moral and spiritual instruction, comprising a longish introductory section and twenty separate discourses. *The Treasure House* belongs to the category of advice literature, long a staple of Persian poetry and prose. Its immediate model was Sana'i's *Hadiqat al-Haqiqat (The Garden of Verities)*, but the vivid and engaging language of Nizami's parables and homilies sets them apart from the dry didacticism of Sana'i's poem.[7] Among western students of Persian, the *Treasure House* has found few admirers, but it is highly regarded in its homeland and was imitated by such eminent successors as Amir Khusraw, *Matla'-i Anvar (The Dawn of Lights)*, Khaju Kermani, *Rowzat al-Anvar (The Garden of Lights)*, and Jami, *Tuhfat al-ahrar (The Gift of the Noble)*.

Nizami chose to set his second work, the romantic epic *Khusraw and Shirin* (ca. 1180), in the court of the Sasanians, the last great pre-Islamic dynasty. He tells of the difficult and passionate relationship between

Shah Khusraw Parviz and the Armenian princess Shirin. Their story is complex, rich in sudden and unexpected reversals of fortune, and peopled with a large and varied cast of characters; it ends tragically with the deaths of both lovers. The most striking feature of the poem, however, aside from its extraordinarily rich and beautiful language, is the character of Shirin, depicted by Nizami with an exceptional depth of sympathy and understanding. Persian literature before the modern period can boast of few memorable female characters and none to equal the independent and strong-willed Shirin, who by her own exemplary behavior serves as a moral guide for the weak and unreliable Khusraw.[8]

In *Layla and Majnun* (1188), Nizami recasts material of Arab origin already popular in the Islamic world for centuries. *Majnun Layli,* as it was known in Arabic, was not a continuous narrative but a collection of love poems attributed to "the distracted lover (*majnun*)" onto whom anecdotes about his frustrated longing for Layla had been grafted. Nizami undertook the task at the request of the Sharvan Shah Akhsatan, but with some expressed reluctance, perhaps because the story was already so well known and yet belonged to a rather unfamiliar land. In his version, this fragmentary material is assembled into a coherent narrative that established the norm for the many subsequent retellings. The central figure of the poem is Qays, an Arab youth who falls in love with a young woman of a neighboring tribe, Layli. He gives voice to his love in poetry, unwisely mentioning her name, which he allows to circulate in the community. Layli is equally smitten with him, but his violation of propriety ultimately frustrates their hopes of union, causing him to be afflicted with love madness. This madness yields the name, Majnun, by which he is henceforth known.[9] Although Layli is an essential presence in the poem, Majnun dominates the story, and Layli's character is not developed as fully as that of Shirin.[10]

In the *Haft Paykar* (*The Seven Beauties*), Nizami returns to the theme of kingship and the court of the Sasanians. In *Khusraw and Shirin* he traces the slow and uncertain, but ultimately successful, moral education of Khusraw, and the agent of this growth is Shirin. In the *Haft Paykar,* the theme is again the moral education of kings. This time the process is carried a step further, and the hero, Shah Bahram Gur, becomes a ruler who not only behaves appropriately but who has so internalized the principles of just leadership that he embodies the archetype of the king.[11] The hero's guidance again comes from the feminine, but here it is not centered in a single character, like Shirin, but is dispersed among a number of characters.

The narrative has three parts. In the first, young Bahram must triumph over court intrigue to win the throne that should be his by right. In the second, a long, fantastic interlude, he visits seven princesses in seven chambers and receives instruction from each through edifying tales. In the third, a tale of intrigue like the first, Bahram must regain control of his kingdom and rescue it from the depredations of corrupt viziers and hostile neighbors. Whereas in the first episode he succeeds by exercising his martial skills, in the third he wins the day by moral perfection. No summary can do justice to the subtlety and skill with which Nizami crafts this richly symbolic but thoroughly engaging narrative, nor can it adequately convey the beauty of his poetry. Perhaps it will suffice to say that subsequent commentators on the *Haft Paykar* have seconded the praise of Helmut Ritter, who called it not only "the best and most beautiful of Persian romantic epics," but one of the greatest masterpieces of the Indo-Germanic literary tradition.[12] The complexity of Nizami's verse has long served as a barrier to the translation of his work into English, but recently Julie Meisami has published a fine poetic translation of the *Haft Paykar.*[13]

For the book that was his fifth and final work, Nizami chose to recast the life of Alexander the Great, a legendary figure in the East as well as the West, using all the sources available to him. Legends of the exploits of Alexander the Great, known as Iskandar or Sikandar, were common in all the languages of the region. *The Iskandarnamah* (*The Book of Alexander*), like all of Nizami's poems, is filled with wonderful stories and fantastic adventures, but its overriding theme is kingship. Nizami presents Alexander as another embodiment of the ideal ruler. Indeed, in the end, Alexander becomes more than a king: he is a prophet and therefore embodies perfect worldly and spiritual guidance.

The poem is in two parts. The first, the *Sharafnamah,* recounts Alexander's adventures during his extraordinary journey of conquest from Macedonia to India. He appears here less as a conqueror of nations than as a liberator of oppressed peoples—"assisting the people of Egypt in their struggle against the Zangis; rescuing Queen Nushaba from the hands of the Russians; freeing the Persian people from the enslavement of Darius and the Zoroastrian priests ... and assisting in building towns."[14] In the second part, the *Iqbalnamah,* Alexander assembles a magnificent library and surrounds himself with the greatest thinkers of the ancient world. Through his association with them, and through their instruction and guidance, he moves beyond mere kingship to become a sage and prophet. In a word, he is the perfect man and anticipates, both in his worldly conquests and in his mastery of the realms of philosophy and the spirit, the coming of Islam and its prophet.[15]

Considering the importance of Nizami, it is surprising that scholarship on his poetry has, until recently, been so meager. In the nineteenth century, we have Wilhelm Bacher's excellent monograph on Nizami's life and work, previously mentioned, that provided the basis for the articles on Nizami in subsequent European literary histories.[16] In our own century, discussion of Nizami's works has been largely limited to such literary histories.[17] Helmut Ritter, in his excellent monograph published in 1927,[18] broke new ground by taking as his subject the construction of metaphor in Nizami, attempting to explain how Nizami's treatment of various broad categories—nature, man, and man in nature—differs from that of western poets like Goethe, on the one hand, and Arab poets like Ibn Mu'tazz and Abu Tamam, on the other. Beyond that, we have a useful monograph on the poet by Ye. E. Bertel's, that refines and extends the research of Bacher.[19]

Ritter, in collaboration with Jan Rypka, also prepared the first scholarly edition of Nizami's poems.[20] Soviet Azeri scholars publishing in Baku and, more recently, Iranian scholars working in Tehran have prepared other critical editions of the *Panj Ganj*.[21] Until recently, the bulk of scholarship on Nizami has been based not on these editions but on those published by Hasan Vahid Dastgirdi in Tehran in the 1930s. Although Dastgirdi's editions contain only a rudimentary scholarly apparatus, they include extensive and detailed annotations on Nizami's frequently problematic verse.[22]

The publication of Julie Meisami's *Medieval Persian Court Poetry* in the late 1980s substantially advanced the interpretive study of Nizami's poetry.[23] The central chapters are devoted to a long and insightful study of *Khusraw and Shirin, Layli and Majnun,* and the *Haft Paykar.* Meisami's study focuses both on the moral seriousness of romance and on the extraordinary integration of theme and metaphor in Nizami's poetry. Wide familiarity with scholarship on European romance informs her analysis of Nizami and the Persian romance tradition, allowing her to illuminate for the first time many common features linking Nizami's poems with other contemporary romances. In this important sense, her work represents the first significant advance in the field since Ritter.

In the last two decades, as well, J. Christoph Bürgel has devoted a significant portion of his considerable scholarly energies to Nizami and has published a number of studies that illuminate important thematic questions.[24] He has also published poetic translations of *Khusraw and Shirin,* the *Iskandarnamah,* and the *Haft Paykar* into German.[25]

Two studies in Persian that depart from Iranian scholarship's biographical emphasis on Nizami appeared in the late 1980s: Jalal Sattari's study of *Layli and Majnun* and A. A. Sa'idi-Sirjani's comparison of Layli and Shirin.[26] Sattari's monograph examines the tale of the two unhappy lovers stage by stage, as a kind of metatext, moving freely between Arabic materials that preceded Nizami, Nizami's poem, and imitations of his work by subsequent poets, especially those of Amir Khusraw and Maktabi Shirazi. The late Sa'idi-Sirjani, famous for his polemic interpretations of classical literature, reads Shirin and Layli against each other as embodiments of the two societies in which their stories are set.

The 850th anniversary of Nizami's birth was marked by several conferences in Iran (Tabriz) and the United States (Washington, D.C.; Los Angeles). These produced a spate of new scholarship.[27]

The rise of Islam to state ideology after the Islamic Revolution of 1979 has affected culture production in Iran, lending new prominence to religious readings of classical literary texts. This Islamic reading of Persian literature in general and of Nizami's poetry in particular also occurred in the period before the Islamic Revolution, particularly in the works of Muhammad Mu'in and Sa'id Nafisi. Since the revolution, however, a great number of ideologically motivated interpreters such as Muhammad Taqi Ja'fari, Abd al-Husayn Muvahhid, Barat Zanjani, Muhammad Riza Hakimi, Muhammad R. Rashid, and especially Bihruz Sarvatiyan have focused on Islamic and Sufic elements in Nizami's stories, subjecting their topological and allegorical levels to reductivist and predictable Islamic exegesis.

Ja'fari, for example, states that Nizami does not write to demonstrate his art but to express himself at the moment of prayer. According to Zanjani, Nizami's strength in art lies not in storytelling but in the ability to incorporate moral teachings and advice as a means of strengthening Islamic principles and faith. Rashid insists that Nizami's work has Sufi tenets, as does Sarvatiyan, who states that Nizami thinks of one thing only: the world of brotherhood and religious equality.[28] He writes "The philosopher's treasure [Nizami's book] is a book that begins with 'in the name of God the merciful', and the readers have to say 'in the name of God' in order to understand the mysterious secrets and to understand its meaning."[29]

These readings seem to be based principally on the works of medieval biographers (*tazkerah navisan*) like Dawlatshah Samarqandi, Awfi, Bigdili, and Jami, who were convinced of Nizami's membership in one or another Sufi school but provided no reliable evidence of this. Nizami's deep spirituality is always present in his writings, and it would be hard to deny traces of Sufi learning, as well. Such learning was relatively commonplace, however, and its presence is by itself hardly sufficient to establish his membership in a Sufi brotherhood and to promote religious reading as the only plausible interpretation.[30]

The question of the nature of Nizami's relation to Sufism cannot be resolved easily. Adhering too rigidly to any point of view can be problematic, however, as when the editor Pizhman Bakhtiyar eliminates verses that undermine his interpretation.[31] Similarly, some editors such as Sarvatiyan will sift through many manuscripts of a work to come up with a rendition that suits their purposes.[32]

Nizami deals with a variety of themes and motives in his poetry. As we have suggested above, however, the concept of *sokhan,* discourse or eloquent speech, is his overriding concern (see note 1 above). Nizami holds a high opinion of *sokhan,* particularly in its poetic forms, and considers poets to be creative artists with a nearly divine status. In *The Treasure House of Mysteries,* he writes:

Jonbesh-e avval keh qalam bar gereft
harf-e nakhostin ze sakhon dar gereft
pardeh-ye khalvat ke bar andākhtand
jelvat e avval beh sakhon sakhtand
tā sakhon āvazeh del dar nadād
jān tan e āzadeh be gel dar nadād
chon qalam amād shodan aghāz kard
chashm-e jahān rā be sakhon bāz kard
bi sakhon āvazeh-ye ālam nabud
in hameh goftand o sakhon kam nabud
dar loghat-e eshq sakhon jān e māst
mā sakhonim in tal ayvān e māst[33]

(As the pen began its first movement,
it produced the first word and speech.
When they raised the curtain of non-existence,
the first manifestation of existence was word and speech.
Until the word gave voice to the heart,
the soul did not submit its free body to clay.
As the pen began to move,
it opened the eyes of the world with its words.
Without speech the world has no voice,
they have said so much but the word has not diminished.
In the language of love, speech is our soul,
we are speech, these ruins are our palaces.)

In this passage—only part of a large section of the book's introduction devoted entirely to the question of speech—the poet asserts that the world begins and ends with words. Words, indeed, have created not only the world but the soul. Meisami aptly acknowledges the importance of *sokhan* in Nizami's work. She refers to the poet's description of *sokhan* discourse as "flawless soul," one that holds "the key to unseen treasure."[34]

Many passages scattered throughout Nizami's work demonstrate both the importance to him of literary creativity, an importance widely recognized by students of his work, and the wide range of topics incorporated in and given life by his discourse. In short, if we do not restrict the meaning of Nizami's work to that of the theological manifesto, it becomes possible to explore further his influential role as a poetic innovator and his treatment of subjects as diverse as love, the role of women in society, and the nature of kingship.

The chapters included in this volume illustrate not only the great diversity of Nizami's ideas but also his underlying and overwhelming preoccupation with the art of speech. In "A Comparison of Nizami's *Layli and Majnun* and Shakespeare's *Romeo and Juliet*," Jerome W. Clinton draws attention to the very different approaches taken by both Nizami and Shakespeare to describe passionate love itself and to show the impact of lovers on their communities.

In "Layla Grows Up: Nizami's *Layla and Majnun* 'in the Turkish Manner,'" Walter Andrews and Mehmet Kalpakli argue that Fuzuli's Ottoman Turkish version of the story should be read as a revisionist interpretation of the legend that gives Layli new prominence. Kamran Talattof provides a comparative study of Nizami's work in his chapter, "Nizami's Unlikely Heroines: A Study of the Characterizations of Women in Classical Persian Literature," to further better understanding of the attitudes of Nizami, Firdawsi, and Jami toward issues of gender.

Asghar Abu Gohrab in "Majnun's Image as a Serpent," demonstrates that in contrast to the early Arabic sources that refer cryptically to Majnun's emaciated body and his nakedness, Nizami uses images of the serpent, among others, to depict Majnun's physical appearance and his complex character. Julie Scott Meisami devotes her chapter, "The Historian and the Poet: Rāvanī, Nizami, and the Rhetoric of History," to a discussion of Rāvandī's use of quotations from Nizami in the *Rāhat al-Sudūr*.

J. Christoph Bürgel, in his chapter "Occult Sciences in the *Iskandarnameh* of Nizami," discusses Nizami's portrayal of an ideal statesman based on Farabi's concept of political philosophy. According to this book, in addition to military, political, philosophical, and prophetic faculties, a statesman should also understand, among others, astrology, alchemy and magic, and music and medicine—in other words, the three major branches of the so-called occult sciences. In "Nizami's Poetry versus Scientific Knowledge: The Case of the Pomegranate," Christine van Ruymbeke explains Nizami's knowledge of pharmaceutical and medical properties and uses by examining his remarks on certain plants.

Firoozeh Khazrai, in "Music in *Khusraw va Shirin*," propounds the belief that men of Nizami's stature were conversant in most of the sciences of their time, including music. She analyzes the story about Aristotle and Plato as a point of departure for speculating on some sources of the musical sciences of Nizami's day.

In his chapter, "The Story of the Ascension (*Me'Raj*) in Nizami's Work," C.-H. De Fouchécour argues that Nizami has used traditional material belonging to the prevalent religious discourse of his time to create magnificent metaphorical expressions, entirely poetic and complex. Because of this literary richness, Nizami's work has invited numerous adaptations. Finally, the bibliography on Nizami's work will provide essential information about the translation and scholarship of Nizami's work in several Western and non-Western languages.

Notes

1. The word *sokhan* and its derivatives and compound forms such as *sokhandan, sokhanvar, sokhan afarin, sokhan parvar, sokhan ravan, sokhan shinas,* and *sokhan gostar,* all meaning referring to poets are abundant in Nizami's work. On the subject of the importance of *sokhan* in Nizami's work, see Hamid Dabashi, "*Harf-i nakhostin: mafhum-i sokhan dar nazd-i hakim Nizami Ganjavi," Iranshenasi,* vol. 3, no. 4 (Winter 1992), 723-40 and the discussion of this topic in chapter 3 of this volume.

2. No exhaustive study has ever been made of the poets in Persian, Turkish, Pashto, Kurdish, and Ordu (and other languages of the Persianate tradition) who emulated Nizami's example by imitation, but by all indications the figure must be staggering. The extraordinary dissemination of Nizami's *panj ganj* throughout Persian and Persianate literature is a remarkable and largely unexplored phenomenon (cf. Jalal Sattari, note 22 below, p. 18). In the present volume J. S. Meisami opens up a new approach to this question by examining the impact of Nizami's poetry on the Iranian historian Rāvandī.

3. E. G. Browne, *A Literary History of Persia* (Cambridge, 1964) vol. 2, p. 403.

4. Wilhelm Bacher, *Nizami's Leben und Werke und der zweite Theil des Nizamishcen Alexanderbuches, mit persischen Texten als Anhang* (Leipzig, 1871). Bacher bases his study on a careful reading of the poet's own work. Vahid Dastgirdi provides a second exhaustive winnowing of these textual references in the introductory section of his *Ganjinah-i ganjavi* (Tehran, 1928).

5. Christine van Ruymbeke illuminates a point on which Nizami gave preference to poetic metaphor over scientific knowledge in her chapter in this volume entitled, "Nizami's Poetry versus Scientific Knowledge: The Case of the Pomegranate".

6. François de Blois, *Persian literature: A Bio-bibliographical Survey Begun by the Late C. A. Storey,* vol. V, Part 2: Poetry ca. A.D. 1100 to 1225, and vol. V, Part 3: Appendix II-IV, Addenda and Corrigenda, Indexes (London: Royal Asiatic Society of Great Britain and Ireland, 1994 and 1997), "Nizami," pp. 438-95. De Blois includes an exhaustive bibliography of editions and translations of Nizami's work in his article as well.

7. For Sana'i's work in general see J. T. P. de Bruijn, *Of Piety and Poetry* (Leiden, 1983). Chapter 10 is devoted to the *Hadiqa.* The only full English (prose) translation of the *Makhzan,* that by G. H. D. Darab (London, 1945), is virtually unobtainable. However, E. G. Browne offers a brief excerpt in verse in vol. 2 of his *Literary History of Persia* (Cambridge, 1964), p. 404.

8. On the character of Shirin see Julie S. Meisami, *Medieval Persian Court Poetry* (Princeton, 1987), especially chapter 4, "Romance: Character as Moral Emblem."

9. For further discussion of *Layli and Majnun* see the chapters by Clinton, Andrews and Kalpaklï, and Talattof in this volume.

10. Ali Akbar Sa'idi-Sirjani compares the character of Shirin with that of Layli in *Sima-yi du zan* (see note 26 below).

11. For an extensive discussion of the *Haft Paykar,* see Meisami, see op. cit., p. 235, and chapter 5, passim, and the introduction to her translation of it (see note 13 following).

12. H. Ritter, in the introduction to his edition (Prague, 1934). Quoted in de Blois, op. cit., p. 486, n. 1.

13. Nizami Ganjavi, *The Haft Paykar: A Medieval Persian Romance,* translated with an Introduction and Notes by Julie Scott Meisami (Oxford, New York, 1995). Peter Chelkowski gives an extended prose paraphrase of Nizami's three romances in *Mirror of the Invisible World: Tales from the Khamseh of Nizami* (New York, 1975).

14. P. Chelkowski, *Nizami Gandjawi,* EI2.

15. In the present collection, J. C. Bürgel discusses seven narratives included in the *Iqbalnamih.* The starting point of Firoozeh Khazrai's chapter in this volume is one of these same narratives.

16. Wilhelm Bacher, *Nizami's Leben und Werke und der zweite Theil des Nizamishcen Alexanderbuches, mit persischen Texten als Anhang* (Leipzig, 1871).

17. Principal among the Western literary histories are those of Browne, *A Literary History of Persia,* vol. II (London, 1906; reprinted Cambridge, 1964); Rypka et al., *History of Iranian Literature,* revised and expanded English edition (Holland, 1968), and Yarshater et al., *Persian Literature* (New York). In Persian, the standard history is that of Zabihollah Safa, *Tarikh-i adabiyat dar iran.* The most recent edition contains five volumes in seven parts (Tehran, 1362/1988).

18. Helmut Ritter, *Über die Bildersprache Nizamis* (Berlin, 1927).

19. Ye. E. Bertel's *Nizami, Tvorcheskii put' poeta* (Moscow, 1956). See also the chapters on Nizami in his *Nizami i Fuzuli* from his collected works (Moscow, 1962).

20. *Heft Peyker, ein romatisches Epos.* Ed. H. Ritter und J. Rypka (Prague, 1934).
21. For details on editions and translations see de Blois, op. cit., pp. 448-95.
22. Ibid. pp. 450-51.
23. See note 8 above. Meisami has continued her examination of Nizami's works in several essays as well, all published in *Edebiyat: A Journal of Middle Eastern and Comparative Literature.* N.S.: "Kings and Lovers: Ethical Dimensions of Medieval Persian Romance," vol. 1, no. 1 (1987) 1-19; "Fitnah or Azadah?: Nizami's Ethical Poetic," vol. 1, no. 2 (1989) 41-75; "The Theme of the Journey in Nizami's *Haft Paykar,*" vol. 4, no. 2 (1993) pp. 155-72.
24. J. Christoph Bürgel: "Nizami" in *Die Grossen der Weltgeschichte* Band III (Zurich, 1973); "Nizami über Sprache und Dichtung" (xxx); "Die Frau als Person in der Epic Nizamis," *Asiatische Studien* (1988) 42: 137-55; "The Romance," *Persian Literature,* ed. E. Yarshater (New York, 1988), pp. 161-78; "The Contest of the Two Philosophers in Nizamis First and Last Epics," *Yad-Nama in memoria di Alessandro Bausani,* ed. Biancamaria Scarcia Amoretti and Lucia Rostagno (Rome, 1991), 1: 109-17; "Conquérant, philosophe et prophète. L'image d'Alexandre le Grand dans l'épopée de Nezāmi," *Pand-o Sokhan. Mélanges offerts à Charles-Henri de Fouchécour,* ed. C. Balaÿ, C. Kappler, and Z. Vesel (Tehran, 1995), pp. 65-78; "Die Geheimwissenschaften im Iskandarname Nizamis," *Proceedings of the Second European Conference of Iranian Studies,* ed. B. G. Fragner et al. (Rome, 1995), pp. 103-12; "The Idea of Non-Violence in the Epic Poetry of Nizami," *Edebiyat: The Journal of Middle Eastern Literatures NS.* vol. 9, no. 1 (1998), pp. 61-84. Bürgel also makes extensive reference to Nizami in other of his works, most notably *The Feather of Simurgh: The "Licit Magic" of the Arts in Medieval Islam* (New York, 1988).
25. *Nizami: Chosrou und Schirin* (Zurich, 1980), *Nizami: Das Alexanderbuch* (Zurich, 1991), *Nizami: Die Abenteuer des Königs Bahrām und seiner sieben Prinzessinenen* (München, 1997). Bürgel's essay, "Nizami über Sprache und Dichtung," (see previous note) also contains verse translations of excerpts from the *Makhzan al-Asrar.*
26. Jalal Sattari, *Halat-i 'Ishq-i Majnun* (Tehran, 1366/1988); Ali Akbar Sa'idi-Sirjani, *Sima-yi du zan* (Tehran, 1367/1989).
27. Mansur Sarvatiyan, ed., *Majmu'ah-i maqalat-i kungirih-i bayn al-milali-i buzurgdasht-i nuhumin sadah-i tavallud-i hakim Nizami Ganjavi* (Tabriz, 1372/1993). Papers from the conferences in Washington, D.C. and Los Angeles appeared as a special issue of *Iranshenasi,* edited by Jalal Matini (vol. III, no. 4, Winter 1992, Washington, D.C.).
28. Muhammad Taqi Ja'fari, *Hikmat, 'Irfan, va akhlaq dar shi'r-i Nizami Ganjavi* (Tehran: Kayhan, 1991), p. 203. Barat Zanjani, *Laili va Majnun-i Nizami Ganjavi* (Tehran: Danishga-i Tehran, 1990), p. 5. Muhammad R. Rashid, "Ishq va Itiqad dar Makhzan al-Asrar," in *Majalih-i Danishkadih-i Adabiyat-i Firdawsi,* Mashhad. no. 88-9, (Spring 1990), p. 87. Bihruz Sarvatiyan, *Sharafnamah-i Ganjah'i* (Tehran: Tus, 1989), p. 23.
29. Bihruz Sarvatiyan, *Ainih-i ghayb-i Nizami Ganja-i dar masnavi Makhzan al-asrar* (Tehran: Nash-i Kalamih, 1990), p. 129.

30. Cf. Safa, op. cit., vol. 2, p. 798.
31. See *Makhzan al-asrar-i Nizami,* edited by Pizhman Bakhtiyar (Tehran: Peygah, 1988).
32. On this latter point see Mina Muallim, "Guftigu ba Bihruz Sarvatian" [A Conversation with Bihruz Sarvatiyan], *Dunya-i Sukhan,* 41 (1991), pp. 26-31.
33. Bihruz Sarvatiyan, *A'inah-i Ghayb, Nizami Ganjah-'i dar Masnavi Makhzan al-asrar* (Tehran: Nashr-i Kalamih, 1989), p. 78.
34. Julie Scott Meisami, "Fitnah or Azadah? Nizami's Ethical Poetic," *Edebiyat,* N.S. vol. 1, no. 2, 1989, pp. 41-77.

Chapter 1

A Comparison of Nizami's *Layli and Majnun* and Shakespeare's *Romeo and Juliet*

Jerome W. Clinton

Introduction

There is an obvious logic to comparing Nizami's *Layli [Layla] and Majnun* with Shakespeare's *Romeo and Juliet*. Each epitomizes the romance of star-crossed lovers within its own tradition and so invites anyone familiar with both works to read them against each other. To attempt to do so, however, is to find oneself groping for a bit of common ground that is wider and firmer than the thought expressed in the old adage, "The path of true love never did run smooth." Beside the obvious and significant differences of time, language and historical context, there are formal distinctions between them that fundamentally alter how the poet approaches issues of character, plot, and pace. To put this briefly, *Romeo and Juliet* is a play of a very particular kind, a tragedy, and it was written to be seen and heard in a public performance that would last a little under two hours. Nizami's poem is a romantic narrative that was written to be read at a much more leisurely pace, and usually, one assumes, in solitude.

Where the two works meet is in the irresistible passion that drives both pairs of young lovers. And where they differ most is in their presentation of that passion. In *Layli and Majnun* love is an illness that causes as much pain as happiness, while in *Romeo and Juliet* it is the unique source of joy and hope.[1] Moreover, for a work that has the most peaceful of lovers at its center, *Layli and Majnun* appears to argue the traditional view that youthful passion, left uncontrolled, can have a ruinous impact both on the families of the lovers and on society in general. *Romeo and Juliet* on the other hand, whose hero commits murder and which concludes with the tragic death of both lovers, presents love as an antidote for the violence that plagues society.

Background

Nizami's poem, which he completed in 1188, was not the first romance in Persian. Roughly two centuries earlier 'Ayyuqi completed the narrative of *Varqe and Golshah,* and a host of other romances were written and circulated in the long interval that lies between the two—most notably the story of *Zāl and Rudābeh,* in the *Shahnameh* of Firdawsi, and Gorgani's *Vis and Ramin.*[2] Nor is it a new version of a traditional Iranian love story. On the contrary, it was based on a famous eighth century collection of Arabic love poems attributed to "the distracted lover (*Majnun*)" and the anecdotes that grew up around his passion for Layli. In this form *Layli and Majnun* had been widely known and loved in the Islamic world for centuries before Nizami achieved prominence as a poet. It was this well-established popularity that persuaded the Sharvan Shah Akhsatan Manuchehr to commission him to undertake a new, Persian retelling of the story. Nizami formed the scattered anecdotes and verses into a coherent, connected narrative, but one that retains both the episodic nature of the original and its focus on the suffering of the two lovers, especially Majnun.

Nizami appears to have been reluctant to undertake the task at first, but of all his works *Layli and Majnun* is the one that has done most to immortalize his name. Both in language and in narrative form, his rendering of this story, which appeared in 1188, captured the attention of Persian poets and their audiences as no previous romance had done, and it engendered imitations and translations to a degree without parallel in world literature. The first of these, by Amir Khusraw, appeared a century later, in 1300, but his *Layli and Majnun* heralded a virtual deluge of similar works, both in Persian, and in Turkish, Ordu, and the other languages of the Persianate tradition as well, a deluge that continues virtually to the present day.[3]

Similarly, Shakespeare's *Romeo and Juliet,* which gave English the phrase "star-crossed lovers," was hardly the first such story to be given dramatic or poetic form in English, and like *Layli and Majnun,* the story of *Romeo and Juliet* was originally an import. Shakespeare's play was based principally on Robert Brooke's *The Tragicall Historye of Romeus and Juliet* (1562), a poem that found its inspiration in a French translation of a story by the Italian short story writer Matteo Bandello (1485-1561).[4] There may also have been an earlier play based on the same story that has since been lost. At all events, Shakespeare's play quickly became the authoritative version not only of the story of Romeo and Juliet, but of the whole genre of tragic romances. Although it did not, like Nizami's *Layli and Majnun,* engender hundreds of other *Romeo and Juliet*s, it was translated into the other languages of Europe, and inspired versions by artists in other media as well. Shakespeare's *Romeo and Juliet* provided the libretto for Bellini's opera, *I Capuleti ed i Montecchi* (1830), and has inspired classical ballets by Lambert, Prokofieff, Ashton, Tudor, and a host of other choreographers. As with *Layli and Majnun,* the remarkable popularity of *Romeo and Juliet* has survived the wearing effects of time. It is still among the most frequently performed of Shakespeare's plays, and has been filmed many times, most successfully, perhaps, by Franco Zefirelli (1968). Two further witnesses to the cultural impact of Shakespeare's creation are the brilliant modern translation of it by Alan Jay Lerner and Leonard Bernstein, *West Side Story,* and the recent and delightful *Shakespeare in Love* (1998), a film that grounds the origins of the play in a fictionalized romance of the young Shakespeare himself.[5]

Finally, a measure of the impact of both these works on their respective cultures can be seen in the fact that the names of the two lovers have gained a meaning independent of the works in which they appear. That is, "Majnun" and "Romeo" are current shorthand in the Islamic world and the West respectively for a man in love—either a "a young man afflicted with romantic passion" (*majnun*) or a ladies' man (Romeo).

The Discussion So Far

While *Layli and Majnun* and *Romeo and Juliet* have each been widely and extensively edited, studied, and commented on, the only sustained comparison of the two that I have found is that of A. A. Hekmat (1936).[6] Since this study is long out of print in Persian, and has never been translated into a European language, let me summarize it briefly here. The first two of the book's four chapters paraphrase the plots of the two works, the third compares them, and the fourth traces the history of *Layli and Majnun* in Persian literature. The third chapter is the one of interest to us here. Hekmat begins with the declaration that it was the similarities between these two romances that led him to undertake his study, and in the chapter devoted to comparing the two poems, he cites several descriptive passages that point out what he sees as a strong stylistic similarity between them—the complaints of Majnun and Romeo at separation from Layli and Juliet and their lamentations at their gravesides (110-13), the comparisons all four lovers make of their beloveds to nature—to nature's disadvantage (123-28)—and so on. The range of images each poet employs differ a good deal, but both write in an intricate, courtly style that foregrounds the poet's virtuosity. However, as Hekmat points out, this stylistic virtuosity is a more essential feature of the fabric of *Layli and Majnun* than it is of *Romeo and Juliet*.

When he addresses matters of plot and character Hekmat at times attempts to establish a commonality where arguably there is none. "Both heroes make journeys into exile," he says (146), but their journeys have very different functions. Majnun's departure from the city into the desert and solitude is a journey of discovery and transformation, and it marks an important turning point in the story. Romeo's exile from Verona to the neighboring city of Mantua is no such thing. It is a simple plot device that assures that he will not receive Juliet's message explaining her feigned death. For the most part, however, Hekmat is aware that apparent similarities dissolve into fundamental differences on closer inspection.[7] Both sets of lovers die in the end without achieving the enduring earthly union they longed for, but as he points out, where Layli and Majnun simply grow old and die in chaste separation, Romeo and Juliet are led by fate into a tragic double suicide (110). Majnun and Romeo each have friends in whom they confide, and who assist them, but these friends "are of very different kinds and natures (145)." Nofal is no Friar Laurence, and has only violence as a means of bringing the lovers together. In this he has an ambiguous success, and in fact ends by siding with Majnun's enemies against him. One should add here that Layli has no equivalent to Juliet's nurse either to act as confidante or go-between for her, or to lessen her isolation in her father's home. The messages that go to and from the lovers in *Layli and Majnun* are carried by unidentified passers-by who remain in the background of the story (117-19).

Finally, Hekmat sees the conclusions (*natijah*) that the poets wish to draw from their works as very different. Nizami's purpose, he says, is essentially descriptive. He wishes to depict the stages and complexities of romantic passion, and to describe how the lovers annihilate themselves in their beloved, giving up all peace of mind and enduring all manner of torments and difficulties. Shakespeare, in addition to giving a romantic tale dramatic life, draws an important moral lesson at the conclusion of the play. It is the ancient enmity of the two clans, he says, that has demanded payment in the blood of these two youths (148-49). Elsewhere he speaks of Shakespeare's work as more realistic than Nizami's (110,119), and typical of the "western" or "European" view of romance as opposed to the "eastern" or "Asian" one of Nizami (105, 107), although he does not elaborate on what he feels is implied by this distinction.

Love East and West

Hekmat is still well worth reading even after the passage of six decades, and I will be revisiting some of his observations in my own conclusions. His essay ends without fulfilling his promise to clarify the deep affinities and similarities that he senses in the two works, however, and he leaves undefined what he means by the "eastern" and "western" views of unhappy romance. As I have already suggested, I would like to begin my own exploration of these two works by examining the differences in the way romantic love is characterized in them, and also how they address the link between romantic passion and violence.

It may seem strange at first to speak of violence and disruption in the context of *Layli and Majnun.* The first scene of the poem projects a world of peace and serenity. It is set in a school, *maktab,* where Layli and Majnun (then known as Qays) have come as children to begin their education. There is something of the classroom in the leisurely, episodic pace of the poem as well. Throughout *Layli and Majnun* action is subordinated to descriptions of the hero's inner state and of the world he passes through. Majnun's is the dominating presence in the poem, and he, unlike Romeo, is by nature gentle and reflective. We may assume he has all the martial skills appropriate to a young Arab tribesman, but in the poem we see him only as a poet and lover. His principal concern is to give voice in poetry to his love for Layli and to his painful longing for her. When he resorts to violence, he does so only as a last resort, when all the means of distracting him from his love for Layli have been exhausted, and when his wish to marry her has been denied. Even then it is not Majnun but his friend, Nofal, who suggests taking Layli from her family by force. This rejection of physical violence means, among other things, that despite many sad and frustrating episodes, none of the principal characters in *Layli and Majnun* dies except from natural causes. The dominant mode of the poem is pathos, not tragedy. In some manuscripts there is even a postscript scene that takes the sting out of the lovers' separation in this life by suggesting that they have been united in paradise.[8]

For all this, the love of Majnun and Layli is far more disruptive to their families and community than is that of Romeo and Juliet to theirs.[9] Consider what follows from the two lovers' refusal to abandon each other once they must give up any hope of marriage. Their decision leads to the despair and early deaths of Majnun's parents, opens a breach between his family and Layli's, and precipitates two pitched battles between their two tribes. His love for her makes him an outcast from his own community, and Layli's for him makes her a virtual recluse. At her father's insistence she marries Ibn Salam, but theirs is a loveless, sterile union, and her life of childless seclusion is the female equivalent of Majnun's desert wandering. Although Nizami gives some scope to the joy their love brings them, their separation blights that joy, and the dominant theme of the poem is, as Hekmat says, the terrible pain of yearning for a distant beloved.

What precipitates this suffering is Majnun's poetry. Writing poems declaring one's love hardly seems a crime and certainly would not be considered one in Romeo's world, but in Majnun's it is a serious breach of decorum.[10] The problem is not that he writes the sort of ecstatic, erotic poetry that has always been the language of lovers, but that he both names Layli unambiguously as his beloved in his poems and allows them to circulate in the community.[11] This violates a strict taboo and threatens the absolute control that fathers exercised over sexual access to their daughters. It was read as an implicit attempt to usurp the right of choosing a mate from both his and Layli's parents. This makes him a renegade, and that, combined with the increasingly bizarre behavior that his love inspires in him, forces him out of society. The simple acts of composing and circulating his poetry transforms Qays, the handsome, promising youth, into the deranged pariah Majnun.

It is important to emphasize here that there is nothing in the poem to suggest either that Majnun chooses to act as he does, or that he is to blame for the misfortunes that befall him. On the contrary, Nizami makes clear that Majnun is as much a victim of his disruptive passion as are his parents and all the others who are wounded by it. Love is an affliction that overwhelms and transforms Qays, and one that he is powerless to combat. When his father implores him to put aside his mad, self-destructive behavior, he answers that it is not within his power to change.

> What can I do? My fate is dark as pitch.
> I have not reached this place through my own wish.
> I am constrained, shackled by iron chains.
> What use to struggle now? This is my fate.

I can't myself unloose these bonds of mine,
Nor free my body of their heavy weight.[12]

The beliefs that love was an affliction, that the lover was helpless to rid himself of it, and that madmen were not legally responsible, were long established conventions by the time Nizami took up the poem and are very much part of the furniture of the story.[13] The epithet by which Qays the mad lover becomes known tells us as much—*majnun* means literally "possessed by a jinn or demon." The many and strenuous efforts that his family and friends make to free him from this love are further evidence, should we require it, of how implacable the hold of love is. Nizami's near contemporary, Attar, depicts another such lover, Sheikh San'an, who has, like Majnun, been enslaved by love. For San'an this love madness is an even greater disaster since it disrupts a long life of spiritual guidance and exceptional piety. He resists it with all his strength, but is forced to succumb. When at last he is freed of his love madness, it is not by his own efforts, which are unavailing, but through the prayers of his disciples.[14]

Love does not have any tincture of pathology in *Romeo and Juliet*. There is a good deal of overlap between the way that young lovers are depicted in both traditions—distracted, given to poeticizing on the beloved's name, filled with sighs, et cetera. But such romantic excesses were neither an occasion for public scandal in Shakespeare's Verona nor interpreted as the first signs of dementia. They were, to import the language of developmental psychology, age appropriate and a positive sign of emotional development. Moreover, Romeo's giddy infatuation quickly transforms itself into action as he pursues and wins his love.

The association of violence with the romance of *Romeo and Juliet* is virtually unavoidable. The use of "tragedy" in the title is a promise that at least one death will occur in the play, and probably more. The prologue sketches the plot, and the very first scene—a battle in the public square of Verona between young men wearing the livery of the Montagues and Capulets—bears vivid witness to the murderous feud between the two families. Prince Escalus, the ruler of Verona, halts this battle and threatens the two houses with severe punishments should the violence continue. He is clearly unable to compel their obedience, however, and from this point on the threat of some further crisis hovers over the stage even in moments of apparent calm. At the beginning of the third act this violence explodes onto the stage in two duels. In the first Tybalt slays Mercutio, and in the second Romeo avenges that murder by slaying

Tybalt.[15] This unhappy act initiates the chain of events that ends in the deaths of the two lovers. Where *Romeo and Juliet* differs from *Layli and Majnun* is that this violence is not caused by either of the lovers. On the contrary, they demonstrate that their individual love can act as a strong antidote to their families' hatred. Romeo, fresh from a night spent in the arms of his beloved bride, would at first rather appear a coward than fight with his former enemy, Tybalt. He brushes aside Tybalt's insults and implies that he has now become united with him by something of which he cannot yet speak openly.[16]

> I do protest, I never injured thee,
> But love thee better than thou canst devise,
> Till thou shalt know the reason of my love:
> And so, good Capulet,—which name I tender
> As dearly as my own,—be satisfied.
>   (*Romeo and Juliet,* Act III, Scene 1)

Romeo's kinsman and friend, Mercutio, is unaware of the reason for Romeo's strange reluctance to engage Tybalt and, shamed by it, attacks him in his place. Tybalt slays Mercutio, and this murder overwhelms the good effects of Romeo's love for Juliet. He reverts to his role as a scion of the Montagues and revenges Mercutio's death by killing Tybalt. Powerful as romantic love is, it cannot by itself withstand this violent assault. Although Romeo's murder of Tybalt makes it impossible for him to be united with his beloved Juliet, his action does not violate the norms of his society as defined by his family and hers. It is these norms more than his action that are problematic.

Romeo and Juliet are star-crossed not because they can never enjoy each other's love, but because having tasted it, and that within the sanctity of marriage, they are denied the full enjoyment of their love by the misguided and illegal feud of their two families.

For Romeo to declare openly his love for Juliet, and she for him, is dangerous, but for quite opposite reasons. Love in *Romeo and Juliet* is disruptive, too, but the order it disrupts is itself corrupt. If the lovers must rely on secrets and stratagems to consummate their love, it is because the criminal hatred of their parents makes this necessary, not because their love is wrong or inappropriate. The vendetta between the Montagues and

Capulets is condemned by both state and church, while their love has the sanction of the church, although a somewhat ambiguous one. Romantic love is here a mirror that is held up against the existing social order to show its failings. The healing of this breach in society is the one benign consequence of the tragedy.

One striking difference between the two poems is in the respective importance of the female characters. Despite the fact that the movement of women was hardly less restricted in sixteenth century Verona than in eighth century Arabia, Juliet enjoys a real parity with Romeo in the action of the play. Their attraction is mutual, and she both asserts her love vigorously and risks her life to be joined with him. Romeo believes that she has chosen to commit suicide rather than face a life without him, and he follows her example boldly. Moreover, the parity between Romeo and Juliet is continued in the use of a female intermediary, her nurse, to balance that of Romeo's friend Friar Laurence. Male characters predominate in the play, but women play highly visible and determining roles as well. Both lovers deserve the star billing they receive in the title of the play.

In *Layli and Majnun,* by contrast, while Layli initially is as much the focus of the poem as is Qays, her role quickly diminishes until the story becomes almost completely his. One obviously cannot have a romance without a beloved as well as a lover, but throughout the great majority of scenes in *Layli and Majnun* Layli is present only as an idol within the mind of Majnun. In one passage the poet even has him explicitly dispense with the flesh-and-blood Layli. About two thirds of the way through the poem, the wandering lover passes near the encampment of her family one day, and comes upon a scrap of paper with both their names written on it. He slices hers away with his thumbnail. Onlookers ask him why he has done this. His answer makes clear how incidental Layli herself has become the story of his love.[17]

"This text requires a single name, not two,"
He answered them, "Majnun alone will do.
If someone delves within a lover's heart,
He'll find the loved one in its deepest part."
"But why," they asked him, "from among the two,
It's *Layli* who's been cut away, not you?"
"It's wrong," he said, "for her to be the cover
That hides within itself this ardent lover.
I am the veil for what should be internal.
I am the outer shell; she is the kernel."[18]

Layli the person has been replaced by Majnun's idealization of her, an entity that he can sustain quite independently. These lines simply makes explicit what has been implicit all along. As the object of Majnun's affections, an object that he never attains physically, Layli has a role of central importance for the poem, but as a character in the narrative she does not. The role that Layli plays within the poem is the diametric opposite of that of Juliet, whose physical presence is essential at every stage of the tragedy and whose actions shape the drama as much as do those of Romeo. Layli, by contrast, is an essentially passive figure. Only Majnun is given the freedom to express his love actively and to attempt to find ways to be joined with Layli. Nizami never gives Layli an individual voice or allows her to shape the events of the story. Her death is not tragic since Majnun has already internalized her voice and personality, and she herself has become superfluous.[19]

Conclusion

One of the defining differences between premodern and modern literary works is in the ethical relation of the individual and society. In modern works, to simplify a great deal, society is corrupt and the hero must redeem it, or at least maintain his integrity against it. In premodern works, society represents the ethical norm, and the individual must either be brought into conformity with it or expelled from it. In Shakespeare's plays, for example, the character who disrupts the order of society is destroyed if it is a tragedy (Macbeth, Lear, Othello), or laughed into submission if it is a comedy (Malvolio, Katherina). In either case the balance of society is reestablished. *Romeo and Juliet* appears at first to violate this norm and to contain a kernel of modernity in that its two protagonists are clearly more sane and healthy than the society in which they live. But this society—by which I mean that of the Montagues and Capulets—is described at the outset as corrupt. The feud between the two families makes their Verona an island of dysfunction within the sea of normalcy represented by Prince Escalus. Romeo and Juliet behave correctly in opposing their society's dysfunction but violate the norms of the larger society in usurping the authority of their parents to choose whom they will marry. Only when we recognize that the behavior of Romeo and Juliet is inappropriate from the perspective of that larger society can we find any rational justification for the death of two such attractive individuals. The immediate cause of their deaths is their own precipitate actions, although Prince Escalus is right to lay the ultimate responsibility at the feet of the patriarchs of their clans.

This kernel of modernity in *Romeo and Juliet* helps explain the ease with which it has been adapted to the modern world. That is, it expresses the common conviction that romantic love, of lovers who choose each other despite all, can triumph over the cynicism and corruption of modern life. And if family vendettas have moved down the social scale, they haven't vanished. Gangs as bent on mutual destruction as the Montagues and Capulets are not a historical artifact but a present reality.

Layli and Majnun by contrast is fundamentally premodern in its governing ethic. While it is very sad, even pathetic that the lovers cannot marry, it is also appropriate. Layli's father is not condemned for refusing to give her to Majnun. Indeed, Nofal, who, like the reader, feels great compassion for Majnun and would like to help him to gain his love, is ultimately convinced of the rightness of her father's refusal and ends by siding with him against Majnun. Society's health apparently requires that the spontaneous passion of Qays for Layli not be allowed to succeed since it is expressed in an inappropriate way. At the level of narrative, Nizami finds a partial and not altogether happy solution to this dilemma by etherealizing the lovers' bond. If they can meet on the spiritual plane, they no longer require physical union. The moral we are to draw from this, insofar as Nizami intends us to draw a moral, is that true love transcends worldly constraints. As narrative, this solution is less satisfying than one that brings the lovers physically together, whether happily or tragically.[20] But this may be beside the point. In the radical disregard of the poem's hero for worldly concerns, and his focus on a transcendent, idealized beloved with whom he cannot be joined in this life, *Layli and Majnun* anticipates key elements of the mystical narrative, and the secret of its appeal may in part lie here. Majnun's madness, like that of the sufi, liberates him from the ordinary conventions and constraints of society. The passionate intensity of his love for Layli is never limited or shaped by the need to accept the restraints of ordinary, conventional lovers. The freedom to suffer brings other freedoms as well. And in the context of a highly structured and formally constrained society, that freedom may well be seen as worth the price.

Finally, Majnun gives madness a good name. He is a poet before he is a madman, but his madness magnifies his poetic gift and makes his suffering heroic, even legendary, as his poems circulate throughout Arabia. Poets and lovers seek him out in the desert, not to shake their heads over the ruin of his hopes but to wonder at the intensity of his love and devotion. Like the great poets of pre-Islamic Arabia, he achieves a fame that is normally reserved for extraordinary warriors or men of unparalleled generosity, and adds a new meaning to the heroism of romantic love.

Notes

1. On the perception of love as an affliction in Islamic society see Michael W. Dols, *Majnun: The Madman in Medieval Islamic Society* (Oxford, 1992), especially his discussion of *Layli and Majnun* in chapter 11, "The Romantic Fool" pp. 313-19.
2. For a discussion of the early development of the romance in Persian see Julie S. Meisami, *Medieval Persian Court Poetry* (Princeton, NJ, 1987), especially chapter 3.
3. The extraordinary dissemination of Nizami's *panj ganj* throughout the Islamic world is one of the most remarkable phenomena of world literature, and the case of *Layli and Majnun* is the most startling of these. There are translations *cum* imitations of it in all the major languages of the Islamic ecumene, often multiple versions, and in many of the minor ones as well. Cf. *Madjnun-Layla* in the *Encyclopedia of Islam,* 2nd edition.
4. *Romeo and Juliet* in *The Oxford Companion to English Literature* (Oxford, New York: Oxford University Press, 1985).
5. Written by Marc Norman and Tom Stoppard, produced by Edward Zwick, directed by John Madden (1998).
6. A. A. Hekmat, *Romi'o va zhuliat-i viliam shakispir muqayisah ba layli va majnun-i nizami ganjavi.* Beroukhim, Tehran 1314/1936.
7. Chapter three, pp. 104-55. See especially his comments on pp. 110, 147, 148.
8. See, for example, "In a dream Zayd sees Layli and Majnun in paradise." Nizami Ganjavi, *Layli va majnun,* ed. Bihruz Sarvatiyan (Tehran, 1347), p. 347.
9. Meisami expresses this idea most emphatically, saying that "all who are touched by Majnun's passion are either altered or destroyed by it. Majnun's passion, like a consuming flame, feeds on itself and seeks to destroy everything in its path; for, like the raging fire to which it is repeatedly likened, it knows no bounds, no limits, and is beyond control." (*Medieval Persian Court Poetry,* pp. 178-79). Her comments are quoted with approval by Dols, op. cit., p. 323.
10. Y. Dunayevskiy, "Nezami," Literatura Irana. X-XV vv. (*Vostok,* sbornik vtoroy) (Moscow–Leningrad, 1935), p. 263. Cited in Rypka, *History of Iranian Literature* (Dordrecht, Holland, 1968), p. 211.
11. Dols, op. cit., p. 332.
12. Nizami Ganjavi, *Layli va majnun,* ed. Behruz Servatian (Tehran, 1347), p. 122, lines 9-10. All references to the text are to this edition.
13. Dols, op. cit., pp. 333-35.
14. Farid al-Din Attar, *Mantiq at-tayr.* Edited by S. Gowharin (Tehran, 1356/ 1978). Translated by Afkham Darbandi and Dick Davis, *The Conference of the Birds* (Penguin Books, 1984).
15. The centrality of violence in *Romeo and Juliet* is reflected as well in the modern recasting of the story as the musical *West Side Story.*

16. Shakespeare, *Romeo and Juliet,* Act III, scene 1.
17. "... Majnun seems to be more in love with the idea of Layli than the person ... " J. C. Bürgel, "Romance," in E. Yarshater, ed., *Persian Literature* (New York, 1988).
18. *Layli o Majnun,* pp. 214-15, lines 8-12.
19. Kamran Talattof gives a substantially different reading of Layli's character in his chapter in this volume.
20. Perhaps we should read later versions of *Layli o Majnun* as evidence that later poets also found this solution unsatisfactory. See, for instance, the chapter by Walter Andrews and Mehmed Kalpaklī in this volume.

Chapter 2

Layla Grows Up: Nizami's *Layla and Majnun* "in The Turkish Manner"

Mehmed Kalpaklı and Walter G. Andrews

Introduction

Sometime in the last fifteen years of the twelfth century, the Shirvanshah Akhsatan made a request of the poet Nizami:

> Mīkhāham ke konūn be yād-e majnūn
> rānī sokhan cho dorr-e maknūn (48)[1]

> I wish you now in Majnun's recollection
> to speak poetic words like pearls of perfection

At the same time the ruler also made it quite clear what the language of this recollection should be:

> dar zīvar-e pārsī vo tāzī   īn tāza 'arūs rā ṭerāzī (49)

> In jewels of Persian and Arabic too
> adorn this bride so fresh and new

But he also goes on to say what language he does not want the poet to use—apparently alluding to Mahmmūd of Gazna's legendary cheapness in the matter of Ferdawsī:

torkī şefāt vafā-ye mā nīst   torkāna sokhan sazā-ye mā nīst (49)

Not in the Turkish way do we keep a promise
   so writing in the Turkish manner doesn't suit us

This couplet seems to indicate that the Sharvanshah could have asked Nizami to write in Turkish and that the poet could have done this. But alas—or fortunately, depending on your point of view—the ruler preferred Persian. So a vastly influential tale was born, and the first complete Turkish version of the story had to wait for almost three hundred years.

By the early fourteenth century, the Turkish rulers of Anatolia were out from under the shadow of Maḥmūd's stinginess and somewhat less inclined to demand poetry in Persian. At this point the Layla and Majnun story begins to appear in Turkish mystical romances.[2] A Mevlevi dervish poet from the town of Kırşehir, known only by the name Gülşehrī included a seventy nine couplet telling of the tale in his Turkish version of the *Mantıku't-tayr* completed in 1317. Another dervish from Kırşehir, 'Āşık Paşa, the grandson of a dervish immigrant from Khorasan, also included a thirty couplet version in his *Garipnāme* written sometime before 1333.

There does not appear to have been a complete Western Turkish version of the Layla Majnun story on the model of Nizami until the latter part of the fifteenth century. In 1478 in Konya, the poet Şāhidī, completed his Layla and Majnun *mesnevi,* which he had begun in Istanbul under the title *Gülşen-i 'uşşāk.* It was presented to Şāhidī's patron Cem Sultan who, coincidentally, became the subject of a romantic love story of his own. Having lost the sultanate to his brother Bayezit, he fled to France as guest, hostage, and later prisoner of the Knights of St. John, and there, according to a popular legend in parts of France, was involved in a hopeless love affair with a French chatelaine.

Şāhidī links his version directly to Nizami. He says in his introduction:

Dile cün hātif-i cān itdi terġīb   vücūda gelmege bu naẓm-ı tertīb

When the unseen advisor made my heart wish
   that this verse composition would come into being

Heves atına bindi tutdı meydān   hevā ṭopına geldi urdı cevgān

desire mounted its horse, and took the field
and approached the ball of passion and struck with the mallet

K'idüp tezyīn 'işḳuñ gülsitānın   yaza Mecnūn u Leylī dāstānın

That it might adorn the rose-bower of love
and write the legend of Majnun and Layla

Diyüp Rūmī zebān ile kelāmı   Niẓāmī naẓmına gire niẓāmı[3]

That it might speak its words in the Turkish tongue
and order it after the verses of Nizami

The poet also mentions Amir-e Khosraw's version (composed in 1299)
as a model but in the end goes beyond all his predecessors. His version is
the longest we know of, with a total of 6,446 couplets, and contains several
scenes that do not appear in his models. For example, there is even a scene
in which Majnun disguises himself as a sheep and goes to visit Layla.

At about the same time, in the court of Hüseyin Baykara in Herat, the
great Chagatay poet, Nevāyī was composing his own Eastern Turkic version, which was completed in 1483—a year before his companion Jāmī
completed his *Layla and Majnun* in Persian. Nevāyī begins by mentioning the usual models:

ʿIşḳ icre necük ki ol yegāne bu ḥüsnde āfet-i zamāne

Because this one was unique in love,
and that one, in beauty, all others above

Efsāneleri cihānda nāmī naẓmeylep īusrev ü niẓāmī (86)[4]

Hosraw and Nizami both gave birth
to the fame of their story on the earth

Nevāyī goes on to explain in his conclusion that although the story of
Layla and Majnun is famous, Turks have been deprived of its beauties
and for this reason he is taking the lead in writing a Turkish version.

Ger nükteleri cihānnı tuttı   ġavġāları ins ü cānnı tuttı

Since the world by its niceties was taken
  its tumult humans and genies has taken

Çün fārisi erdi nükte şevķı   azraķ edi anda türkī zevķı

Since the pleasure of its fine points was Persian
  for Turks its joys had a much diminished version

Ol til bile naẓm boldı melfūẓ   kim fārsī anglar oldı maḥẓūẓ

In that tongue the poetry was writ
  that Persian speakers might take joy in it

Min türkce başlaban rivāyet   ķıldım bu fesāneni ḥikāyet

It was I who began to tell the tale in Turkish
  and made a story out of this legend

Kim şöhreti cün cihānġa tolġay   Türk elige daġı behre bolġay

So that its fame might fill the world
  and the Turks might have a share in this

Necün ki bu kün cihānda etrāk   köp-tür īōş-ṭāb' u şāfī-idrāk (380-81)

Because there are today in the world many
  Turks of pleasant natures and pure understanding

In the West, the name associated most closely with the Layla and Majnun story in Turkish is that of the sixteenth century Iraqi poet Fuzūlī. Fuzūlī's version is an acknowledged masterpiece. It harks back to Nizami, but in the manner of *imitatio/nazire* rather than translation. It contains its own peculiar imagery, an unusual excitement, and pathos. In addition, the ghazals and quatrains written as the voice of Layla and Majnun give it a special emotional and psychological depth and poetic richness.

Born in Kerbela, Fuzūlī was among the scholars and intellectuals of Iraq who rushed to greet the triumphant Sultan Süleyman when he entered Baghdad in the winter of 1533-44. By Fuzūlī's own account, at this time he met some of the noted Ottoman poets who had accompanied the Sultan on campaign—most likely, Yahyā Beg and Hayālī Beg. One day while somewhat intoxicated in the *majlis,* they got around to discussing poets and Fuzūlī became vocal in giving his opinions. The Ottomans took this as an occasion to put the Azeri poet to the test. As Fuzūlī puts it in the introduction to his *Leyla ve Mecnun:*

Luṭf (ile/eyle) didiler ey süīan-senc   fāş eyle cihana bir nihān genc

Do us a favor, they said, oh weaver of poetry
   reveal to the world a hidden treasury

Leylī Mecnūn ʿacemde cohdur   Etrākda ol fesāne yoīdur

In Persian *Layla and Majnuns* are many
   among the Turks there are not any

Taḳrīre getür bu dāstānı   ḳıl tāze bu eski būstānı (46/32)[5]

So, you, this legend firm establish
   this ancient orchard now refresh

But Fuzūlī is reluctant—not about writing a romance in the Ottoman style, which he likely felt he could do in the same way as he produced *divan*s in Turkish, Persian and Arabic—but, in the same vein as Nizami, he says, this subject is a difficult one and not suited to lighten the heart of the listener:

Sevdāsı dırāz u baḥri kūtāh   mazmūnu fiġān u nāle vü āh

Its crazed passion is long and the meter short
   its conceits, cries and wails of every sort

Bir bezm-i muşībet u belādır   kim evveli ġam soñı fanādır

A gathering of calamity and affliction
   which begins in grief and ends in annihilation

Ne bādesine neşāṭdan reng   ne naġmesine feraḥdan āheng (46/33)

In its wine no coloring of pleasure
   in its song no harmony of joy

And he goes on to underscore his agreement with Nizami to the extent of quoting him directly:

Billāh ki ne īōş dimiş Nizami   bu bābda īatm idüp kelāmı

By God, how pleasantly Nizami said it
   the final word on this subject he said it

Asbāb-e soīan naşāṭ o nāzast   zīn har do soīan bahāna-sāzast

The essentials of poetry are joy and coquetry
   out of these two is made the reason for poetry

Maydān-e soīan farāī bāyad tā ṭabʿ dar ū honar nomāyad

The playing-field of poetry ought to be wide
   that one's nature show its talent there inside

Dar germī-ye rīg u saīṭī-ye kūh   tā cand soīan ravad ba-enbūh (47/33)

That in harshness of peaks and the heat of sand
   poetic words in abundance may walk the land

This reluctance, although it has a conventional side, is significant and we will dwell on it further below. At this point it is enough to mention that Fuzūlī picks up on the Sufi/mystical reading of Nizami and carries it off in a general direction taken by post-Timurid Perso-Ottoman poetry. One of the features of this direction is that its mysticism maintains a consistent balance between the activities of the actual, physical world and the mystical interpretation of those activities. That is, the mystical interpretation is always in force, but there is also—or usually—an actual party, an actual beloved, real kisses, and a rose garden one can touch and smell. When Fuzūlī says "whatever (truly) exists in this world is love"

('Išḳ imiş her ne var 'ālemde) behind it is a rejection of a "real world" in which his hopes never flowered.[6] The petty local rulers of his land would not or could not support a talented poet and the Ottomans, despite having the ability and making grand promises, never produced any such support. His feelings of loneliness, friendlessness and his identification with Majnun all seem to be informed as much by longing for the patron he never found as by his other—mystical—longing. For example, as he says in a famous ghazal:

> Ne yanar kimse bana āteş-i dilden özge
>   ne acar kimse ḳapum bād-ı ṣabādan gayrı[7]

> No one burns for me but flames of the heart
>   no one opens my door but the wind from the east

We emphasize this point because of the tendency of learned interpreters to discover only an abstract, spiritual message in this kind of poetry. Fuzūlī's *Leyla ve Mecnun* is certainly "mystical," more so even than Nizami's. And this seems to be what makes it "serious" poetry to some. But, as we will see, it also carries a secular theme of impossible love/thwarted love that is consistently noted by a host of other interpreters.

There were a huge number of Layla/Majnuns on the Fuzūlī-Nizami model with a conventionally mystical tone in Ottoman Turkish. However, there were also innumerable popular versions—from poems to folk tales to shadow puppet plays—in which the themes of hopeless love, over-whelming love, lost love, the nature of "true" love are referenced with only the slightest, conventional gestures toward a transcendent reading. This is how the metaphor of Layla and Majnun comes forward in time. A very modern poet sensitive to Ottoman themes will write to Layla in the voice of Majnun:

> Ben artık bulunduğum şehirden gittim
> İnsan kuş misali.
> Sen hâlâ
> O kalabalık evde olmasın,
> Gelip gidenin cok mu bari?

Uzgünüm Leylâ
Dünya hâli![8]

I have gone from the city where I was.
A person is like a bird.
And you, still,
Must be in that teeming house.
Are they many who come and go there?
Leylâ I'm sorry.
It's the way of the world.

(Behcet Necatigil)

The founder of the popular *arabesk* music tradition in Turkey, Orhan Gencebay, has a song entitled *Leyla and Mecnun* that in translation goes like this:

This wailing for years endured with no reply
Such a wailing that the hearer could but cry
Full of longing, full of trial, love, and pain
Such a love as never could be lived again

My love's tears are my only hope now
The bloody tears I shed, loneliness and sorrow
At the resurrection I'm yours, yours Layla

Death is no ending for us
Who loves is deathless, Layla
We exist so long as the world endures and we love, Layla

We became a legend in pain and in trial
Ever they asked, "Majnun, where is your Layla"
I said, my Layla's in my daytime and in my night
In my fate, in my fate, in my wailing and my last breath[9]

A contemporary pop idol, Rafet El-Roman, was asked by a reporter if his song entitled "Leyla" was named after "another of his lovers." "No," he replied, "It is true that most of my songs are taken from bits of my life. But not all of them. In 'Leyla' I wanted, by way of music, to bring to a new generation the story of Layla and Majnun."[10]

It is no surprise that Layla and Majnun live on as a metaphor in a world that has not lost its fascination with hopeless love. What we will suggest in this chapter, however, is that today's "secular" reading of the story converges in a meaningful way with a reading that is already "present" in Nizami. This is to say that Nizami's tale gives rise to a history of readings that cause us to doubt the usefulness of the common binary, either/or, secular or religious formulation. Even when the story seems overtly to focus on and foreground the mystical interpretation, the mystical and the mundane are often inseparably intertwined.

We will also suggest that the secular reading surfaces most obviously in the growth of the character of Layla. In our reading this growth begins with the "addition" to Nizami's text, the section that contains the final meeting in the desert between Majnun and Layla who has at last been freed of family obligations by the death of her husband. Both Dastgirdī and A. S. Levend consider this episode to be the work of a later and inferior poet.[11] Dastgirdī does not include it in his edition nor is it included in either the English and German translations by Gelpke or in A. N. Tarlan's modern Turkish translation.[12] In the light of our contention that this "addition" is the beginning of an expansion of the story's secular dimension, it is interesting that the episode *is* included in the edition of Bihruz Sarvatiyan who seems to be quite firmly in favor of a spiritual/mystical reading.

We are reluctant to comment at all about the "authenticity" or "authorship" of this addition—it makes no difference to our argument. Nor are we interested in contentions about the quality of its writing, except perhaps to point out that the "inferiority" of later participants in a text is one of the conventional tropes of scholarship descended from romantic notions about "originality." What we would like to exemplify in a brief "close reading" of a small portion of the "post-Nizami" text are the directions in which the text grows and the way in which Nizami's text seems to make that growth inevitable.

Leyla Grows Up

Despite its status as an undisputed masterpiece and model, the short "authentic" text of Nizami's *Layla and Majnun* has a terribly unsatisfactory ending. Layla's husband dies, leaving her free to do as she wishes, at which point she abruptly lies down and dies apparently of lovesickness for Majnun. As true as this sudden pining away is to the general "death by love" theme of the tale and its 'Udhrī-tainted sources, it makes little sense and gives no satisfaction. On what basis do we assert this? Well, we begin by taking seriously Nizami's own doubts about the story. He seems to indicate that there was a limited taste in his time for the very constrained 'Udhrī story type that focuses on the anguish of impossible love within a time-space setting where the "catching" of love and its inevitably fatal consequences are functionally simultaneous except for episodic delays that are resolutely ahistorical and bring no growth or development in anything other than the intensity of passion. Next we take into account the centuries-long concern to "repair" the story beginning with the "added" episode, which if not Nizami's own repair is close enough that it was accepted as such without question by many of his successors—at worst, a case of story-sense triumphing over "textual criticism."

The part of the added segment that we will focus on can be summarized as follows: Instead of simply dying after the death of her husband, Layla experiences a sunrise that resembles the rebirth of her hopes and, like any sensible woman, sets out to take advantage of her dearly bought freedom. "With tears in her eyes and fire in her heart" (310) no longer fearing her parents, she returns to her father's house where she sits in her room and makes plans for a union with Majnun, a union that has unmistakable physical connotations. No longer a passive object, she calls her friend Zayd to her and says, *K'-emrūz na rūz-e entezārast / rūz-e talab-e veşāl-e yārast,* ("Today is not the day for waiting / it is the day for seeking union with the beloved.") *"Bar khīz"* she says, "Rise up, the world is pleasant, rise up ... " (311) She then launches into a cluster of very sexually suggestive images: *ham-'āba-ye sarv kon caman rā / dar dasta-ye lāla kaş saman rā,* ("Make the cypress bed-made of the meadow / bind the jasmine in a bunch with the tulip,") *ān āhū-ye naġz rā be-şast ār / v'ān nāfa-ye moşk rā be-dast ār,* ("Bring that lovely ghazal under the thumb / And bring to hand that sac of musk") (311). She then puts together an appropriate outfit for the now ill-clad Majnun and sends Zayd into the desert to tell him the good news. In time, the overjoyed Majnun wanders to her tent accompanied by an army of wild animals, both predators and less threatening beasts. When she hears the news of his arrival, she rushes from her tent oblivious to the wild beasts and falls at the feet of her beloved "like grass at the base of a tall tree." The two are so overcome by love that they both fall unconscious in the middle of the road. Their companions rush up to see if they are alive or dead, and several are immediately torn to bits by the wild beasts who continue to protect the privacy of the unconscious pair. Thus they remain for half a day and when they revive, still struck dumb by the intensity of their passion, Layla shyly takes her bewildered lover by the hand and leads him into her tent.

The animals now ring the tent in a curious scene emphasizing the power and dangerousness of these beasts, who "would tear a fly to pieces should it come into their midst." The poet/narrator also points out that it is because Majnun's love is "true/spiritual/*ḥaqīqī*, free of lust or base desire, that the beasts are tame in his presence: *z'ān az dadagān badī barū nīst / k'ālāyeşi az dadī darū nīst,* ("The wild beasts had no enmity toward him / For there was no mixture of animality within him") (314). Majnun appears to have externalized his animal/physical self; it rings him about and protects him but is not a part of him anymore.

In the tent, Majnun is silent while Layla cradles him in her arm, her hand a collar about his neck, her hair cascading down over him like a shirt. She entices him with longing glances, and both are rendered witless by their passion. They remain in this embrace, the two as one, for a full day and night. When they recover, Majnun rushes out of the tent and Layla follows to find him sitting in the road before her dwelling. There the two lovingly confront one another, unable to speak for the intensity of their emotion. Finally, after at least a day and a half of stunned silence, Layla takes the initiative and, casting a sharp glance, speaks to Majnun:

> K'ay sūsan-e dah zabān ce būdat   k'andīşa-ye man zabān robūdat
> Bolbol ke sokhan segāl bāşad   bī gol hama sāla lāl bāşad
> Çun bīnad rūy-e gol be bostān   gūyad na yaki hazār dastān
> To bolbol-e bāġ-e rūzgārī   man bā to co gol be sāzgārī
> Emrūz ke hast rūz-e payvand   bar dorz-e dahān nehādayī band
> (317)

Oh iris of ten tongues what's with you
     that thought of me has stolen away your tongue?
The bulbul that speaks in poetry
     for a whole year stays mute without a rose
But when it sees the rose bloom in the garden
     it speaks not one but a thousand tales
You are the bulbul in the garden of this world
     I am attuned to you like the rose
And today, which is the day of union
     you have put a clasp on the casket of your tongue

In response to this quite reasonable question, Majnun goes into a lengthy discourse on why his love has become so pure that it no longer needs an object. When he finishes, Layla looks at him so longingly that he screams, tears his clothes, faints, and finally escapes into the desert.

In contrast to the perfect passivity of the "early" Layla who is the pawn of her parents throughout and who, in the end, simply lies down and dies, this Layla acts decisively in a way that makes sense for someone in love. She no longer fears her parents' displeasure; she makes and executes a plan to reunite with her beloved, and she does her best to bring him to his senses. What is more, in the context of this worldly good sense, Majnun's behavior begins to appear indefensible, cruel, and even ludicrous. That is to say, when he is kept from his beloved by outside forces, including the world's misinterpretation or its censure of his overwhelming passion, Majnun is a tragic figure even without any hint of mystical sublimation. But when the possibility of a legitimate (or even illegitimate) union with the object of his affection presents itself, the only way to preserve his role as the hero of this story is to raise the mystical interpretation to the surface.

This move is still not without its core of ambiguity. In the added segment, Majnun, as we have pointed out, is quite overtly "split" into a spiritual self, which remains (tenuously) in his body, and an animal self, which is exteriorized and identified with the band of wild and vicious animals. Layla, however, remains whole. She is not overtly presented here as the locus of "animalistic" passions (as Jāmī seems to do later), nor do her passion or her sensuality (which are both quite evident in the "added" segment) seem separable from her essence. She does what we would expect someone to do in her circumstances. She is like us (in our nonmystical lives, at least). In fact, she appears to foreground the discomfort many Muslims (and others) have with notions of spiritual celibacy—the supposed celibacy of Jesus, for example—that were so clearly rejected by the Prophet. The later Layla is a good, faithful, chaste woman who deserves a normal married and sexual life.

Keeping this much about the Nizami text in mind, we would like to launch ourselves on the historical trajectory of the "added text" and examine where it takes us in the case of an (or an-other) Azerī master-poet, this time, written in the Western Turkish/Ottoman mode of the high sixteenth century. As we have mentioned, Fuzūlī sees himself directly in the line of Nizami. In his poem, gestures toward his illustrious predecessor are overt and sincere. Nonetheless, his version of the tale is substantially different from Nizami's in several significant respects. Using the story-segment that corresponds to the "added text" as an example, we will go on to examine some of these differences.

One general difference having a significant bearing on issues of "voice" is the inclusion of lyric poetry in the romantic *mesnevi*. As we know, the earliest of Persian romances, Ayyūqī's *Varqa va Golşāh* (written sometime before 1030 C.E.) contained several monorhyming ghazals. This usage was picked up by Ayyūqī's Turkish imitator, Yūsuf-i Meddāḥ, in his own (1342 C.E.) romance by the same title. However, the practice of including lyric poetry in the romance never caught on in Persian, while in Turkish it flourished. Nizami, for example, follows the model of Gorgānī and does not include any in his romances, even when writing about Majnun whose fame derives from his skill as a lyric poet and whose story was concocted as a setting for a collection of lyric poems. On the other hand, Fuzūlī's *Layla and Majnun* contains 22 ghazals, 2 murabbā's, and 2 münācāt. Of these poems, 9 are in the voice of Layla (although one is recited to Majnun by Zayd).[13]

Because the lyrics imply a single, emotionally involved speaker rather than a more or less omniscient narrator, they generally have the character of dialogue or monologue and impart a sense of immediacy. In Fuzūlī this lyric character seems to affect the narrative style as a whole, whereas in the Nizami addition, the majority of lines are devoted to descriptions and interpretations of the actions, motives, and feelings of the characters. In Fuzūlī, descriptive passages are relatively few and are, for the most part, limited to one or two lines of transition between large stretches of speech often capped by a lyric outburst. As a result, Layla, to whom the "added Nizami segment" granted the power of active agency, acquires, in Fuzūlī, a powerful "voice" and lyric sensibility much the equal of Majnun's.

The effect of this emphasis on speech is that the story reads more like the script of a play (wherein the descriptive passages fulfill the secondary role of stage directions) or even of a musical play in which the ghazals take the place of breaking into song at significant moments. How this works and how Fuzūlī departs from Nizami can be exemplified by a brief summary that will end by focusing on a speech of Layla's.

Upon the death of her husband Layla returns to her father's home where she outwardly mourns Ibn Salām and inwardly mourns Majnun. In the dark night of her grief she first addresses the morning, asking it for relief. Finding none, she then prays to God asking "Either give me the endurance to bear my torment / or torment in proportion to my endurance" (*Yā vir meñā miḥnetümde tāḳat / yā tāḳatum olduǧunca miḥnet*) (249/190). She goes on to express her fear that the intensity of her passion will overwhelm her modesty and chastity: "My fear is this that (my) chastity be trampled upon / that (my) mental state not conform to commandment" (*Ḳorīum bu ki 'işmet ola pāmāl / Fırmāna muvāfıḳ olmıya ḥāl*) (249/190). She ends with a *münācāt* and while she is still praying the journey bells ring and the whole family sets out in a caravan.

It is interesting to note here that Fuzūlī restores to the story some features associated with its supposed origins that are obscured in Nizami: his main characters are lyric poets and their verses adorn the story. Layla is obviously a nomad; the family packs up and goes without any particular destination. As the story continues, she mounts her she-camel, which becomes "intoxicated with the wine of her love" (251/192). When she sees the camel so joyously giddy she tells it her problems, asks it to take her to the country of Majnun, and then on the way passes out from the intensity of her grief. When she awakes she has become separated from the caravan and wanders about until she runs across a grieving stranger. She asks who he is and he answers, "Majnun." "Oh no" she says," Majnun has a fairy's face, an alluring body, and you are crazy and woebegone, your face is torn, your body bent. Majnun is mighty you are wretched. Majnun is a poet; where is your poetry?" (254/195). Majnun replies that the true lovers are silent but Layla is not accepting any such mystical excuses and insists on a poem telling what has befallen him. Majnun relents. He briefly tells his tale, summarizing the story to this point, and ends with a ghazal beginning:

Alas that the heavens never once turned as I foresaw
    never drove off separation's pain with the balm of union

*Āh kim bir dem felek rāyumca devrān itmedi
    vaṣl dermāniyle defʿ-i derd-i hicrān itmedi* (257/197)

Finally recognizing him, Layla bursts into tears and begs to be forgiven, explaining how her sorrow has blinded her to the real world. She ends by addressing her soul: "Oh soul that has waited so long for him / that has ever begged to see the beloved. You have reached him, come, emerge from the flesh / go to the beloved, cut off the mingling with me" (*ey cān ki cekerdiñ intizārı / görmek dileyüp hemişe yārı Yetdiñ aña gel çık imdi tenden / git yāra kes iïtilāṭı menden*) (260/200).

After she recites a ghazal, Majnun indicates that he does not recognize her. He says that her eloquence refreshes his soul, that he is gladdened by her presence, that she seems familiar. He asks where she is from, by what roads she has traveled here. "If you are a poppy, from what mountain / if an iris from what garden?" (*ger lāle iseñ ne dāġdansın / v'er sūsen iseñ ne bāġdansın*) (261/202). He then ends this brief section with another ghazal, beginning:

> öyle ser-mestüm ki idrāk itmezem dünyā nedür
> men kimem sāķī olan kimdür mey ü ṣahbā nedür
> gerci cānāndan dil-i şeydā icün kām isterem
> ṣorsa cānān bilmezem kām-ı dil-i şeydā nedür (262/203)

> I am so drunk, I can no longer tell what this world is
> who I am, who the saki, what the white and red wine is
> Though I beseech the beloved for what this love-crazed heart desires
> if the beloved asks, I do not know what the love-crazed heart's desire is

Before going on to Layla's reply, which we will examine in detail below, let us look at a few of the major divergences from the Nizami addition. It is striking that there is a change in the spatiotemporal setting—what Bakhtin called the *chronotope*. The Nizami text elides any significant historical development: there is no noticeable growth or development in the lovers between the initial "falling in love" and the final "dying of love." The characters do not age. Most of the events that befall them do not have any special connection to a time sequence except to delay the inevitable conclusion. The spatial setting is similarly restricted. There is no deviation from a division into interior spaces (house/tent, Layla, family, friends) and exterior spaces (desert, Majnun, animals). This is very much a lyric chronotope, and as such it links the story to its legendary origins in the chronotope of the ʿUdhrī ghazal. In Fuzūlī's version, there is a restoration of a sense of time passing. The characters age and change. Not only does the mad Majnun not recognize his beloved, but his not-so-mad beloved does not recognize him. They are changed people in a way that is only hinted at in the Nizami addition by the new public assertiveness of the widowed Layla. In this kind of time, their last meeting occurs in a desert setting that has no interior space. There is no "Layla's tent," no retinues, no helpers, no "organizing," or ordering of space. They are simply cast loose in each other's presence.

It is also quite striking that the animals too have disappeared. The boundaries between animality and spirituality have been reabsorbed into the two individuals and are expressed more ambiguously in the inner conflict of Layla between her modesty and her desire. The dangerousness of the outside becomes the dangerousness of the inner, psychological struggle that is most manifest in Layla. In the same manner, the differences between Layla and Majnun diminish. They are both poets; they both express their love in powerful voices; they are both, in a sense, maddened and "wandering" both physically and spiritually. And there is none of the extravagant "being struck dumb" by passion. The two lovers encounter each other and sort out their identities and relations themselves without being rendered unconscious and thus being made objects of description or narration.

Returning to the story, what follows is a translation of the entire segment containing Layla's response to Majnun's request that she identify herself.

> Layla said, oh my spirit's near companion
>   desire of the entranced and wounded heart
> Good news! Destiny has granted your desire
>   filled your cup with the wine of merriment
> Good news! What you seek is divinely given
>   in the end you profited from passion
> Good news! Your wish has been attained
>   God has united you with what you seek
>
> I am Layla, object of your souls' yearning
>   desire of your forlorn and feeble heart
> Ever were you full of longing for beauty
>   ever were you needful of union
> Now that the vision has been granted you by God
>   don't be remiss and make excuses, beware!
> Consider union with me yours for the taking
>   come, be near me, don't waste the chance
> My heart is a pledge to union with your body
>   as for my life, it is given as a trust to you
> Now that it's in your power, don't be neglectful
>   come, hold what is pledged to you, take up your trust
> If you are ill, I am your physician
>   if you're a lover, I am your beloved
> Come, be a lawful guest at the feast of union
>   for a moment be my close companion
> Give luster to the narcissus with a poppy
>   adorn the lily with a fresh fragrant herb
> Make turquoise near companion of the ruby
>   make a meal for the parrot of purest candy
> Graft the red-bud to the rose
>   bring Hızır to the water of life

And if you are not an enamored lover
    if you are unwounded by grief and woe
Don't show the signs by feigning them
    don't make a disgrace of us both
Show me some idea, a sign or signal
    else shame us both before all people
Oh rose, is this not shameful for me
    that you will not be my companion?
That I present to you the sun of my cheek
    and you display no warmth in return
That I hold a cup and say come take it
    and you don't rise forthwith to your feet
I have experienced much and it seldom happens
    that a lover be coy with his beloved
That a rose display its loveliness
    and the bulbul see it and pay no heed
By some means that heart-adorning idol
    also composed a curious ghazal

(This ghazal is in the voice of Layla)

Oh you who drives me mad with love what is this disdain of me
    why is it you do not ask what is the state of this crazy heart

If you don't acknowledge me in public you are excused
    but what is it that you don't know me in the secluded places

It's easy, if you don't know how I feel and show me no compassion
    but what is it if you know my feelings and are heedless still

They call the outcries of the bulbul a salute to the rose
    but what is this outcry, when he sees the rose and feels no attraction

That fairy surely pays no respect to avoiding shame
    oh Fuzūlī, I do not know, what is the fault in avoiding shame
(262/204-263/206)

    As this passage begins, Layla is overjoyed, as is indicated by the opening cluster of three lines all beginning *müjde,* "good news!". She displays a perhaps naive faith that things will now turn out for the best. She has prayed to God, asking that she may find her beloved and her honor be preserved. And it appears as though her prayers are answered. She finds

Majnun in the desert as if by a miracle … and now all that remains is for the two to be lawfully joined, as it seems God intended. However, from the increasing intensity of her entreaties, it becomes clear that Majnun is not responding. Finally she warns and commands him in an exasperated tone:

> Now that the vision has been granted you by God
>   don't be remiss and make excuses, beware!
> Consider union with me yours for the taking
>   come, be near me, don't waste the chance (263/204)

To Layla, he is in peril of rejecting that which God has offered him. And she, in her inability to move him, succumbs to the danger she foresaw and prayed to be delivered from—the danger that her passion would overwhelm her modesty and good sense.

What follows are four lines that seem to pick up on (and perhaps interpret) the suggestive garden imagery of a line from Layla's conversation with Zayd in the "added text:" *ham-ī"āba-ye sarv kon caman rā / dar dasta-ye lāla kaş saman rā,* ("Make the cypress bed-mate of the meadow / bind the jasmine in a bunch with the tulip") (311). We must remember that in the Nizami addition, Layla's sensuality and seductiveness are represented mostly through the description of her embraces, caresses, tender and longing glances. In Fuzūlī, however, her behavior is condensed into speech, and she makes a startling offer:

> Come, be a lawful guest at the feast of union
>   for a moment be my close companion
> Give luster to the narcissus with a poppy
>   adorn the lily with a fresh fragrant herb
> Make turquoise near companion of the ruby
>   make a meal for the parrot of purest candy
> Graft the red-bud to the rose
>   bring Hızır to the water of life (263/205)

What a contemporary audience would have made of this passage is no mystery. The word translated above as "close companion" is *hem-dem,* which more literally means "sharing breath" in the sense of coming close, face to face, lip to lip. The narcissus is Layla's yellowed eye and the poppy, Majnun's bloody red one. Her hair is a fragrant lily, his a hyacinth cascading down over hers. (Remember Layla's hair covering him like a hair shirt in the Nizami addition.) The poet, Majnun, is a parrot with a blue, turquoise beak that is brought together with her ruby lips. The parrot will eat of the lip's sweet candy enabling him to speak sugared words. The judas tree or red-bud branch, turgid with small red blossoms, is obviously phallic and its "grafting" onto the delicate folds of the rose is a graphic metaphor for sexual intercourse. As Hızır—the undying phallus—wanders in the darkness, he/it is brought to the "water of life" or the semen that creates immortal generations.

Even this stark and shockingly sexual proposal quite clearly meets with no suitable response. The "tongue-tied with passion" theme of the Nizami addition is replaced by Majnun's (off-stage) inability to respond to her increasingly urgent and, in a sense, sacrificial pleas. Finally Fuzūlī's Layla comes to the same point as the Layla of the addition, but having sacrificed her modesty to a far greater degree. In the addition (as cited above), Layla chides her lover for not speaking when any reasonable poet/lover would—and thus she keeps herself contained within the world of "poetic" expectations. In Fuzūlī, she chides him for not acting, for leaving her in the position of having abandoned her modesty (and chastity) for nothing, for having shamed her by his indifference. There is nothing ethereal or transcendent or other-worldly about her offer. Unlike the addition text, which consistently overlays a mystical interpretation from the viewpoint of an omniscient poet/narrator, in this monologue Fuzūlī's Layla speaks without outside comment, interpretation, or censure. It appears that even the mysticism of the passage has matured. It is integrated almost seamlessly with the worldly tale. The physical passion and the spiritual passion are not clearly divided by symbols into the spiritual/mystical and physical/animal; they persist naturally as two sides of the same coin. In addition, Majnun, in his response to Layla, does not censure her or accuse her of improper behavior. His refusal does not suggest that her proposal is unacceptable but only that he has degenerated to the point at which physical union is no longer possible for him.

> Majnun said, oh idol so like a fairy
>> don't set fire to this wisp of chaff
> Your image is enough to set me aflame
>> I no longer have strength for union with you (265/207)

He has arrived at a stage at which the only possible consummation is a spiritual one. Having absorbed her essence, he no longer has any need of her.

> Alas for the soul, for it is the soul
>   that pleasures in the cheek of the heart-stealer
> As for me, long since have I lost my soul
>   it is a different soul that inhabits my body
> Now the soul in my body, the light in my eye
>   the blood in my heart is all you (266/208)

As for Layla—this more mature, intelligent, and aware Layla—she does not go off defeated, frustrated, unfulfilled to die like a petulant teenager. She is fully capable of understanding what has happened to Majnun. I am aware of what has become of you, she says, and it is a good thing. "I was grief stricken and you made me glad; you set me free from love of this world" (270/212). *You made me glad.* When Fuzūlī's Layla, in the end, dies, she dies having experienced a spiritual/mystical insight similar to Majnun's. Physical existence is no longer meaningful to her, and she casts it off—not bitterly or overcome by disappointment but gladly.

In the "short version" of *Layla and Majnun,* Nizami inscribes his doubts about the story both at the beginning and the end. At the beginning his doubts and dissatisfactions with the story are articulated quite overtly, as we have indicated. At the end, the abrupt death of Layla, unmotivated except in so far as it is forced by the ʿUdhrī chronotope, also underscores the weaknesses of the inherited tale. It is our suggestion that the growth of the story, beginning with the "added text," is a consequence of Nizami's doubts and follows the trajectory that he built into his telling.

This is to say, repeating what we said earlier, that Nizami leaves his tale spectacularly incomplete. The abrupt death of Layla underscores the role of the ʿUdhrī "beloved" as merely an object, an object presented solely so that a hopeless and extravagant love can be constructed about it. As such an object, Layla can simply be discarded without substantial motivation if this is necessary to add another, final level of intensity to Majnun's already hyperbolic passion. She exists only for his passion.

But Nizami finds this story-type unsatisfactory and by foregrounding the unsatisfactory development of Layla's character in the ending of the short text, he creates an empty space for his successors to fill. Thus, by

Fuzūlī's time the possibility exists—a possibility that we believe Fuzūlī realizes spectacularly—to create a Layla who is (at least!) as complete and real a character as Majnun, whose story is intertwined with Majnun's in a way that thenceforth blends spiritual and physical love and makes them inseparable. From this point on, any lover, be it Rafet El-Roman or Eric Clapton or any man or woman in the world, mystic or no can identify with Layla and Majnun. This is Nizami's gift to humankind, reluctantly granted but the kind of seed that genius often plants even unawares.

Notes

1. Nizami, *Layla va Majnun,* Bihruz Sarvatiyan, ed. (Tehran: Intisharat-i Tus, 1364 [1986]). All quotations from Nizami will be from this text unless otherwise noted and will be cited by page number only. All English translations in this chapter are by Walter G. Andrews, who is obligated to Hadi Sultan-Qurraie for help with the translation of several passages from Nizami.
2. Agah Sırrı Levend, *Arap, Fars, ve Türk Edebiyatlarında Leyla ve Mecnun Hikâyesi* (Ankara: Türk Tarih Kurumu, 1959).
3. Levend, *Arap, Fars, ve Türk,* pp. 110-11.
4. All quotations from Nevāyī are from the edition of Ulku Çelik, ed., *Alī-şīr Nevāyī Leylī vü Mecnūn* (Ankara: Atatürk Kültür, Dil ve Tarih Yüksek Kurumu, 1996). Citations are by page number in this edition.
5. All quotations from Fuzūlī's *Layla and Majnun* will be taken from the texts of Hamid Araslı, *Leylā vü Mecnūn* (Baku, 1958) and Fuzuli, *Leyla ile Mecnun,* Necmettin Halil Onan, ed. (Istanbul: Maarif Basımevi, 1956). Citations will be given by page number from both texts in the form (Onan/Araslı).
6. Kenan Akyüz, Süheyl Beken, Sedit Yüksel, Müjgan Cumbur, eds., *Fuzūlī, Divanı* (Ankara: Akcağ Yayınları, 1990), p. 306.
7. See, Ali Nihat Tarlan, *Fuzuli Divanı Şerhi III* (Ankara: Kültür ve Turizm Bakanlığı Yayınları, 1985), p. 186.
8. Behcet Necatigil, "Sevda Peşinde," (originally published in a collection called *Kapalı Çarşı) Bütün Eserleri: Şiirler 1938–1958* (Istanbul, 1995), p. 42.
9. Orhan Gencebay, *Leyla ile Mecnun,* Kefvan Plak_ılık, Istanbul, n.d.
10. Rafet El-Roman, *Bah Ueşehir Magazin* No. 11 (Spring 1996), p. 25.
11. Vahid Dastgirdi, ed., *Namah-i Layli va Majnun Nizami Ganjavi* (Tehran: Muassasah-i Matbuat-i Ilmi, 1972). Levend, *Arap, Fars, ve Türk.*
12. Rudolf Gelpke, ed. and trans., *The Story of Layla and Majnun* (Oxford: Cassimer, 1966). A. N. Tarlan, ed. and trans., *Fuzuli: Leyla ile Mecnun* (Istanbul: M. E. B. Şark-İslam Klâsikleri, 1943).
13. Robert Dankoff, "The Lyric in the Romance: The Use of Ghazals in Persian and Turkish Mas̱navīs," *JNES* 43:1 (1984), pp. 9-25.

Chapter 3

Nizami's Unlikely Heroines: A Study of the Characterizations of Women in Classical Persian Literature

Kamran Talattof

Women are featured in the works of three major classical Persian poets, Nizami Ganjavi (1140-1202), Abul al-Qasim Firdawsi (932-1020), and Abd al-Rahman Jami (1414-92). These poets' portrayals of their female characters vary considerably; however, because all three have written love stories, it is possible to compare them. Certain stories are common to at least two of these authors. Their stories include common characters, often based on historical figures. Moreover, Nizami was inspired by Firdawsi in a significant way and refers to his work, while Jami was inspired by Nizami and refers to him. Perhaps for these reasons, prominent scholars of classical Persian literature, including Meisami, Bürgel, and Moayyad, have compared some of these female characters. The existing literature on the topic, however, does not provide reasons for such diverse characterizations, but merely offers engaging descriptive analyses. This comparative study of the portrayals of women will seek to clarify the ambiguity surrounding the ideological and literary positions of these poets to explain the diversity in their presentations of the female. Such clarification carries broad significance, for in postrevolutionary Iran, the interpretation of these poets' works has become the subject of intense debate among cultural and literary critics, many of whom are widely divided over Islamic discourse and state ideology. Although Nizami's work has always been subject to a variety of opposing readings in Iran, these differences have become political in recent years. Encouraged by the ruling elite, advocates of the state ideology use these poets' works to further their own ideological objectives. An analysis of their portrayals of women shows that the three poets do not belong to the same ideological paradigm, and that religious interpretations limit the understanding of their literary significance.

Nizami's work, in particular, has been the subject of notably contradictory readings. While Muslim scholar A. A. Sa'idi Sirjani has read Nizami's works from a non-ideological point of view, a host of other Muslim critics offer merely religious readings of the poet's work. Such varying approaches have produced highly diverse images of the poet's beliefs and attitudes. For example, Sa'idi Sirjani, pointing to Nizami's positive portrayals of characters such as Shirin and Layli [Layla], presents the poet as progressive and culturally liberated, especially in regard to women's issues.[1] But Sarvatiyan, a prolific scholar bringing a peculiar Islamic point of view to the poet's work, claims that the writer promoted the Islamic *hijab* (veiling of women) and implies that Nizami's female characters do not necessarily represent women but are rather symbols, codes, and secrets that often carry religious meanings.[2] Sarvatiyan also states that Nizami has portrayed human nature and sensuality as deceitful procurers, and wisdom as a wealthy world traveler.[3] Sarvatiyan's conviction is most probably based on a story in the *Iskandar Nameh* (*The Book of Alexander*) in which Alexander tries to convince the women of the city of Qifchaq to wear the veil. However, in addition to all the historical inconsistencies and ambiguities that mark this last work of Nizami, as Jalal Matini states, Nizami's voice in this story is neutral and stops short of corroborating Iskandar's views.[4] Moreover, he disregards the fact that even in the *Iskandar Nameh,* women are portrayed as free members of society who participate in all sorts of activities. They play music, fight on the battlefield, and provide deep insight into social and philosophical issues. As with Sarvatiyan, Fatimah Alaqih offers a traditional interpretation of women's roles in Nizami's writings when, in a critique of *Khusraw and Shirin,* she concludes that Shirin appears in the story simply to exalt the spirit of Farhad, a male character deeply in love with her.[5] Alaqih disregards the central significance of Shirin in the story and the fact that in his narrative Nizami often disassociates himself from characters who struggle with virtues. Alaqih's interpretation of women in Nizami's works stems from her belief that women in gnostic lyric poetry form the basis for the ascension of gnostic men's spirits.[6] In general, these interpretations display the problematics of the discourse on sexuality in Iran, as the interpreters try to disassociate Nizami from this aspect of human activity. Nizami, as a Muslim poet, did render religious themes, but postrevolutionary religious critics attempt to portray those themes according to the exigencies of their own time.

I maintain that Nizami, reflecting on human love, offers a favorable and consistent concept of love and its diverse forms in his presentation of female characters. He portrays these characters in their roles as lovers, heroines, rulers, and even educators and challengers of men, as he places them in a variety of contexts. Given the patriarchal nature of twelfth-century Iranian society, such a portrayal of women seems anachronistic, unlikely, and puzzling. Comparing Nizami's characterization of women with that of Firdawsi, who wrote approximately two centuries before him, and Jami, who appeared approximately three centuries after him, will further illustrate Nizami's unique position. Although these and many other classical poets, as Meisami asserts, may in one way or another address themes in their love stories such as self-knowledge, ethics, and the protagonist's suitability as a lover and king, they differ in the way they characterize women.[7] Firdawsi seems to follow the logic and necessities of epic writing in his characterization of women, and female characters are not, therefore, the focus of the stories in the *Shahnameh* (*The Book of Kings*). The women in Firdawsi's work are described in terms of their relationship to the heroes. Jami, embracing the dominant traditional culture, portrays women in a highly negative, unflattering manner.[8] In his work, homosexual love, relatively common in certain Sufi expressions, overshadows his characterization of women. I have no quarrel with either those who view the artistic and historical importance of Firdawsi's work as equal or superior to Nizami's or those who feel that Jami's work is sufficiently significant to count him as one of the great Persian poets of the classical period. This is all true. My contention relates to the relevance of the characterization of women to the genres and discursive contexts of the three poets. And such an approach is especially problematic when a distinction should made between women in Jami's allegorical work and the notion of women presented by orthodox Islam.

Nizami was born in Ganja, now in the Republic of Azerbayjan. He received an excellent education in several branches of science and learning. Women, love, and relations between men and women are among his major themes. Through his treatment of such themes, he brings a progressive and humanist approach to the characterizations of Shirin from *Khusraw va Shirin* (*Khusraw and Shirin,* 1180), the female characters in *Haft Paykar* (*The Seven Beauties,* 1197), and Layli from *Layli va Majnun* (*Layli and Majnun,* 1188). Aware of the position of women in pre-Islamic Iran and the cultural context of his own time, Nizami demonstrates familiarity with the psychological aspects of women's experience.

Khusraw and Shirin and *The Seven Beauties* portray several women in pre-Islamic society while *Layli and Majnun* presents a woman within the social context of the early Islamic period.

Khusraw and Shirin recounts the love between the Sasanid King Khusraw Parviz (590-628) and the Armenian, or possibly Zoroastrian, Shirin. It is a complicated story. Shirin, an affectionate, strong, and honest woman, plays polo, goes on picnics with her maids, and swims naked in ponds. She hears about Khusraw, sees his picture, falls in love with him, and rides to the capital, Mada'in, without an escort, to meet him. She discovers that Khusraw is an irresolute and inadequate person and challenges him, attempting to make a responsible and caring man of him. Many years go by, and Khusraw changes to some extent. After they marry, she continues to ascend morally and spiritually by good deeds and thoughts, both of which are basic principles of Zoroastrianism. When Shiruyeh kills Khusraw and tries to marry Shirin, she commits suicide.[9] Throughout the story, Nizami portrays Shirin with affection. He shows enormous sensitivity to the happy and tragic aspects of her life. Some scholars believe that Shirin, in fact, represents Nizami's wife, Afaq.[10] However, he portrays other women in the story as equal, and in some cases superior, to men—capable even of ruling a country. As we shall see, Nizami's sympathetic portrayal of Shirin as affectionate, strong, and straightforward can be better appreciated by contrasting it with Firdawsi's version of the story, in the *Book of Kings,* in which Shirin is assigned negative characteristics.[11]

The characterization of each woman in *The Seven Beauties* also highlights Nizami's unique, humanistic, and eloquent representation of women.[12] The "frame story" of the book revolves around the Sasanid king Bahram, and includes seven stories told to the king by seven princesses of seven climes on each of the seven days of the week, and in seven different beautiful and colorful domes.[13] Each tale describes fulfilled or thwarted love. The Slavic princess tells of a beautiful, wise, and learned king's daughter who concludes that no ordinary man deserves to be her husband.[14] Suitors wishing to gain this princess's hand in marriage, however, encircle the castle, and she tires of rejecting them. Frustrated, she moves to a strong fortress on a high mountain pushing its head into the clouds, where she can dwell and be spared the great plague of burdensome suitors. She arms the castle with numerous talismans to keep away men of inferior intelligence. Any man able to navigate the deadly traps and find the castle entrance will be made to answer four riddles to discover whether he is worthy of her love. Such a man must therefore be of noble lineage, brave, strong, sufficiently cunning to disarm the talismans and find the entrance, and clever enough to solve the riddles.

Suitors try to reach the castle but fail and lose their lives. One young prince comprehends the vast amount of knowledge needed to win the princess. He goes away to study and learn the necessary skills and wisdom. After a long journey, he returns, successfully enters the fortress, and solves the riddles. The princess finds him worthy of marriage. They make love:

> gāh rokh buseh dād o gāh labash
> gāh nārash gazid o gāh rotabash[15]

> Now he kissed her cheek, at times her lips. Sometimes he tasted
> her pomegranates [her breasts], and sometimes her dates [her lips].

The princess is an admirable character—beautiful, wise, knowledgeable in the sciences, and discriminating in the choice of a husband. Even the way she speaks to her father reflects confidence in her abilities: "Dearest Father, forgive me, but I must leave you. Provide me with provisions for travel."[16] Rarely in stories of the same period did daughters have the tenacity, let alone the resources, to reject a system in which patriarchs arranged women's marriages. The princess's search for wisdom in both herself and her husband forces a comparison with men who act without thinking. Nizami further demonstrates their inferiority by presenting the princess's ultimate victory. Furthermore, the concluding love scene nullifies any notion that Nizami's metaphors represent religious symbols and refutes the claim that Nizami's story describes a metaphorical union between God and humankind, as traditional interpretations suggest. This scene does not support Jafari's notion that love in Nizami's work is directed to God, nor does it bear out Sarvatiyan's statement that Nizami's female characters represent not real women but symbols, codes, and secrets, often carrying religious meaning.[17] Although Nizami uses a good number of metaphors to refer to the female body, "cheek" and "lips" are too literal, and pomegranates too obvious, to be dismissed as just symbols.

In the story told by "the Persian princess," a group of women feast and drink in a garden. Two who are responsible for guarding the area during the party capture a young man trying to enter the garden through a breach in the creek. They discover that he owns the garden and that the party is taking place without his knowledge. The women allow the garden's owner to enter, and he sits in a hidden corner, watching the group as they revel and play music. One girl discovers the man's presence and becomes interested in him. They fall in love and attempt several times to make love, but without success. The party ends, and the girl's father and others later find out about the incident. However, the women are not punished or accused of wrongdoing. Some, in fact, seem to understand the passionate girl and her desire. The girl is not contrite and feels no reluctance or restriction in talking about herself, her feelings, or her ill-fated attempts to make love with the man. In the concluding scene, the community helps the young couple marry.[18] Although Nizami explains the necessity of marriage for legal intercourse, he again represents female desire, even outside wedlock, as neither sinful nor blasphemous. Because they describe their inner feelings, the female figures are more expressive, eclipsing the male characters. Such portrayals of women and the centrality of their roles lend the poet's work an anachronistically modern quality, as his contemporaries do not share such an approach.

Yet another story from *The Seven Beauties,* entitled "Dastan-i Bahram ba Kanizak-i Khish" ("The Story of Bahram with His Slave-Girl"), features a female character named Fetneh, who rejects traditional, patriarchal customs. Like Shirin, Fetneh, one of King Bahram's slaves, is also present in Firdawsi's *Book of Kings,* where, as will be seen later in more detail, she appeared in a radically different light. The differing treatments of this character by Nizami and Firdawsi reflect fundamental differences in their genres and portrayal of sexuality.

In Nizami's version of the story of King Bahram's slave-girl, the woman is renamed Fetneh (meaning revolt or sedition) from Azadeh (meaning free or noble), her name in Firdawsi's version.[19] Fetneh rebels resolutely against the traditions and institutions of King Bahram's court: hunting does not impress her, so she repudiates a cherished court custom. She then uses her wits to stay alive and challenge the king's beliefs.

Fetneh has the opportunity to accompany the king on one of his ceremonial hunting trips to witness the great skill with which he kills his prey. She avoids praising the king's hunting skills. Then she downplays the king's amazing performance in hunting an onager, stating that it only takes practice to shoot the animal so skillfully, and that she really does not consider it an art. The king is filled with rage and asks one of his army commanders to kill her. Fetneh reasons with the officer, persuading him to spare her life so that if the king later regrets his harshness, the officer will not be in trouble. The commander sends her to a faraway place where, as part of her work, she carries a calf on her shoulder up sixty stairs to the palace roof every day. Because of this, she becomes so strong that she is able to carry the animal even after it is a fully-grown ox. Meanwhile, Bahram remains under the sad impression that Fetneh was executed. One day, however, he visits the palace and sees her carrying the ox. He tells her that with practice, everything is possible. Fetneh reveals her identity. He is happy that she is still alive and apologizes to her. Fetneh in turn apologizes and attempts to justify her comments on the hunting trip. Nizami's Bahram is wise enough to see that Fetneh was right; by marrying her, he acknowledges her superior wisdom.

Nizami wrote during a period when women were strongly believed to be impaired in intelligence (*nāqes ul-aql*). His humanistic approach to rhetoric and his understanding of women as equals sets him apart from the dominant literary discourse of his time. In fact, Bürgel and Meisami have also pointed to Firdawsi's and Nizami's differing portrayals of this character as a means of underscoring their contentions about Nizami's work and personality. Bürgel states that "seldom is the humanism of Nizami more palpable than in the alterations he made in this story."[20] Meisami states that "the story is paradigmatic, demonstrating Nizami's conception of his poetic task and his specific intent in *The Seven Beauties,* displaying the devices used to achieve his ends, and clarifying both his relationship to his surfaces and his departure from the epic tradition embodied in Firdawsi's (ca. 1010) *Book of Kings,* on the heroic values of which both this episode and the poem as a whole provide a commentary."[21] In general, Meisami's study sheds light on the moral seriousness of romance and on the integration of literary elements in Nizami's poetry.[22]

In Nizami's tragic romance, *Layli and Majnun,* Layli's father removes her from school to prevent her from seeing her childhood love, Majnun, originally named Qays until he goes mad (*majnun*). He later forbids her to think of Majnun and gives her hand in marriage to an older man, Ibn-al-Salam. Majnun goes mad and wanders in the desert, living with wild animals. During the lovers' separation, Majnun's parents and Abd al-Salam die, but the situation does not improve. Finally, after a miserable life, Layli dies while speaking about Majnun to her mother. Upon receiving news of her death, Majnun goes to Layli's tomb and dies there.

Nizami illustrates how social restrictions prevent Layli from speaking out. Throughout the tale, we hear little from Layli directly because she has no one to trust and is afraid to reveal her love for Majnun to others. She hides her pain, even from her parents, to avoid disgracing her tribe. So she suffers, laments, and finally dies completely unfulfilled. Layli is correct in believing that she would damage her family by disobeying tradition, which holds that love outside marriage, or even marriage not arranged, constitutes a sin. Yet Layli's last words to her mother reveal not only her love for Majnun but also her condemnation of those cultural restrictions. In her confession to her mother, she states, "I am dying because this is not a life." It is a critical indication of the emotional deprivation enforced by the cultural constraints of that time.

Even under such miserable conditions, Layli does not submit to her fate easily; in fact, she resists vehemently.[23] She shows more emotional fortitude than Majnun, for she complains less about her own misfortune. She writes a letter to Majnun and suggests plans to escape with him.[24] She condoles Majnun when his father dies. She writes to Majnun about their love and their circumstances. This letter demonstrates Layli's superior strength; unlike Majnun, whose behavior demonstrates his surrender, she suffers as much pain or more, yet continues to function within society and bravely refuses sexual intercourse with her husband. The letter, written in the form of an elegy, also shows Nizami's empathy for Layli. Although she is not as outspoken as Nizami's other female characters, she is portrayed as a victim of the traditional culture and a prisoner of male dominated society, making Nizami's characterization of Layli as impressive as his characterizations of other women.

Nizami approaches the subject of sex in keeping with the settings of his stories, which he actually refers to occasionally as *Havas Nameh*, (*The Book of Passion* [*or Lust*]). In the stories of Shirin and the characters of *The Seven Beauties*, set in more open societies, Nizami explores the complexities of this subject. He avoids sexuality in the story of Layli, because in her conservative society she was deprived of any realization of her sexual self, and therefore no lovemaking scene is described and no words of passion with sexual connotations are exchanged between the lovers.

We hear little direct testimony from Layli because, as Nizami mentions in introductory verses, the social context gives him little room to describe her appearance. The way he describes Layli is different from the way he describes his ideal protagonist, Shirin. Nizami wrote *Layli and Majnun* reluctantly, on the court's command and not by his own choice.[25] He had to elaborate about how after the conquest of Iran by Islam, the season for earthly love was gradually lost to the desire for repentance and salvation. In *Layli and Majnun,* he criticizes a society steeped in tradition. Despite the lack of desirable context, he weaves another artistic love story, portraying a deprived Layli, deeply in love, who has no choice but to surrender, yet she passively resists. She does not completely give in to her fate. She never submits to the husband she does not love, although Islam stipulates that a wife must yield to the husband's sexual demands. On one occasion, she even punches her husband, knocking him down. In that society, the perception of love was different from that which Nizami portrayed in *Khusraw and Shirin* and *The Seven Beauties*. In these works, in the context of what he presents as pre-Islamic open society, men and women seem to be more equal, and women have the right to enjoy life, love, and sex. He selectively promotes personal and cultural freedom in both works.[26]

Nizami's liberal portrayal of sexuality is also demonstrated through the use of metaphors for male–female relationships, carnal love, and men's and women's sexual organs. In *The Seven Beauties,* he refers to women's genitals as *ganj* (treasure), *ganj-e dor* (treasure of pearl[s]), *ganj-e gohar* (treasure of gem[s]), *khazineh* (treasury), *ganj-e qand* (treasury of sugar), and *dorj-e qand* (jewel box of sugar).[27] He also refers to the hymen and virginity as the *kan-e la'l* (mine of rubies), *dar-e ganjkhaneh* (treasure house door), *qufl-e zarrin* (golden lock), *mohr-e gohar* (jewel seal), and *mohr* (seal). Regardless of his occasional resorting to a male-constructed notion of virginity, these references to love and sex do not specifically denote any particular Sufi trend. Interestingly, they are entirely ignored in Sufi or religious interpretations.

How may such openness and progressive characterization be explained? And if Sufism did not provide the driving force for Nizami, what inspired him throughout his career and what links his diverse works in *Five Treasures?* Bürgel's contention—that Nizami was concerned with promoting humanistic values—contributes to an understanding of the diversity and depth of the poet's work.[28] However, I believe that Nizami shows sensitivity to a variety of social and cultural issues. Living in a multicultural society, he made use of a unique opportunity to embed elements that elevate in his works: universality of human experience, tolerance, and lessons from history. Equally important, I argue that Nizami was preoccupied with more than issues of jurisprudence, or any other Islamic concerns, but with the art of speech itself. For him, this art was the sublime. These characteristics explain why a Marxist, a Zoroastrian, a feminist, and a Muslim theologian may all find ideologi-cal interest there. It is because his work is art before anything else. Nizami's language is not faithful to matters of fact, as is most evident in *The Book of Alexander,* for example, where he brings together in one room Alexander, Plato, Balinas, Socrates, Thales, Hermes, and Aristotle. His interests influenced his language as they developed throughout different periods of his life. And this influence is precisely what makes him a distinct rhetorician, far from an ideologue, boasting that he could have written *Layli and Majnun* in fourteen nights instead of four months.

Of all these issues, however, he devotes his *sokhan* (eloquent rhetoric) particularly to love and women in his poetry. His education, his liberal position on social issues, his vast knowledge of diverse societies, and his personal experiences lead him to present progressive views of women. And in presenting this liberal interpretation of love and of women's social roles, he subverts the dichotomy of love and morality. He celebrates the union of good and happiness: to be good does not mean to suppress passion. In accomplishing these ideas, he has benefited from a strong imagination and wealth of metaphors. These aspects have influenced poets after him and distinguish his work from that of Sana'i and Firdawsi, who to a limited degree influenced him.[29]

Nizami's preoccupation with *sokhan* and his desire to perfect it led him to read, to speculate, and to acquire knowledge of other cultures and religions. He deals with a variety of themes and motives; however, the concept of *sokhan* (pronounced *sakhon* or *sokhon* in the classical period) recurs throughout his work. *Sokhan* literally means "speech," "words," or "discourse." Dabashi stresses the importance of language and the concept of *sokhan* in Nizami's work, believing that these provided Nizami with an identity.[30] He states that for Nizami, being is conceived by *sokhan*, which is used "not only to convey the meaning but also the creation."[31] I would like to think that *sokhan* has a rather broader meaning and implication for Nizami, that *sokhan* could be conceptualized as eloquent rhetoric (always expressed in the form of poetry) in his overall literary discourse. His books include more than one hundred verses that begin with this word, and many more contain it. In addition, his poetry is replete with derivatives, such as *sokhandan* or *sokhanvar,* meaning a person who demonstrates an oratorical, eloquent, and poetic manner when writing or speaking, and compound words such as *sokhan afarin, sokhan parvar, sokhan ravan, sokhan shinas, sokhan gostar,* all meaning an eloquent rhetorician who values words, an excellent writer or orator. Nizami holds a high opinion of *sokhan,* particularly in its poetic forms, and considers poets to be creative artists of nearly divine status.

Because *sokhan* is so important to him, Nizami assigns the poet a high status in *Layli and Majnun,* as well. He ranks his verses with the Quran, an ambitious aspiration for his time, particularly as such a claim stands against Islamic belief that the Quran could not and cannot be written or imitated by a human being. In *The Book of Honor,* he compares himself with kings. In *The Book of Happiness,* he considers himself a great poet, imitated by others.

Moreover, Nizami offers a liberal understanding of Islamic discourse that does not limit his learning from other cultures. His impressions and his love for the Prophet as expressed, for example, in *Layli and Majnun,* are mingled with his other cultural impressions. Departing from a Manichaeist or Zoroastrian dichotomy of good versus evil, he subverts the prevalent dichotomy of love and morality by presenting both as good. In his view, to be a good rhetorician required flexibility, sensibility, and responsiveness to a given situation. Nizami's interest in ancient Iranian culture and in philosophy, and his peculiar interpretation of Zoroastrian teachings as illustrated above, may further explain his liberal approach to women and sexuality. Indeed, his understanding of these teachings was more philosophical and therefore different from their idealization by many authors of books of kings in preceding centuries, especially in books written about the history of kingdoms in Iran. Moscati describes ancient Iranian civilization as follows:

> [T]he function of ancient Iranian civilization is principally historical and religious in its nature. In the historical field, the tolerant liberalism which combines different people into an harmonious empire has repercussions incalculable in their extent upon the maintenance of civilization. ... In the religious field Zarathustra's teaching achieves the highest point of ancient oriental intellectualism. In his conception of the universe, the forces of logic are already active. The one task remaining is to give them their own autonomous life.[32]

Dustkhah states that in Zoroastrianism, according to the god Ahuramazda, the female angel Anahita is equal to the male Mehr, and woman is an equal companion of man. In fact, in the Zoroastrian religious text, *Gathas,* Zoroaster lets his daughter, Puruchist, decide who should become her husband.[33] We hear an echo of this in a verse from Yasna 53, "I tell these words to these girls who are being married and to you."[34] Thus, both women and men are addressed in scripture equally. We hear an echo of these influences in Nizami's writing.

Nizami refers to this ancient culture frequently. Even in *Makhzan al Asrar* (*The Treasure House of Mysteries,* 1163), he calls upon the Prophet, "*Su-ye Ajam rān, maneshin dar arab / zardeh-ye ruz inak o shabdiz-e shab* (Do not stay in Arab land, come to Iran / here are the light and dark steeds of night and day)."[35] Indeed, one of his friends criticized him for reviving Zoroastrianism by writing *Khusraw and Shirin.* Instead of answering the critique, Nizami read some of the verses to his friend and made him praise the poet for the beauty of the poem. This is probably a hint from Nizami himself as to how he expected his poetry to be read.

Once again, I would like to mention that the dichotomy of good versus evil is a major theme in his works and sometimes constitutes the only theme, as in the section of *The Seven Beauties* entitled "Khayr va Shar" (The Virtuous and the Evil), which may help explain Nizami's underlying philosophical beliefs.[36] He contends with the concept of good versus evil as he portrays the evolution of characters such as King Khusraw or the warrior Alexander from their youth. Bürgel states that as the characters mature and gain knowledge and experience, they begin to show a desire for goodness. Nizami may have derived this binary pattern and epistemological element from Zoroastrian dualism. His positive characters always seek to ascend, cognizant of philosophy and sometimes of prophecy.

Therefore, the poet's acceptance of the concept of duality leads for example to the portrayal of Shirin as a good Armenian and virtuous Muslim at the same time. Or it enriches his writing when he talks about himself as half *serkeh* and half *angabin*.[37] Another binary opposition surfaces in Nizami's description of his own destiny. In *Iskandar-Nameh* (*The Book of Alexander*, 1200) he writes about how he explores new artistic areas:

> beh har moddati gardesh-i ruzegār
> ze tarze degar khāvhad āmuzegār
> sar āhang-e pishineh kaj ro konad
> navā'i degar dar jahān no konad
> be bāzi dar āyad cho bāzigari
> ze pardeh borun āvarad paykari
> bedān paykar az rāh-e afsungari
> konad modatti khalq rā delbari
> cho piri dar ān paykar ārad shekast
> javān paykari digar ārad be dast[38]

> With each turning of the wheel of Time,
> the teacher wants it a different way.
> He makes the previous opening of the song go a different way,
> and the song is renewed in the world.
> When the players begin the game,
> another figure will appear from behind the curtain.
> With that figure, in a magical way,
> he will steal peoples' hearts for a time.
> When that old figure becomes decrepit,
> a young figure will appear.

Through dichotomies, Nizami presents his protagonists as constantly working to improve their attitude. As honest, combative individuals, the female characters are more successful in expeditions and as they attempt to amend themselves, provide a model for the dishonest men.[39]

His sensitivity may also derive from his experiences of being in love and married three times. In *The Book of Alexander,* Nizami gives a chronology of his life and the deaths of his wives. Writing stories, he says, is pleasurable, although sometimes difficult, and can ease his sorrow. This again attests to the importance of women in his life.

> ma rā lāle'i torfeh hast az sokhan / keh chun no konam dāstān-e kohan
> dar ān 'id kān shekkar afshān konam / 'arus-e shekar - khand qorbān konam
> cho halvā-ye Shirin hami sākhtam / ze halvāgari khāneh pardākhtam
> cho bar ganj-e Layli kishidam hesār / degar gohari kardam angah nesār
> konun niz chun shod arusi besar / beh rezvān sepordam 'arusi degar
> nadānam keh bā dāgh-e chandin 'arus / cheh guneh konam qesseh-e rum o rus
> beh ar nāram anduh-e pishineh pish / bedin dāstan khosh konam vaqt-e khish[40]

I have a strange destiny in speech
whenever I write an old story anew.
In that celebration when I pour the sugar,
I lose a sweet, smiling bride.
When I made the *halva* of Shirin
I had to give away the *halva* in my house.
When I enclosed the treasure of Layli,
I gave away another jewel.
Now that the wedding is over,
I give another bride to Paradise.
With my grief for each bride, I don't know
how I can write the story of Byzantinum (Rome) and Mordvins (Russia).
It is better that I not recall this past sorrow
so that I can enjoy myself with this story.

According to his chronology, he lost his wife Afaq as he wrote the story of Shirin, his second wife when he completed Layli's story, and then he lost his last wife. The deaths of his wives signify important turning points coinciding with the completion of one work and the start of another. The above passage ties together four major aspects of Nizami's life: his cultural knowledge, the beloved women in his private life, the cherished female figures in his fiction, and *sokhan*. His celebration of the creation of Shirin turns into lamentation over the death of his first wife, Afaq. The pattern repeats two more times, and yet he continues to seek a remedy for his grief in his art: *sokhan.*

Firdawsi is known for his monumental epic poem, the *Shahnameh* (*The Book of Kings*), which consists of some fifty thousand couplets. This book is a literary representation of ancient Iran and its dynasties. Based on material from mythical, heroic, and historical periods of Iranian history, Firdawsi's *Book of Kings* presents a mixture of epic and love stories, versified in lucid language that uses nearly exclusively Persian words. Women constitute about one fifth of the characters in Firdawsi's *Book of Kings.*[41] Presented as lovers, wives, servants, and even brave warriors, these characters are fully developed, with beauty, coquettishness, and kindness. They are compared to the sun, stars, gardens, flowers, trees, and idols.

However, these women do not figure as importantly as male heroes and always occupy peripheral roles. Moreover, some characters such as Sudabeh, Zanbandavi, and Malikhah are portrayed as villainous, impetuous, or at best, hypocritical.[42] Even positive female characters such as Sindukht, Rudabeh, Tahmineh, Farangis, Jarireh, Manizheh, Gordafarid, Katayun, Gurdieh, Shirin, and Rushanak are either beguiling and fallible, or are good only because they act like men. This does not mean that Firdawsi's book is antifemale. Nor does it mean that the poet practiced male dominance in his personal life. As is evident in the book, he benefited from his wife's cooperation in the versification of the stories. Moreover, as mentioned before, his female characters are certainly more memorable than those described in the sources Firdawsi used. It simply means that because of the nature of epic writing, allegorization of these women serves the purpose of mere symbolic glorification of the men who possess them. Such glorification of the possession of women is characteristic of most epics. The epic, a long narrative poem recounting glorious heroic deeds of national heroes, deals with myths, heroic legends, history, religious tales, and edifying morals. As with Firdawsi's book, such legendary narratives gained central importance during a time when nations had to struggle for a national identity. Indeed, during a critical period following the Muslim conquest of Iran, several authors such as Daqiqi, Moayyad Balkhi, Ahmad Balkhi, Mansur Razzaq, and Asadi Tusi wrote their own versions of *The Book of Kings* or similar books. It was a time when small dynasties tried to link their lineage to the great pre-Islamic dynasties.[43] A main function of this genre was to glorify the past and thereby present an ideal model of a heroic society. In such a genre, women are present to preserve the heroic lineage, to be abducted by the victorious force, or to be recovered by the heroic men of their family. This perhaps explains the difference between Nizami's understanding of Zoroastrian teachings, as least as regards women, from that of Firdawsi. In any case, the women close to the heroes are portrayed as sublime and superior models in beauty and servitude to their men.[44]

Additional evidence suggests that this characterization of women is dictated by the genre of *The Book of Kings*. The love scenes and lyrics that embellish the book show Firdawsi's loyalty to his sources. As Meisami has noted, Firdawsi himself acknowledges the "truthfulness of his presentation."[45] The book is based for the most part on a prose *Shahnameh* that was itself based on a translation of the Middle Persian history of the kings of Persia, *Khvatay Namak* (*The Book of Kings*). Before Firdawsi, another poet, Daqiqi, had versified this history but because of his early death he finished merely 1,000 verses. Firdawsi's perception of his sources is not, however, as creative as Nizami's. Disparaging remarks about women are common, although nonheroic characters such as the King of Yaman, King of Hamavaran, or Afrasiyab express them. Such expressions are rare in Nizami's work. By allowing these men to speak, Firdawsi remains faithful to his art. He creates a masterpiece from the historical documents in his possession.[46]

Moreover, in Firdawsi's stories, in contrast to Nizami's, women more often fall in love with men first. The reason for this might well be that the male hero must remain as "righteous" as possible. Each of these love stories functions as an introduction to an epic in which the real themes are birth, life, battles, or the death of a hero. The "Rudabeh and Zal" love story, for example, is an introduction to Rostam's birth. And of course, in terms of its historical and fictional significance, the birth of Rostam is not comparable to Rudabeh's love experience. She is only a peripheral character, a good example of many such characters. Tahmineh's expression of love for Rostam functions as an introduction to the birth of Sohrab, another significant highlight of the epic. Love acts only as a catalyst for tragedies, and women do not play an essential role. Such a subordinate role for women is not only apparent in a structural and thematic sense but is also often expressed in verses such as "*zānan rā bovad bas hamin yek honar / nashinand o zāyand shirān-e nar* (For women, it is enough to have just one art, To sit down and give birth to male lions)."

Tahmineh, who serves the tragic story by giving birth to the hero, exemplifies such female characters. Rostam spends a night at the court of Samangan. There, Tahmineh, who had fallen in love with Rostam based on rumors about him, attempts to seduce him so that she can have his child: "*Va digar keh az to magar kerdegār / neshānad yeki kudakam dar kenār*" (Further, perhaps The creator / would place your child in my womb).[47] Rostam is amazed by her beauty and spends a night with her and she gives birth to Sohrab. He grows into a strong and brave man and is killed mistakenly by his father in a long, tragic battle. Tahmineh's assertions therefore only serves the purpose of setting up the tragedy of Rostam and Sohrab. The fact that she initiated sex is inconsequential. Once the child is born, she all but vanishes. Her goodness is assured because, as Firdawsi's Shirin says, "a good woman gives birth to a boy."[48]

Quite unlike Nizami's portrayal of the same character, Firdawsi's Shirin is delinquent and weak as well. In *The Book of Kings,* she appears on Khusraw's way to remind him of their former love in order to manipulate him. He is portrayed as morally weak, promiscuous, and responsible for the death of innocent people. Shirin, now Khusraw's lover, poisons Maryam—the king's princess—out of jealousy. Shiruyeh, Maryam's son, appears justified in berating Shirin now as a murderer:

> hameh jādu'i dāni o bad kho'i
> beh Iran gonahkār tar kas to'i

> you only know witchcraft and bad behavior
> you are the most sinful person in Iran

Shirin defends herself and denies any wrongdoing, including the poisoning of Maryam. With some flattering moves, she persuades Shiruyeh (now king after the death of Khusraw) to think better of her.

Azadeh, one of King Bahram's female slaves, is a beautiful harpist who accompanies Bahram on a hunting trip. Bahram, the good hunter, shoots two gazelles very skillfully in the way Azadeh had requested. However, instead of praising the king's skill, she criticizes him for hurting the poor animal. Bahram kills her brutally under his camel's hooves and seems to be justified because she challenged his authority. He concludes that he should never have taken a slave girl on a hunting trip. Meisami aptly indicates that Firdawsi's includes this story to epitomize his epical and heroic values, such as brevity and hunting skill, and for this reason the description of Azadeh's story is short.[49] As can be seen, Nizami's departure from Firdawsi's depiction of this woman is radical. For Nizami, the story of Fetneh is, in Meisami's words, "an emblem of the larger cosmic circle, symbol of the forces of wisdom, justice, and love that maintain the order and harmony of that circle."[50]

Among all these figures, Sudabeh may well represent the first evil female character. Not confined to this story alone, she embodies all "beguiling women," drawing on the trope of women's guile in classical Persian tales. She is the daughter of the king of Hamāvarān, who decides to throw off the yoke of Persia. Kay Kavus, the Iranian king, attacks the unruly Hamāvarān region and captures it. He takes Sudabeh, intending to bring her back to Iran to marry her as tribute and to guarantee peace between the two countries. Bitter over the defeat, Hamāvarān's king conspires to imprison Kay Kavus. Sudabeh remains loyal to her husband and accompanies him into prison until Rostam, the book's foremost hero, saves them. Several years later, Sudabeh falls in love with her stepson, Siyavosh, a handsome, artful, and popular man, the product of the king's casual sex with another woman. She unsuccessfully tries to trick Siyavosh into sleeping with her by seduction and threats, and even attempts to marry off one of her daughters to him to provide further opportunities. However, the good Siyavosh abstains and does not deviate from the righteous path. Finally, she desperately besieges him. "*Sarash rā tang begreft o yek pusheh chak / bedād o nabud agah az sharm o bāk*" (She held his head and undressed. She had no shame or fear). Siyavosh resists and manages to set himself free. She causes a scene by tearing her dress, beating herself, and accusing Siyavosh of making advances toward her and of an assault that killed her unborn child, although she was not pregnant. After a second accusation and in order to find the truth, King Kavus makes a huge fire and asks Siyavosh to pass through, believing that if Siyavosh is telling the truth in denying the accusation, he will emerge from the fire unharmed. Siyavosh passes the test successfully and volunteers to fight the Turks, only to be banished to a foreign land, where he is killed. Sudabeh herself ultimately dies at the hand of Rostam for contributing to the death of Siyavosh. Sudabeh's trickery is contrasted with the honesty and grace of a hero for whose death Rostam never forgives her.

The tale hardly leaves any alternative reading of Subadeh's character. She represents ultimate guile. She betrays her father, her husband, her country, and her love. In small and remote villages of Iran, Siyavosh remains to this very day the ultimate symbol of martyrdom for truth and righteousness. Rostam, the mighty symbol of national consciousness, who considers Siyavosh his own son, kills Sudabeh by cutting her in half with his sword. King Kavus watches the killing passively.

In short, Firdawsi does not seem to have needed to express the sensitivity toward women and women's issues later exhibited by Nizami. Firdawsi was much preoccupied with reviving the Persian language and with other issues related to writing a national epic. Moreover, he may have lacked the sort of personal experience that enabled Nizami to show such perceptiveness and sympathy toward issues of gender. Although Firdawsi's wife was apparently quite literate and played music, and although he describes her beautifully in the beginning of the story of "Bijan and Manizheh," telling us that his poems depended on her contributions as she read the sources to him while he versified them,[51] it seems unlikely that she played as important a role in his life as Afaq played in Nizami's. Other than this, little is known about Firdawsi's life and his relationship with his wife. Nizami Aruzi, a twelfth-century writer, states that Firdawsi was a landowner with sufficient income to support his only daughter. What is clearer is that he advocated the dominant movement among writers: to contribute to the revival of what they perceived as Persian society through this art. In writing epic poems, he remained faithful to his sources and followed the conventions of the genre.

Jami, a poet of the last years of the Timurid epoch, is considered the last great classical poet. A leader of the Naqshbandi order of dervishes, he devoted his life to saintliness and the study of Arabic and Persian and became a critic, a prolific writer, and a biographer of Sufi personalities. His works include the *Baharistan,* "a memoir of famous Persian poets"; *Lava'ih* (*Splendors* or *Flashes*), a collection of articles concerning the principles of mysticism; *Ashii'at al-lama'at* (*Rays of the Flashes*), elements in the Fakhr al-Din Iraqi book *Lama'at: Sharh az Shuruh-i Qarn-i Hashtum Hijri;* work on the *Nai-nama of Jalal al-Din Rumi, Nafahat al-uns* (*Breaths of Fellowship*), a biography of 614 Sufi saints; and the translation of the *Tabaqat al-sufiyya* by Mohammad b. Husain Sulami of Nishapur. His *Masnavi haft awrang* (*Seven Thrones*) includes several historical romantic poems. Referred to as "khatam al-shu'ara" ("the last of the poets"), the prolific Jami is known as an imitator even though he shows creativity in characterizing figures such as Yusuf and Salaman, portraying them quite skillfully. He primarily imitated Nizami both in form and motifs, going so far as to borrow entire stories, such as *Layli and Majnun.* Women characters are also present in his work. Generally, the earlier classical works influenced literary activities during the fourteenth and fifteenth centuries, and poets such as Sa'di and Nizami were widely imitated.[52] However, in contrast to Nizami, Jami's main thematic concerns revolve around Islamic jurisprudence, *hadith,* morality, and, most important, Sufism. Such differences between Jami and Nizami—and Firdawsi—reflect the different times and places influencing these poets' work. Jami lived in a time and place in which he could easily enjoy the generosity and favor of the rulers of three dynasties, Āl-i Kart, Timurids, and Gurkans, all of whom supported poets. Yet for most of this time, disorderliness marked the period.

Disturbances that can be dated back to the Mongol invasions, and which finally developed into the disruption and disorder of the period after Shah Rukh's death, occasioned a serious decline in civilization and deterioration in thought. At the beginning of this period a few of the scholars, poets and writers of the interval between the Mongol Il-Khans and the Timurids were still alive and affording contributions to science and literature. But apart from these few, and with the possible exception of those who had gathered at the court of Sultan Husain Baiqara at Herat and who were didactic rather than original, we hardly hear of any important or justly celebrated men of learning or science until the latter part of the 9th/15th century.[53]

However, "with the coming of Timur, Herat experienced the beginning of a new age. It was an age of splendor that witnessed the city's rise to an apogee in cultural achievement that has only on rare occasions been equaled in urban history."[54] And during Husain's reign (1469-1506), Herat reached its cultural peak. During this time, "it was the most refined city in Asia, the center of Persian and Turkish culture, and the capital of a prosperous province."[55] All these factors helped in shaping poets' literary enunciations. Jami also lived in a period when Sufism was a major ideological discourse. The purpose of art had come to mean making sense of all earthly aspects of life in terms of Sufi theology. Poets especially were expected to recast earlier literary monuments in this new mode. Jami's creativity was manifested in the way he reinterpreted, redefined, and rewrote the love stories of Nizami and other stories that he found interesting.[56] This new mode influenced the way he characterized women.

In Jami's work, negative characteristics and generalizations define women. Their major attributes include betrayal, deceit, and disgrace. *Salaman and Absal* exemplifies Jami's attitude. A powerful and prosperous Greek king wished to have a son but wanted to refrain from having contact with women, whom he and his vizier believed were all lustful and inferior. Finally, the wise vizier finds a solution: *"notfeh ra bi shahvat az sulbash gushād / dar mahalli joz rahem ārām jāy dād,"*[57] (Without lust, he released the sperm from his backbone / and laid it in a place that was not a womb). The king assigns an assertive nanny, Absal, to care for the child. The child grows up to become the handsome Salaman, whose beauty is equated to that of Joseph. These two fall in love, and the king's attempt to separate them and to convince his son to stay away from women fails. Salaman and Absal fight against all odds to save their love. The force of morality and the continuity of the kingdom are too powerful to defeat, however. At the end, Absal dies and Salaman takes up the "righteous path" of his father. From the beginning Jami seems to uphold the king's perspective by portraying Absal as beguiling and deceptive.

Even in describing Salaman's falling in love with her, Jami's eloquent language carries a sense of condemnation of the woman:

Chon Salaman bā hameh helm o vaqār / kard dar vay eshveh-ye Absal kār
dar del az mozhgān-e u kharāsh khalid / vaz kamand-e zolf-e u mārash
    gazid
z-abrovanash tāqat-e u gasht tāq / vaz labash shod talkh-e shahdash dar
    mazāq
narges-e jādu-ye u khābash bebord / halqeh-e gisu-ye u tābash bebord
ashk-e u az ārezash golrang shod / ayshash az yād-e dahānash tang
    shod
did bar rokhsār-e u khal-e siyāh / gasht az ān khāl-e siyah, halash tabāh
did ja'd-e bi qararash bar ozār / z-arezuy-e vasl-e u shod biqarār
shoqash az pardeh birun āvard lik / dar darun andisheh mikard nik
keh mabādā cheshm-e u ta'm-e vesāl / ta'm-e ān bar jān-e man gardad
    vabāl
ān namānad bā man o omr-e derāz / mānam az jāh-o jalāl-e khish bāz
dowlati kān mard rā jāvid nist / bekhrad ānra qiblah-e omid nist[58]

When, for all Salaman's self-control and propriety,
Absal's coquetry did its work on him,
the prick of her eyelashes pierced his heart,
the snake of her tress's lasso bit him,
his strength was bowed by her eyebrows,
her lips made honey bitter to his palate,
her magic narcissus-eyes robbed him of sleep,
the ring of her curls robbed him of power.
Then his tears flowed bloodstained over his cheek,
the memory of her mouth strangled his joy.
He saw her restless ringlets on her cheek,
he became restless with the desire to embrace her.
Yearning brought him out of the veil, but
inwardly he still mediated well,
thinking, 'if—God forbid!—I once taste the savour of union
that savour will prove fatal to my soul.
That will not remain with me, and all my life
I shall remain deprived of rank and majesty,
A happiness that endures not eternally
is not the wise man's altar of hope.[59]

Jami's language here is shrewd. He unnecessarily exaggerates the association of love and pain that is a characteristic of the classical period.

It is not clear whether the poet is carried away by his rhetorical power or is communicating a literal pain that his male protagonist somehow endures upon falling in love. Absal's eyelashes pierce Salaman's heart, her tress's lasso bites him, her eyebrows subdue his strength, her lips make honey bitter to his palate. Given the idea that the "savour of union" with her will "prove fatal" to Salaman's soul, it is not unlikely that in Jami's discourse on sexuality, women may cause pain. This is a constitutive element of love and sexuality in religious discourse of this period in the medieval Islamic world.

Eventually, after going through a rough time, they decide to jump into a huge fire that Salaman has set for this purpose. However, the king, who has been secretly watching them, saves Salaman and allows Absal to burn. Soon after, Salaman, with the help of the vizier's new trick, manages to forget about her. In a section of the book entitled "In Condemnation of Women, Who Are the Focus of That Passion Upon Which the Child's Existence Depends" (*dar mazammat-e zanān keh mahal-e shahvatand moquf alayh-e velādat-e farzand ishānand*), Jami lists women's deficiencies:

zan che bāshad nāqesi bāshad dar aql o din / hich naqs nist dar ālam chonin

dur dār az sirat ahl-e kamāl / nāqesān rā sakhreh budan māh o sāl

pish kāmel kān beh dānesh sarvar ast / sokhreh-e nāqes ze nāqes kamtar ast

bar sar-e khāwn-e atā-ye zul manan / nist kāfer ne'mati bad tar ze zan

gar dahi sad sāl zan rā sim o zar / pāy dar zar gir u ra tā beh sar

jāmeh az dibā-ye shostar duziyash / khāneh az zarrin lāken afruziyash

la'l dar āvize-ye gushash koni / sawb-e zarkesh setr shab pushash koni

ham beh vaqt-e chāsht ham hengām-e shām / khwānash āra'i beh gunāgun ta'ām

chun shavad tashneh ze jām-e gohari / ābash az sar chashmeh-ye kosar dahi

miveh chun khāhad ze to hamchon shahān / nār-e yazd āri o sib-e Esfahan

chon fotad az dāvari dar tāb o pich / jomle inhā pish-e u hich ast o hich

guyadat key jān godāz-e omr kāh / hich chiz az to nadidam hichgāh

gar che bāshad chehreh-ash lawh-e safā / khalist ān lawh az harf-e vafā

dar jahān az zan vafādari keh did? / ghayr-e makkāri o ghaddāri keh did?

salhāst dast andar āghushat konad / chon betābi ru farāmushat konad

gar to piri yar-e digar bāyadash / hamdami az to qavitar bāyadash

chon javāni āyad u rā dar nazar / jay-e to khāhad keh u bandad kamar[60]

What is woman? A thing deficient in reason and faith;
there is nothing so deficient in the whole world.
Know, then, that it is far removed from the conduct of perfect men
to be, month and year, the plaything of defective creatures;
in the eyes of the perfect man, a leader by his knowledge,
the defective's plaything is inferior even to the defective.
At the table of munificence of the bountiful man
there is no ingrate worse than a woman.
If you should give a woman silver and gold a hundred years,
smother her from head to foot in jewels,
stitch for her robes of the brocade of Shushtar,
furbish her house with pots and pans of gold,
hang on her ears pendants of ruby and pearl,
fashion for her night-covering cloth of spun gold,
alike at breakfast time and at supper
adorn her table with every kind of viand,
when she is thirsty, in a jeweled cup
offer her water drawn from Khizer's fountain,
when she craves fruit of you, like a monarch
bring her pomegranates of Yezd and apples of Isfahan—
the moment she is twisted up in a quarrel
all these things count with her for nothing, nothing;
she says to you, "Why, you soul-melter, you life-lessener,
I've never, never had anything out of you."
Though her cheek be a tablet of purity,
that tablet is utterly bare of the word Fidelity.
Who ever saw faithfulness in a woman in this world?
Who ever saw anything but craftiness and treachery?
For years she will put her hand in your bosom;
the moment you turn your face away, she forgets you.
If you are old, she must needs have another lover,
a companion more vigorous than you;
as soon as a young man catches her eye
she will have him, to serve her in your place.[61]

The story of *Salaman and Absal* has a Greek origin. It would have been available to Jami through Ibn Ishaq's Arabic translation of the original Greek as well as through the references to the story in the works of Ibn Sina, Fakhr al-Din Razi, and Nasir al-Din Tusi.[62] It nonetheless includes a large amount of Jami's own amplification. Moreover, it is well situated in his general discourse on Sufism and what threatens it: "womanly guile."

The story, as Jami indicates at the end, can be interpreted allegorically from a Sufi point of view. In Bürgel's word, "the fact that the mystical spirit, long present in the ghazal, has earned a permanent place in romance is verified by this epic and others such as those by 'Arefi (*Halnama*) and Helali (*Shah va gida*).' "[63] In *Salaman and Absal,* and similarly in *Yusof and Zulaykhā*, the demands of romance writing are eclipsed by the poet's ideological orientation and his perception of women. Even to the extent that these works can be considered works of romance, the misogynistic characterization of women discourages the reading of works within this genre, as least in the way it is possible to read similar stories by Nizami as works of romance. The poet's ideological points of view weigh centrally in the story, making a Sufi reading of it more possible. That Salaman is not born of a woman can be interpreted as a reflection of the need to create the most pious heir possible for the king. At the conclusion of the story, the fire does not burn Salaman, though he is in it just long enough to be purified. As Hadland Davis expresses it, "little by little Salaman came to regard his old earthly love as 'The bondage of Absal,' a thing merely of the senses, whereas by his new knowledge, this love, belonged to the 'Eternity.' And so this beautiful little poem, to put it as briefly as possible, tells of the love that binds and fetters and is corruptible, and of that other Love that is incorruptible."[64] More significantly, many critics have indeed read the story as Sufi symbolism related to wisdom, moral truth, and self-control. However, such reading does not change the fact that it contains the poet's general notions that women are "deficient," "ingrates," "bare of … fidelity," and full of "craftiness," and "treachery." As Jami frequently asserts in the stories, it is his true belief that women are unfaithful, weak, and crafty by nature. This attitude is pervasive throughout his poetry. In *Salaman and Absal,* Absal represents ardent sexual desire and bestial, carnal love while the king represents reason, and Salaman the immortal soul.

Two points should be mentioned here before I procede to Jami's other works. First, Jami is not the only poet in the classical period to hold a negative view of women. Such allegorical use of women's images as symbols of unreliability was not only pervasive in Iranian medieval literature but also in many other parts of the world. Second, Jami's understanding of Islam and Sufism is not necessarily representative of the official view of these discourses.[65] Muslim scholars such as Ibn Hisham, Ibn Hajar, Ibn Sa'd, and al-Tabari presented a radically different portrayal of women.[66]

The theme that love between men is more important than love occurring between men and women is fully developed in the stories of Farid al-Din 'Attar (d. 1230), such as *Mahmud and Ayaz.* In the case of Jami's anecdotes (*hikayat*), his distrust of women turns into disinterest. To convey a message regarding the *qiblah* (the direction to which Muslims turn in prayer), Jami versifies the same short love story three times, insinuating that love for a boy (or young man) may be mystical and might be interpreted as love for God. In a piece entitled "Story of that Young Beloved and the Amorous Old Man," Jami portrays a young man who is loved by an old man.[67] G. H. Yusufi has also analyzed this piece.[68] A young man sits on the eaves of a roof, and his beauty and coquetry kill those who fall in love (or long for union) with him. An old man with gray hair approaches the boy on the roof and declares his love for him. The young man tells the old man to look in the other direction to observe his brother, who is one hundred times more beautiful than he. As soon as the old man turns around and realizes that the brother is not there, the young man pushes him off the roof. The boy expresses his private thoughts: "If he loved me why did he want to see another face?" The poet then steps into first-person narration, concluding the poem with a vow to close his eyes on those who are not his friends lest he should weep blood day and night. If he did not benefit from the union, he would be mournful of the separation.

Jami has included a similar story in *Subhat al-Abrar* (*Rosary of the Pious*), a collection of poetry about moral and Islamic issues, under the title of "Qiblah of Love," this time with no direct reference to the gender of the beauty. He refers to this beloved as a "*chardah-saleh mahi*" (a fourteen-year-old moon), a metaphor used most often for the young female lover. However, he immediately uses masculine adjectives such as "*nojavan*" (youth), leaving little doubt that he is talking about a male moon. Here Jami does not use a female figure to convey his mystical message that the *qiblah* in Islam and the *qiblah* in love function to focus attention on and solemnize the beloved.

Both of these stories and another similar to them then beg the question, why are beloveds amoral only if they are women? We know that the modern concept of homosexuality was not a determining factor in such portrayals and the debate on sexuality in classical period is extensive. "The Islamic view of the couple based on the pre-established, premeditated harmony of the sexes presupposed a profound complementarity of the masculine and the feminine. This harmonious complementarity is creative and procreative."[69] However, what J. W. Wright Jr. states about homoeroticism in Arabic literature may have some implications in classical Persian literature. He writes that reading homoerotic texts "reveal complex parody and satire through which artists and writers metaphorically strengthen their social and moral positions vis-à-vis that dominant Islamic polity."[70] He views homoeroticism "as a reflection of sublime and often subversive ideals" and believes it "represent[s] a metonymical complex of beliefs and reactions."[71] For Jami, as a Sufi, then the love of God is the greatest love achievable on earth. Carnal love, on the other hand, is of value only if it signifies the greater divine love. The beauty of the boy signifies the "light of God." Just as there is only one Mecca, there is only one true love, and if one truly believes in one God, one looks in Mecca's direction. Therefore, the beloved could be anyone, but Jami prefers young men.

However, it is quite possible to argue that homosexuality may serve to represent a criticism of some deviation from the true Sufi path. Analyzing a few homoerotic poems, Sprachman writes, "Like Sanā'ī's version of the homoerotic take, Sa'dī's plays on the hypocrisy of Sūfīs who are more interested in self-satisfaction than self-denial."[72] And that "His primary purposes are to entertain and to poke gentle fun at outwardly ascetic but inwardly hedonistic Sūfīs." The absence of women in this story, nevertheless, further signifies the poet's indifference to them. Sarvatiyan's aforementioned statement about the symbolic value of women in Nizami's work could have been a profound assertion had he applied it to Jami's work. Both women and young men in the writings of Jami serve as symbols and designate broader religious and cultural issues.

Jami's *Yusof va Zolaykha* (*Yusof and Zolaykha,* 1509) might seem to be an exception to his negative portrayal of women. This story is based on the biblical (*Genesis,* chapter 39) and quranic (sura 12) love story that has inspired several other poets, including Gurgani, to rewrite it. It also resonates to the story of Sudabeh and Siyavosh in Ferdowsi's work. Jami's version is arguably the best in terms of fluency, clarity, and poetic expression. Yusof, sincere and righteous, but lonely, is his father's most beloved son. His jealous brothers torture him for a long time before selling him off to slavery in Egypt. There, the gluttonous, self-indulgent Zolaykha, the wife of Egypt's ruler (Aziz-e-Mesr), buys Yusof at an auction. Deeply in love after having several dreams about him, she tries all her tricks to gain Yusof's love and to sleep with him. When she fails, she conspires to send him to prison. After he is freed, he continues to remain moral and virtuous. He leads Zolaykha to believe in God. Upon God's order, he enters into union with her. Following an inspiring dream, Yusof decides to leave this world. He receives an apple from Gabriel, smells it, and dies. Zolaykha, who suffers tremendously from his death, goes to his tomb and lies there without saying a word. She then dies, in an ending similar to that of *Layli and Majnun.* In this story, as Merguerian and Najmabadi write of its Quranic version, "Yusof, through the concept of *Jamal* [beauty], stands in for the Divine; Zolaykha, through '*Ishq* [love], for a Sufi burning with desire for union with the Divine."[73] These authors also note that "even in the story's happy closure, it is Yusof and his sexual desire that are rewarded. In fact, one could argue that in an important sense and despite that clarity with which the Qur'an says 'she desired him,' Zolaykha remains the 'object of desire' in narratives—namely, the desire and drive of the narrative to produce Yusof's victory over her temptation and his own sexual desire, thus establishing his merits as a righteous prophet."[74]

In Jami's version, Zolaykha is not so different from Sudabeh except that she interferes with a prophet. And Yusof does not share Siyavosh's fate. That Yusof is a prophet accounts for the work's significance not only as a symbolic reference work but also as a story that ends happily. Zolaykha stands for the untrustworthy female and the temptation that men must resist by virtue of their wisdom. More importantly, a prophet is, after all, supposed to proselytize, and this is what he achieves in the end. Zolaykha improves, but Sudabeh is cut in half.

It is worth emphasizing that Jami's antipathy toward women causes him to depict them negatively even when the stories are not originally his. He often expresses his views directly rather than through characters, leaving no room for literary interpretation. In, *Subhat al-Abrar,* he discusses the dichotomy between men and women, "*Buvad mardāneh zani dar musel sar-e jānash behaqiqat vāsel / hamcho khorshid mu'annas dar nām lik dar nur-e yaqin mard-e tamām.*"[75] (There is a manly woman [a woman as man] in Mosul, her head and soul reached to truth/like the sun, feminine in name, but a complete man in knowledge.) That is, only men can recognize truth and obtain knowledge. Such perceptions underpin Jami's overall portrayal of women and gender.

In sum, it should be mentioned that all three authors, as Muslims, were sensitive to Islam, women questions, and literary issues. The exigencies of their genre, the dominant cultural discourse, and the impact of the general understanding of Islam in their time, however, influenced their impressions.

Although Nizami characterizes women in positive ways, he also alters his sources to present perhaps the most amiable and charming portrayals of women from a humanistic and liberal point of view in the classical period. If these images are occasionally tinted by a vice, it points to the presence of a reality about these women's charming complex situations and a multidimensional portrayal of their characters. Such vices and flaws are portrayed within the context of human ascension to higher virtue. His poetry is a reflection of his character, his ideas, and his high esteem for the women with whom he was involved. It points to his deep understanding of the human psyche and the role culture plays upon it. His poetry is also a reflection of his time in that this period was marked by a renewed attempt to redefine the concept of Iranian-ness more from a philosophical point of view. It is a reflection of his place, an area marked by tolerance of several cultures. Nizami's love stories are therefore unique in terms of female characterization and he stands out as an anachronism among the great Persian poets of different periods of classical literature for his progressive and positive characterizations of women.

In contrast to Nizami, Firdawsi remains perhaps more faithful to his historical sources and portrays women according to the logic of the epic stories he versifies. In his monumental work, he seems to be more concerned with the culture and the genre he writes in than with the problematics of gender representation; the genre carries out the labor.

Five centuries after Firdawsi and three centuries after Nizami, Jami inherited the rich literary tradition they left behind and creatively altered it to produce new masterpieces. He nevertheless represents a regression in this area and denigrates the moral and intellectual capacity of women. Thematically he had a new fixation: the problematics of ideological representation of Sufism. He was deeply submerged in the discursive exchange, which did not necessarily prompt him to be sensitive to the cause of women or to portray them realistically.

Notes

Three anonymous readers have read an earlier version of this chapter. I am indebted to them for their criticism and comments. I am also grateful to the writings and insights of Julie S. Meisami and J. C. Bürgel.

1. Ali Akbar Sa'idi Sirjani, *Sima-yi du zan: shirin va layli [Layla] dar khamsah-i nizami ganjavi* (Tehran: Nashr-i Naw Avaran, 1991).

2. Bihruz Sarvatiyan, *A'inah-i ghayb, nizami ganjah-'i dar masnavi makhzan al-asrar* (Tehran: Nashr-i Kalamih, 1989), 37, 40.

3. Bihruz Sarvatiyan, ed. *Makhzan al-asrar-i nizami,* Makhzan al-asrar / ba muqabilah-'i davazdah nuskhah, tashih va ta'liqat hamrah ba vazhah va amsal va hikam (Tehran: Tus, 1984), 283.

4. Jalal Matini, "Azadigi va Tasahul-i Nizami Ganjavi," in *Iran-Shinasi,* 4, 1 (Spring 1992), 1-20.

5. Fatamah Alaqih, "Sima-yi zan az didgah-i Nizami," in *Farhang* 10 (Fall 1992), 317-30.

6. Ibid.

7. Julie S. Meisami, "Kings and Lovers: Ethical Dimensions of Medieval Persian Romance," in *Edebiyat* 1 n. 1 (1987), 7.

8. J. C. Bürgel offers a comparison of romance writing in the work of Gorgani, Nizami, Amir Khosrow Dehlavi, Jami, and others. See J. C. Bürgel, "The Romance," in E. Yarshater, *Persian Literature* (New York: Bibliotheca Persica, 1987), 161-79 and "Die Frau als Persien in der Epik Nizamis," *Asiatische Studien* 42: 137-55.

9. For a treatment of this text as a work of drama, see Peter Chelkowski, "Nizami: Master Dramatist," in E. Yarshater, *Persian Literature* (New York: Bibliotheca Persica, 1987), 190-213.

10. Abd al-Majid Ayati, *Dastan-i khusraw va shirin; surudah-i nizami* (Tehran: Shirkat Kitabhay-i Jibi, 1974), 27-29.

11. Ibid.

12. For a recent translation of *Haft Paykar* in English, see Nizami Ganjavi, *The Haft Paykar: A Medieval Persian Romance,* translated with an Introduction and Notes by Julie Scott Meisami. See also G. E. Wilson's translation of *The Haft Paykar* (The Seven Beauties), (London: Late Probsthain and Company, 1924).

13. Elements such as colors, numbers, and weekdays play important roles in this book and indicate Nizami's awareness of some of the sciences of his time. See Meisami, *The Haft Paykar: A Medieval Persian Romance* and Georg Krotkoff, "Colour and Number in the Haft Paykar," in *Logos Islamikos: Studia Islamica,* ed. by Roger M. Savory and Dionisius A. Agius (Toronto, Canada: Pontifical Institute of Mediaeval Studies, 1984).

14. Peter Chelkowski argues that Puccini's Turandot is very likely rooted in an Iranian original and in Nizami's Haft Paykar. See "Āyā uprā-yi turāndut-i Puchini Bar Asas-i Kushk-i Surkh-i *Haft Paykar*-i Nizami Ast?," in *Iran-Shinasi* vol. 3, no. 4 (Winter 1991), 714-22.

15. Nizami, *Haft Paykar,* ed. Dastgirdi (Tehran: Ibn-i Sina, 1955), 233.

16. Ibid.

17. See Muhammad Taqi Jafari, *Hikmat, Irfan, va Akhlaq dar Shir-i Nizami Ganjavi* (Tehran: Intisharat-I Kayhan, 1991) and Bihruz Sarvatiyan, *A'inah-i ghayb, nizami ganjah-'i dar masnavi makhzan al-asrar* (Tehran: Nashr-i Kalamih, 1989), 37, 40.

18. Nizami, *Haft Paykar,* ed. Dastgirdī (Tehran: Ibn-i Sina, 1955).

19. He has renamed other female characters such as Ferdawsi's Qaydafeh to Nushabeh in the Sharafnameh.

20. J. C. Bürgel, "The Romance," in E. Yarshater, *Persian Literature,* 161-79.

21. Julie S. Meisami, "Fitnah or Azadah? Nizami's Ethical Poetic," in *Edebiyat* N. S. vol. I, no. 2, 1989, 41-77.

22. Julie Scott Meisami, *Medieval Persian Court Poetry* (Princeton, N.J.: Princeton University Press, 1987).

23. For a more detailed discussion of Layli's character, see A. A. Sa'idi Sirjani, *Sima-yi du zan* (Tehran: Nashr-i Naw, 1989), 24.

24. Barat Zanjani, *Layli va majnun-i nizami ganjai* (Tehran: Tehran University Press, 1990), 113.

25. Jan Rypka, *History of Iranian Literature* (Dordrecht, Holland: D. Reidel Publishing Company, 1968), 211.

26. The Sasanian (224-642) empire was the last to rule ancient Iran, and its defeat by the Arabs marks the beginning of the medieval period in the history of Iran and the Middle East in general.

27. Arjang Maddi, "Bar rasi-i suvar-i khiyal dar haft paykar," *Farhang,* 10 (Fall 1992), 331-408.

28. See J. C. Bürgel, "The Romance," in E. Yarshater, *Persian Literature* (New York: Bibliotheca Persica, 1987), 161-79.

29. Nizami compares his *Treasure House of Mysteries* to Sanai's *Hadiqatu' l-haqiqat* (*The enclosed garden of the truth*) and occasionally compares his romances to Firdawsi's *Shahnamih* (*Book of Kings*).

30. Hamid Dabashi, "Harf-i Nakhostin: Mafhum-i Sokhan dar Nazd-i Hakim Nizami Ganjavi," in *Iranshenasi* vol. III, no. 4 (Winter 1992), 723-40.

31. Ibid., 733.

32. Sabatino Moscati, *The Face of the Ancient Orient* (Chicago: Quadrangle Books, 1951), 111.

33. Jalil Dustkhah, *Avesta* (Tehran: Murvarid, 1983), 9.

34. "Yasna," 53.

35. Nizami Ganjavi, *Kulliyat-i khamseh-i hakim nizami ganjah-i,* ed. Dastgirdī, fourth edition (Tehran: Amir Kabir, 1987), 23.

36. From *Haft Paykar*. Nizami Ganjavi, *Kuliyat-i khamseh-i hakim nizami ganjah-i.*

37. *Khusraw va shirin,* Nizami Ganjavi, *Kuliyat-i khamseh-i hakim nizami ganjah-i.*

38. From *Haft Paykar,* 1168.

39. In *Layli and Majnu,* he passionately talks about his mother too.

40. Nizami Ganjavi, *Kuliyat-i khamseh-i hakim nizami ganjah-i,* ed. Dastgirdī, 1196.

41. Dabir Siyaqi counts up to 32 women who are named in the *Shahnameh* and adds that Firdawsi refers to more than 35 other women without naming them. M. Dabir-Siyaqi, "Chihrah-i Zan dar Shahnamah," in *Kitab-i Paz* (20-78).

42. Obviously, this is not to suggest that Firdawsi does not portray men negatively.

43. Shahrukh Miskub, *Milliyat va zaban* (Tehran: Karavan, 1989), 23.

44. For more information on the genre of the epic, see C. M. Bowra, *Heroic Poetry* (London: Macmillan; New York: St. Martin's Press, 1961).

45. Julie S. Meisami, "Fitnah or Azadah? Nizami's Ethical Poetic," in *Edebiyat,* 1, n. 2 (1989), 44.

46. For English translations of Firdwasi's work (in part), see Firdawsi, *The Epic of the Kings: Shah-nama, the National Epic of Persia,* translated by Reuben Levy (London: Routledge & K. Paul, 1967); Firdawsi, *The Legend of Seyavash,* translated with an introduction and notes by Dick Davis (London; New York: Penguin, 1992); Firdawsi, *The Tragedy of Sohrab and Rostam: From the Persian National Epic, The Shahname of Abol-Qasem Ferdowsi,* translated by Jerome W. Clinton (Seattle: University of Washington Press, 1996); *In the Dragon's Claws: The Story of Rostam and Esfandiyar*, translated by Jerome W. Clinton (Washington, DC: Mage Books, 2000). And for information about this work, see E. G. Browne, *A Literary History of Persia,* 2 vols.; J. Rypka et al., *History of Iranian Literature* (Dordrecht: D. Reidel, 1968); Dick Davis, *Epic and Sedition: The Case of Ferdowsi's Shahnameh* (Fayetteville: University of Arkansas Press, 1992); Olga M. Davidson, *Poet and Hero in the Persian Book of Kings* (Ithaca: Cornell University Press, 1994).

47. Firdawsi, Abu al-Qasim, "Rostam va Sohrab," *Shahnameh,* ed. M. A. Furughi (Tehran: Intisharat-i Javidan, n.d.), 83-98.

48. See M. Islami-Nudushan, "Mardan va Zanan-i Shahnamah," in Nasir Hariri, ed. *Firdawsi, zan, va tirazhidi* (Babul, Iran: Kitabsara-yi Babul, 1986).

49. Julie S. Meisami, "Fitnah or Azadah? Nizami's Ethical Poetic," in *Edebiyat* N. S. vol. I, n. 2, (1989), 46.

50. Ibid., 63.

51. Abu al-Qasim Firdawsi, *Shahnameh,* 195.

52. For more information, see Parvin Shakiba, *Shi'r-i farsi az aghaz ta imruz* (Tehran: Hirmand, 1992) and *Nigahi guzara bar vizhagiha va digarguniha-yi shi'r-i farsi* (Piedmont, CA: Shirikat-i Kitab-i Jahan and Iran Zamin, 1987).

53. Peter Jackson, ed. *The Cambridge History of Iran,* vol. 6, The Timurid and Safavid Periods (Cambridge: Cambridge University Press, 1986), 913.

54. Shannon Caroline Stack, *Herat: A Political and Social Study* Ph.D. Dissertation, University of California, Los Angles, 1975, 241.

55. Terry Allen, *Timurid Herat* (Wiesbaden: LRV, 1983), 15.

56. In some of his other works, especially those that deal with Sufism more directly, he imitated Attar.

57. Abd al-Rahman Jami, *Masnavi-i Haft Awrang,* ed. M. Mudarris Gilani (Tehran: Sa'di, 1958), 331; *Salaman va Absal,* edited and introduced by Muhammad Rawshan (Tehran: Asatir, 1994), 118.

58. Ibid., 341.

59. Jami, *Salaman and Absal,* trans. Edward Fitzgerald, edited and with a literal prose translation by A. J. Arberry (Cambridge: Cambridge University Press, 1956), 174-75.

60. Abd al-Rahman Jami, *Masnavi-i Haft Awrang,* 330.

61. Jami, *Salaman and Absal,* trans. Fitzgerald, 160.

62. See Abd al-Rahman Jami, *Masnavi Haft Urang,* 28.

63. J. C. Bürgel, "The Romance," in *Persian Literature,* no. 3, Ehsan Yarshater, ed. (New York: Bibliotheca Persica, 1988), pp. 175-77. See also note number 7.

64. Hadland F. Davis, *Wisdom of the East: The Persian Mystics, Jami* (London: John Murry, 1908), 23.

65. For more information on women in Islam see, Amina Wadud, *Qur'an and Woman: Rereading the Sacred Text From a Woman's Perspective* (New York: Oxford University Press, 1999); Anwar Hekmat, *Women and the Koran: The Status of Women in Islam* (Amherst, N.Y.: Prometheus Books, 1997); Haideh Moghissi, *Feminism and Islamic Fundamentalism: The Limits of Postmodern Analysis* (London; New York: Zed Books, 1999); Fatima Mernissi, *Women and Islam: An Historical and Theological Enquiry.* Trans. Mary Jo Lakeland (Oxford: Basil Blackwell, 1991); and M. E. Combs-Schilling, *Sacred Performances: Islam, Sexuality, and Sacrifice* (New York: Columbia University Press, 1989).

66. Fatima Mernissi, *Women and Islam: An Historical and Theological Enquiry.* Trans. Mary Jo Lakeland (Oxford: Basil Blackwell, 1991), viii, 126, and 128.

67. Abd al-Rahman, Jami, *Silsalat-al-zahab* (*Golden Chain*) in the collection *Masnavi-i Haft Awrang* (Tehran: Kitabfurushi-i Sa'di, 1972).

68. Gulam Husayn Yusufi, *Chishmih-yi rowshan* (Tehran: Ilmi, 1970), 269-78.

69. Abdelwahab Bouhdiba, *Sexuality in Islam* (London: Saqi Books, 1998), 30.

70. J. W. Wright, Jr. and Everett K. Rowson, *Homoeroticism in Classical Arabic Literature* (New York: Columbia University Press, 1997), xv.

71. Ibid., xv and 3.

72. Paul Sprachman, "Le beau garcon sans merci: The Homoerotic Tale in Arabic and Persian," in J. W. Wright, Jr. and Everett K. Rowson, *Homoeroticism in Classical Arabic Literature*, 196.

73. Gayane Karen Merguerian and Afsaneh Najmabadi, "Zolaykha and Yusof: Whose 'Best Story'?" *International Journal of Middle East Studies,* 29, no. 4 (November 1997), 485-508.

74. Ibid.

75. Jami, A., *Subhat al-Abrar,* 495.

Chapter 4

Majnun's Image as a Serpent[1]

Asghar Abu Gohrab

In contrast to the early Arabic sources such as Ibn Qutaiba's (213-276/834-897) *Kitāb ash-shi'r waash-shu'arā,* Abu'l Faraj al-Isfahānī's (d. 356/967) *Kitāb al-aghānī,* and Ibn Dāwūd al-Isfahānī's (255-297/868-910) *Kitāb az-zahra,* which refer cryptically to Majnun's emaciated body and his nakedness, the Persian Majnun is depicted with particular attention to his physical appearance. Among the various characterization of Majnun created by different Persian poets such as Amīr Khusrau, 'Abd ar-Rahmān Jāmī, Maktabī and Hātifī, Nizami's Majnun is the most complex and, at the same time, the most intriguing figure. This is the first portrayal of the historico-legenderic Majnun that unites all his character traits in an artful and uniform fashion. In fact, after some centuries of scattered anecdotal notices about Majnun, it is through the skillful hands of Nizami that Majnun comes to life and acquires the status of an ontological character, living on in the mind of the reader. Nizami establishes a picture of Majnun that has been a source of inspiration for subsequent poets who tried their hands at writing their own versions of the poem.[2] Although it is true that Nizami pays relatively little attention to Majnun's facial appearance compared to his psychological profile and his mental state, there are a number of scattered outward descriptions of Majnun that are indispensable for a sound interpretation of Majnun's character.

The purpose of this chapter is to demonstrate how Majnun is depicted by means of ophidian imagery. In order to inquire into various aspects of this imagery, a brief note about the symbolism of the serpent in classical Persian is required. In mystical love poetry, the beloved's lock, *zulf,* is often likened to a serpent. In *Anīs al-'ushshāq,* Sharaf ad-Dīn Rāmī (d. 795/1393) defines forelock as "the hair which circles the cheeks like a serpent in the bed of roses."[3] When the lover tries to steal a kiss from the beloved's lips, the serpent bites his heart; the antidote is the beloved's sweet saliva. Here it will suffice to give only two examples, one by Shams ad-Dīn Muhammad Hāfiz (d. 1390) and one by Khajū-yi Kirmānī (1281-1352) respectively:

> *dil-i mā rā ki zi mār-i sar-i zulf-i tu bi-khast*
> *az lab-i khud ba shafā-khāna-yi taryāk andāz*

> (O beloved) from your lips cast our heart, which is wounded by the serpent of
> your forelock's tip, into the healing-house of antidote.[4]

> I said: "I am the day;" she said: "Do not boast of this day";
> I said: "I am the night;" she said: "Do not lengthen the tale";
> I said: "I am your forelock;" she said: "Do not twist around the serpent":
> I said: "I am your beauty spot;" she said: "Go and do not play with the precious stone."[5]

Unlike the majority of the Western literature in which the image of the snake is associated with the Bible and sin, the position of this creature in Persian literature is ambivalent. The serpent occurs only once in the Koran, in connection with Moses' staff, which turned into a serpent (20:20) and has no malignant connotation.[6] Percy Byshe Shelley's positive symbolic use of the snake in *The Revolt of Islam* and in his other works such as *Prometheus Unbound* is an exception within the Western literary tradition; in the former poem, he depicts an "unimaginable fight" upon the ocean between an eagle and a serpent, presenting the latter as a symbol for good and the former for evil.[7] Although Shelley's image is probably derived from works such as *The Iliad, The Aeneid,* and *The Metamorphoses,* the impact of oriental literature cannot be excluded.[8]

In Persian literature, the emphasis is put both on the malevolent and benevolent nature of reptiles. In Sa'd ad-Dīn Warāwīnī's (d. 854/1450) *Marzbān-nāma,* there are five stories about snakes.[9] The most impressive one is the account of the snake that interprets dreams. This snake is portrayed as a pious believer who teaches a weaver the science of dream interpretation. In the account of a conjurer and a serpent, the latter pretends to be dead by remaining motionless in order to escape from the conjurer. The author relates the serpent's inaction to the prophetic tradition, "die before you die" and to the extinction of concupiscence, *nafs-i ammāra*. In Abū Tāhir b. Ḥasan-i Tarsūsī's *Dārāb-nāma,* the hero, Dārāb, is confronted with a benign dragon who helps him to find his abducted mother, Humāy.[10] In *Kalīla and Dimna* (completed ca. 1145)— a version of which is known in the West as *The Fables of Bidpay,* by Abu'l Ma'ālī Nasr Allāh ibn Muhammad ibn 'Abd'l-Hamīd Munshī— snakes are used as representatives for the four humors of the body that support life:

A certain person fled from a rutting camel and out of necessity, jumped into a well while grasping two branches which grew on the top of the well. He secured his feet somewhere, but when he looked better, he noticed that he had placed his feet on the heads of four snakes which had poked their heads from their holes. Then when he looked at the bottom of the well, he saw a harrowing dragon with his mouth open, waiting for his fall. Then, he looked at the top of the well, and saw two rats, one black and one white, chewing eagerly the stem of the branches. Meanwhile, in this horrible situation, as he was searching for a measure to emancipate himself, he noticed a bee-hive before him, which contained some honey-dew. He ate a bit of the honey and became so occupied with its sweetness that he neglected his own situation.[11]

The well represents the world, the branches life, and the two rats day and night; the four snakes symbolize the four humors, and the sweet honey stands for the passing delight and temptation of this world that eventually leads to destruction, and the dragon represents death.[12]

One of the most impressive presentations of the serpent occurs in the hagiography of the great mystic Abū Sa'īd Abu'l Khair (357-440/978-1061) entitled *Asrār at-tauhīd,* written by his grandson Muhammad Munawwar. In one of his biographical anecdotes, in order to punish one of his brutal disciples, Abū Sa'īd sends the latter to a valley to encounter a serpent. Abū Sa'īd speaks of this huge black serpent as one of his "friends" and when he talks with the disciple in question, the latter actually thinks that his master is sending him to another *pīr,* or "spiritual guide." Abu Sa'īd says: "This serpent has been our friend for seven years and we found much comfort and relaxation from each other's companionship."[13] This particular snake recurs in two other places and frightens the shaikh's disciples, but the shaikh reminds them that the serpent is his close friend.[14] It is not clear, however, whether this specific serpent is the same beast that is used by Bāyazīd as his whip while riding on the back of a lion, a scene depicted numerous times by miniaturists.[15] In addition, in Farīd ad-Dīn 'Attār's (537-627/1142-1229) hagiography, *Tadhkirat al-aulīyā,* there is a marvelous description of a benign serpent which appears from time to time and fans the mystical lovers "with a branch of narcissus held in its mouth."[16] In Muhammad Bukhārī's bulky commentary on Kalābādhī's *Kitāb at-ta 'arruf li-madhhab ahl al-tasawwuf,* there is also a story about a beneficial serpent, that saves the life of a mystic:

I heard Abu'l-Ḥasan al-Fārsī saying: "I became so extremely thirsty in a desert that I could not move any more. I had heard that the eyes of thirsty people burst before they die. I was waiting for the bursting of my eyes when I suddenly heard a voice. I turned my face and saw a white serpent, as bright as pure silver, approaching me. I ran fearfully because fear had engendered power in me. Then due to weakness I walked slowly while the serpent was still after me. In this way I walked, till I reached water. The voice grew silent and I could not see the serpent."[17]

In Sufism, the serpent symbolizes, on the one hand, the ominous carnal desire, *nafs-i shūm,* and the world.[18] On the other hand, it stands for treasure and the revelation of the inner being of the mystic; it is the symbol of change and transformation as well as the union with one's inner self. In the same way that the serpent sloughs off its old skin and appears shining in its new dress, the mystic annihilates his lower soul and lives eternally by undergoing a metamorphosis. To conclude our brief ophidian survey of Persian, a last example of the ambivalent nature of the snake will be provided from Shams of Tabrīz's *Discourses.* Here a kind of two-headed serpent, that has a head at either end, is presented to illustrate the ambiguous symbolism of the serpent:

The world is a treasure and the world is a serpent. Some people play with the serpent and some with the treasure. He who plays with the serpent, must bare his heart to its bite. It bites with its tail and it bites with its head. When it bites with its tail, you will not awake, and then it starts to bite with its head. People who have turned their back on the serpent, and have not become proud of its precious stone, *mār-muhra,* and its love, *mihr,* have taken elderly reason as their guide—because reason regards the glance of the serpent as an emerald. As the dragon-like serpent noticed that elderly reason conducted the leadership of the caravan, it became dejected, despised, and discouraged. In that ocean (of the world) the serpent was like a crocodile forming a bridge under the feet of reason.

Its poison turned into sugar, its thorn into a rose. It was a highway robber, but it grew to be a guide. It was the cause of fear, but it grew to be the cause of security.[19]

The image of Majnun as a serpent occurs several times in Nizami's *Laili and Majnun* and bears a highly symbolic significance. Not only is the image intertwined with Majnun's nakedness and physical weakness but it also points to the fact that Majnun is possessed by a *jinn*. Jinns can assume every form, especially that of serpents, lizards, and other creeping creatures.[20] Outwardly Majnun is as emaciated as a snake and inwardly he is possessed by a jinn who is inclined to assume the form of a serpent. The first reference to Majnun as a serpent occurs in chapter 20 in which a passerby from the tribe of Banī Sa'd spots Majnun and reports to his father. Here, the passerby first gives a physical description of Majnun and then compares him and his twisting and coiling movements to a serpent:

47. As the passer-by set his eyes on Majnun,
    he saw a nice face with a good shape.
48. He asked him from hither and thither,
    but he received nothing save silence.
49. When he lost his hope of communicating with him,
    he passed him by and went his way.
50. He went from there to Majnun's native land,
    and informed Majnun's tribe of him:
51. "There, in that particular ruined place,
    he is creeping like a serpent over a stone.
52. He is insane, in pain and distressed,
    and like a demon, he is far from the eye of man.
53. Due to wounds, his soul is pierced;
    the marrow of his bones can be seen."[21]

Moreover, in chapter 19, when Majnun's father brings him to the holy Ka'ba in order to heal his lovesickness, as soon as the word "love" leaps onto his father's lips,

24. Majnun jumps like a snake from his coil,
    grasping the coil of the Ka'ba's locks with his hand.

25. While he holds the coil [door-knocker] to his bosom,
     he cries: "Today, I am like the coil upon the door."

In these distichs, Nizami presents the Ka'ba as feminine and its door-knocker is likened to the beloved's coil of hair. In early Arabic sources such as Abu 'l-Faraj al-Isfahānī's *Kitāb al-aghānī*, Majnun's visit to the Ka'ba is mentioned.[22] Here, Majnun only holds the coverings, *astār,* of the Ka'ba praying to God to cure him. Concerning the above couplets, Anna Livia Beelaert notes that the association of the door-knocker to curly locks "may well have [been] invented" by Khāqānī, a poet of the Azarbaijan school, but the comparison of the Ka'ba to Lailī is Nizami's invention.[23] Not only did Nizami use this fertilizing image in *Lailī and Majnun,* but he composed a beautiful ode (*qasīda*), in which he elaborated the image and exploited all its elements in a coherent way.[24] Nizami's ode is one of the exceptional instances in which the image of the beloved woman is most coherently and exhaustively dealt with; it can be regarded as an indispensable source for the analysis of this religious imagery in love poetry. In *Lailī and Majnun,* Nizami compresses the whole image into a single couplet. What is important in this image is that not only is the Ka'ba compared to a bride, but more importantly the union between the lover and the beloved is portrayed. To become a coil of the beloved's hair is a popular Sūfī imagery for union, *visāl,* expressing the lover's longing to become a lock of the beloved's hair. By becoming a strand of the beloved's hair, the lover symbolically unites with the beloved; the image also stands for the lover's emaciated body which has become as thin as a lock of hair. N. Pourjavady holds that the origin of this image goes back to Muhammad Ma'shūq of Tūs, a mystic from whom no extant text is handed down; only a number of biographical notices are recounted by 'Attār.[25] The image originates most probably in Ahmad Ghazālī's (d. 520/1126) *Sawānih al-'ushshāq,* in which, after delineating the concepts of *fanā,* or annihilation of the lover and his *baqā,* or subsistence, in the beloved, Ghazālī offers the following quatrain:

Since I suffered so much hardship from your locks,
I have become a strand of hair in those two curly locks of yours.
Why should I wonder from now on, if I become one of your locks?
What matters if there be a strand of hair more or less in your tresses?[26]

In the following couplet, Hāfiz alludes to Majnun's station, *maqām,* of union by the image of becoming a lock of the beloved's hair:

hikāyat-i lab-i shirin kalām-i farhād ast
shikanj-i turra-yi lailī maqām-i majnun ast

Farhād's talk is about the tale of sweet/Shirin's lips;
the curl of Lailī's hair is the station of Majnun.[27]

Majnun desires to annihilate his ego and to find union with his beloved by becoming a coil of her hair. By personifying the Ka'ba as a beloved and by likening Majnun to a serpent, Nizami opens another perspective for the interpretation of the poem.

The image has another layer of interpretation as well, namely the analogy of the serpent holding watch over a treasure. This particular image occurs frequently in *Lailī and Majnun;* Majnun is compared to a serpent holding watch over Lailī, the treasure. In Sufism, the snake symbolizes the existence of the traveler on the mystical path. Sūfī poets occasionally referred to the existence of the mystic and the truth by employing the image of the snake and treasure. In his voluminous *Sūfī Symbolism,* Jawād Nūrbakhsh gives only a couplet from Muhammad Shirin Maghribī (d. 810/1408) to elucidate this aspect of the mystical symbolism of the snake:

Unless you slay the serpent of existence, you cannot find the way to the
    treasure;
because your existence is a snake upon His treasure.[28]

Applying this symbolism to Nizami's romance, Majnun can be taken as a sentinel guarding Lailī by his existence. Majnun has a strong desire to annihilate himself in order to obtain the treasure.

Majnun's comparisons to the snake have no malignant connotations: his appearance as a snake and as an emaciated person dwelling in a cave or a ruined place, *kharāba,* correspond, on the one hand, to the image of a mystic living in such places. Instances of mystics living in these kinds of dwellings occur endlessly in various genres: from mystical texts such as 'Attār's *Tadhkira* to historico-legenderic books such as the *Dārāb-nāma*.[29] Here, I mention only one example from the genre of romantic poetry. At the beginning of Vahshī Bāfiqī's romance, *Nāzir and Manzūr* (*Regarder and Regarded*), the fathers of the pair of lovers come across a "ruined place in which was hidden a treasure, an illumined mystic whose tongue was the key to the treasure of the gnostic knowledge." On the other hand, Majnun is compared to a serpent that guards the treasure, Lailī. In chapter 62, as soon as the news of Lailī's death reaches Majnun's ear, he rushes madly to her grave and

42. rolls in the same way as a serpent,
    or a worm coiling beneath the earth.
43. With a thousand toils, he coiled himself around
    the grave-stone like a serpent on a treasure.

After a long elegy on the death of his beloved, Majnun uses the same image, comparing himself to a snake and Lailī to a treasure. Moreover, he takes Lailī to be his "companion of the cave," *yār-i ghār,* an allusion to the historical journey of the Prophet from Mecca to Medina during which he had to take refuge in a cave with the first Caliph, Abū Bakr. This comparison, which carries a spiritual implication, is another aspect of the terminology used by Majnun to describe Lailī. Religious terminology and phraseology in relation to Lailī abound in this poem:

67. The cavern is always the home of a snake;
    O Moon, why has the cavern become your residence?
68. I will lament in your cave, for you are my beloved;
    you are the companion of the cave, (*yār-i ghār*), how can I not
        weep?
69. You turned out to be a treasure in the earth;
    If you are not a treasure, why are you then thus [in the earth]?
70. Every treasure, which is in a cave,
    has a serpent upon its skirt.
71. I am a serpent which is the sentinel of your grave
    watching the treasure on your grave.

In chapter 64, in which Majnun breathes his last breath on Lailī's tomb, he is likened to a snake anew:

> 6. While weeping because of grief,
>   Majnun approached that earthly bride.
> 7. He fell on the ring [tomb] of that enclosure;
>   his vessel fell in turbid water.
> 8. He rolled like a wounded ant;
>   he twisted like a bitten snake.

It should also be added here with regard to Lailī that her emotions and her isolation are also likened to a snake in at least three places. In chapter 39, Lailī's unexpressed feelings and her veil are compared to the writhing of a snake whose head has been cut off and put into a sack. By this vivid image, Nizami depicts Lailī's feelings in her immurement. Now and then, she secretly comes to the roof or the veranda hoping to hear a word from her chaste lover:

> 19. Indoors wrapped in her veil upon the roof,
>   she lived like a snake deprived of its head.

In chapter 52, Lailī's sorrow for Majnun is also expressed by snake imagery; the snake twists its tail in pain:

> 2. Due to the sorrow for her beloved, she became like the tail of a snake;
>   it means "to be trapped by a thousand-fold sorrow."

In chapter 48, being agitated by the fact that Lailī lives with Ibn Salam, Lailī's imposed husband, Majnun addresses her in these words:

> 17. O, while you are a treasure in the hands of the rivals,
>   you grow into a snake in the hands of the friends.

The image of reptiles is prevalent in the poem. In chapter 32, after having released a herd of gazelle, Majnun bewailingly rambles the desert, and as soon as he sees a cave he

44. Bemoaningly creeps into the cave,
    like a lizard which is bitten by a snake.

In chapter 39, in which Majnun's physical appearance is described, he is again compared to a serpent. This is the scene in which Majnun's father visits him:

20. He saw Majnun, but not in a way his eyes desired to see him;
    As he saw Majnun, his heart rose from its place.
21. Without a frame, he looked at a moving soul,
    [a bunch] of bones shrouded by skin.
22. A destitute in the world of existence;
    absconding from the road of idol-worshipping.
23. Like a stick [figure] in the shadow-play;
    a lock of hair escaped from the mouth of death.
24. Running on the earth faster than a dog;
    being more hidden than the inhabitants beneath the earth.
25. The cauldron of his frame had became cold,
    falling on his brain, he swooned away.
26. Twisting himself in his agony like a serpent;
    no covering on his head while slumbering away.

In chapter 41, in which Majnun's father delivers a long tirade, admonishing him not to be like a serpent but rather like a rose, the image of the serpent recurs again:

35. He is a serpent and not a nimble man,
    who leaves the treasure and feeds on earth.[30]
36. Eat happily, for you are a world-glowing rose;
    be not like a serpent which feeds on earth.

In chapter 46, in which an old man filled with light brings a message from Lailī to Majnun, the image recurs once again. Having abandoned men's association and now abiding with beasts, Majnun is at first afraid to communicate with this man, but later he welcomes the messenger and gives the reason for his fear:

15. I, who have been bitten by a snake, am afraid of a rope;
     what a snake, Lo, it was a dragon.

The image of the snake employed in this couplet is ambiguous and can allude to men, from whom Majnun flees, to love, which has bitten Majnun's heart, and also to Lailī, who in Majnun's view turns into a serpent when she is in the reach of "the hands of the friends."

In conclusion, Nizami applies various symbolical aspects of the serpent to Majnun. Although at one level, the poet points to Lailī's lover as being *majnun*, "possessed by a jinn," and thus assuming the form of a creeping creature, at another level, through the serpent imagery, Nizami displays Majnun's strong longing for union with Lailī. Furthermore, the image not only points to Majnun's emaciated body, but it also presents Majnun as a guard over a treasure, Lailī. Moreover, the image implicitly evokes the prophetic tradition "die before you die." In other words, Majnun desires to peel off his phenomenal existence and to live a life detached from materialism. In sum, the use of such imagery dramatizes something of Majnun's inner feelings and highlights the correlation between the external and the internal attributes of a character. In fact, the external appearance and attributes of a character are often symbolic indications of his internal state. Such an image shows that an analysis of Majnun's physical appearance is a prerequisite in acquiring a better insight into his psychologically complex character. Further research on other aspects of Majnun's physical appearance is, however, required to provide more information about Nizami's Majnun.

Notes

1. This chapter has been written at the State University of Leiden as a part of a Ph.D. research project with the financial support of the Netherlands Organization for Scientific Research (NWO).

2. P. Chelkowski in the *Encyclopedia of Islam* (hereafter referred to as *E. I.*), s.v. Nizami Gandjawī; also consult J. T. P. de Bruijn in *E. I.,* s.v. Madjnūn Laylā.

3. Sharaf ad-Dīn Rāmī, *Anīs al-'ushshāq,* ed. A. Iqbal, Tehran: 1325/1946, p. 6. For more information about the content of this book, see G. M. Wickens in *Encyclopedia Iranica,* s.v. 'Anis al-'Oshshāq; also compare E. Bertels and J. T. P. de Bruijn in *E. I.,* s.v. Rāmī Tabrīzī.

4. *Diwan-i Hafiz,* ed. P. Nātil Khānlarī, Tehran: Khārazmī Publisher, 1362/1983, p. 532.

5. *Dīwān-i ash'ār-i khājū-yi kirmānī,* ed. A. Suhailī-yi Khānsārī (Tehran: Pazhūhishgāh Publishers, 1369/1990), p. 540. The "precious stone" alludes to the Persian belief that there are black stones in the heads or brains of large serpents.

6. For the image of the serpent in Arabic literature, see J. Ruska in *E. I.,* s.v. *Hayya*; also see L. Kopf in *E. I.,* s.v. *'Af'ā.*

7. The enmity between an eagle or falcon and a serpent occurs a number of times in classical Persian. Maulānā Jalāl ad-Dīn Rūmī recounts in his *Mathnawī* the story of an eagle that takes away the shoe of the Prophet in which a black serpent was hidden. *Mathnawī-yi ma'nawī,* ed. M. Isti'lamī (Tehran: Zawwār Publishers, 1372/1993), vol. III, ll. 3240ff.

8. See *The Complete Poetical Works of Percy Bysshe Shelley,* ed. N. Rogers, vol. II (Oxford: Clarendon Press, 1975). The aerial fight between the eagle and the serpent occurs in stanzas VIII-XIV. It might be added here that Shelley himself was nicknamed the "Snake" by a number of his friends. In the *Revolt,* Shelley employs the Zoroastrian myth of the creation of Ohrmazd and Ahriman as the framework of his poem. For a discussion on Shelley's use of the Zoroastrian mythology, see Carlos Baker, *Shelley's Major Poetry: The Fabric of a Vision* (Princeton: Princeton University Press, 1948), esp. pp. 64-70.

9. Sa'd ad-Dīn Warāwīnī, *Marzbān-nāma,* ed. K. Khatīb Rahbar (Tehran: Marvi Publishers, 1373/1994), pp. 101-104, 234-46, 576-616.

10. *Dārāb-nāma,* ed. Z. Saf (Tehran: 'Ilmī and Farhangī Publishers, 1374/1995), vol. I, pp. 341-42.

11. Nasru'llāh b. Muhammad b. 'Abdul-Hamīd Munshī, *Kitīāb-i Kalīla wa Dimna,* ed. A. Qarīb (Tehran: Sa'dī Publishers, 1369/1990), pp. 50-51. This story is recounted by Muhammad ibn 'Abdullāh al-Bukhārī in *Kalīla wa Dimna,* which is published under the title of *Dāstānhā-yi Bīdpāy,* by P. Nātil Khānlarī and M. Raushan (Tehran: Khārazmī Publishers, 1369/1990), pp. 69-70.

12. The theme of a *mast camel* is repeated in modern Persian novels as well: Mahmūd Daulatābādī in his *Jā-yi khālī-yi salūj (Salūj's Vacant Place)* elaborates this theme to a high degree of perfection. See M. Daulatābādī, *Jā-yi khālī-yi salūj* (Tehran: Buzurgmihr Publishers, 1368/1989), p. 1273ff.

13. *Asrār at-tauhīd fī maqāmāt ash-shaikh Abī Sa'īd,* ed. M. R. Shafī'ī Kadkanī (Tehran: Agāh Publisher, 1371/1992), pp. 99-101.

14. Ibid., pp. 100, 150. There are a number of reports that Sūfī masters tested their disciples by sending them to wild beasts that turn out to be good friends of the master. See for instance 'Attār's *Tadhkirat al-aulīyā,* ed. R. A. Nicholson, (Tehran: Manūchihrī Publisher, 1370/1991), p. 153.

15. *Asrār at-tauhīd*, p. 253. In this scene, Bāyazīd is riding upon a lion while holding a serpent as a whip in his hand. This story is also retold by Maulānā Rūmī; see *MM*, vol. VI, ll. 2133ff.

16. 'Attar, op. cit., p. 46. The same image recurs on p. 184; also compare Abu'l-Ḥasan 'Alī ibn 'Uthmān al-Jullābī al-Hujwīrī, *Kashaf al-mahjūb*, ed. V. A. Zhukovskii, Intro. by Q. Ansārī (Tehran: Tahūrī Publishers, 1358/ 1979), p. 118.

17. Muhammad Mustamlī Bukhārī, *Sharh at-ta 'arruf*, ed. M. Raushan (Tehran: Asātīr Publishers, vol. IV, 1366/1987), pp. 1792-93.

18. For the symbolism of the serpent in Rūmī's works see, A. Schimmel, *Triumphal Sun.* (London: 1978), p. 112. According to Schimmel, Rūmī takes the snake as man's base soul.

19. *Maqālāt-i Shams-i Tabrīzī*, ed. M. A. Muwahhid (Tehran: Dībā Publishers, 1369/1990), p. 313.

20. See T. Nöldeke in *Encyclopaedia of Religion and Ethics,* s.v. Arabs, p. 669.

21. This and all further citations from Nizami's *Lailī and Majnun* have been taken from the edition of A. A. Ali Asgharzada and F. Babayev (Baku: 1965).

22. Abu'l Faraj al-Isfahānī, *Kitāb al-aghānī* (Cairo, 1346/1928), vol. II, p. 22.

23. For the development of the image of the Ka'ba as a beloved woman and as a bride in Persian literature, see chapter 4 of A. L. F. A. Beelaert, *A Cure for the Grieving: Studies on the Poetry of the Twelfth-Century Persian Court Poet Khāqānī Shīrwānī.* Ph.D. dissertation, Leiden: 1996. Beelaert's chapter originally appeared in *Persica,* 13, 1988-89, pp. 107-123, under the title "The Ka'ba as a Woman: A Topos in Classical Persian Literature."

24. See *Dīwān-i qasāyid wa ghazalīyāt-i nizami-yi ganjawī,* ed. S. Nafīsī (Tehran: Furūqī Publisher), pp. 232ff.

25. See N. Pourjavady, *'Ain al-qudhāt wa ustādān-i ū* (Tehran: Asātīr Publishers), pp. 69-75.

26. *Ahmad Ghazzālī's Aphorismen Über die Liebe.* Herausgegeben von H. Ritter (Istanbul: 1942), pp. 37-38 and 59. For an elaborate mystical interpretation of this image in Ghazālī's treatise, see N. Pourjavady, op. cit., pp. 70-75.

27. *Dīwān,* p. 126.

28. J. Nurbakhsh, *Sūfī Symbolism,* vol. IV (Tehran: KNP, 1369/1990), p. 140. Nurbakhsh unfortunately gives no source for his citation. The couplet belongs to *ghazal* no. 186, l. 14, in Leonard Lewisohn, *A Critical Edition of the Divan of Muhammad Shirin Maghribi* (Tehran: Institute of Islamic Studies, 1993).

29. In the *Dārāb-nāma,* vol. I, pp. 80-82, when the hero flees from his enemies and seeks refuge in a cave, he unexpectedly sees an old ascetic, who claims to be appointed by God to help him.

30. V. Dastgirdī explains this couplet in the following way: "It is well-known that during the winter snakes do not leave their holes and eat earth." See *Lailī u Majnun,* ed. V. Dastgirdī (Tehran: 'Ilmī Publisher), p. 160.

Chapter 5

The Historian and the Poet: Rāvandī, Nizami, and the Rhetoric of History

Julie Scott Meisami

Allin Luther combined an interest in Persian history and historiography with a deep appreciation of Persian literature. He wrote frequently on Muhammad ʿAlī Rāvandī and his *Rāḥat al-ṣudūr wa-āyat al-surūr*. He was also a great admirer of the poetry of Nizami Ganjavi. It seems appropriate to devote this chapter to a subject that also combines those interests and to a writer who shared them: to Rāvandī's use of quotations from Nizami in the *Rāḥat al-ṣudūr*.

I have discussed elsewhere the status of Rāvandī's work as a "hybrid text"[1] and his use of quotations from Firdawsi's *Shahnameh*.[2] In a forthcoming book I deal with questions relating to Rāvandī's style and his purpose in writing the *Rāḥat al-ṣudūr*.[3] Rāvandī himself provides information on his own background and on the circumstances surrounding the work's composition.[4] After his father's death, he was brought up by his uncle Taj al-Dīn Aḥmad, a scholar who enjoyed the patronage of Jamāl al-Dīn Ay Aba, who served the last Great Saljūq sultan, Ṭughril III ibn Arslān (571-90/1176-94), in Hamadan. He visited various cities in Iraq in pursuit of knowledge and studied both religious and secular sciences, in addition to acquiring the skills of calligraphy, gilding, and book-binding by which he earned his living.

In 577/1181 Ṭughril appointed another of Rāvandī's uncles, Zayn al-Dīn Maḥmūd Kāshī, to teach him calligraphy. This uncle introduced Rāvandī into Ṭughril's court, where he applied his gilding skills to decorating a copy of the Koran written in Ṭughril's hand. In 580/1184

Zayn al-Dīn Maḥmūd compiled an anthology of poetry for Ṭughril; this inspired Rāvandī to assemble his own edifying compilation of poetry and prose. The disturbances of the last years of Ṭughril's reign and the chaotic conditions that followed his death in battle in 590/1194, forced Rāvandī to abandon his project; but according to his own statement, he took it up again in 599/1202. The book was finally completed around 601/1204-5 and dedicated to the Saljūq ruler of Konya, Kaykhusraw ibn Qilij Arslān. Luther conjectured that Rāvandī wrote the work in order to obtain a post at that ruler's court through a display of his rhetorical skills;[5] but much of the book must have been completed around a decade earlier.[6]

That the *Rāḥat al-ṣudūr* was intended as an edifying compilation, and not specifically as a history, explains (1) Rāvandī's modifications of the model for his accounts of Saljūq history prior to Ṭughril's accession, Zahir al-Dīn Nīshāpūrī's *Saljūq nama;* (2) his often elaborate rhetorical style (which contrasts with Nīshāpūrī's far less ornamental one); and (3) his liberal use of interpolations. He seems to have intended to write a separate historical work describing the flourishing intellectual milieu of Ṭughril's court. He writes, "If the history of that house and the wonders of that realm were to be written, they would be more than ten *Shahnamehs* and *Iskandarnamehs,*" and asserts that should he live he will "write the history of Ṭughril's reign, and make of it a book in verse and prose."[7] (He also states that he has written a book on the heretical beliefs and scandalous actions of his *bête noire,* the "Rafidis" [Shi'is]).[8] The *Rāḥat al-ṣudūr's* contents are markedly diverse: its lengthy exordium includes praise of God, His prophets, the *Ahl-i Bayt* and other religious figures, and the *'ulama,* and concludes with a lengthy excursus on justice. It is liberally adorned with praise of Sultan Kaykhusraw, including panegyric *qasida*s of Rāvandī's own composition; the historical section on the Saljūqs also mentions and quotes poets who recited at their courts; and this section is followed by chapters on such practical subjects as the etiquette of the *nadīm,* wine, chess, and backgammon, horsemanship and hunting, court protocol, battle and feasting, calligraphy, and so on.

Iqbal counted, among Rāvandī's poetic interpolations, 249 verses by Nizami.[9] Five of these, by my count, are from *Layli u Majnun;* the overwhelming majority are drawn from *Khusraw u Shirin,* and it is upon these that I shall focus here. It is perhaps of interest that given his propensity for quotations illustrative of ethical precepts, Rāvandī does not draw upon the *Makhzan al-Asrar.* It is primarily the *Shahnamih* that serves as the source of such materials, with occasional quotes from other poets such as Sana'i.

A typical example of Rāvandī's use of quotations from *Layli u Majnun* is seen in his account of Chāvlī Jāndār and Khāṣbik Arslān ibn Bulankari.

Khāṣbik had been favored by Sultan Mas'ūd (529-47/1134-52); other amirs, jealous, complained to Chāvlī, whom they turned against him. The Sultan was displeased, and Chāvlī was obliged to apologize; the Sultan then ordered Khāṣbik to demonstrate his skill at horsemanship and polo, so that it would become clear why he was so favored. Chāvlī was amazed at this display; he

> showered Khāṣbik with honors, (giving him) a horse (with) a (jewelled) collar and reins and precious coverings, and sent him (back) to the Sultan.
> That service which your fortune will maintain:
> in doing it, don't loosely grip the rein.[10]

The bulk of Rāvandī's interpolations (excepting to some extent, the panegyrics) point to moral lessons or enjoin suitable conduct in specific situations, as does this one, and are often closely linked with the accounts in which they occur. This is the case with many of his quotations from *Khusraw u Shirin;* but here we find other methods of deployment that are less often seen with respect to other materials. We might posit a continuum ranging from general sentential purposes to situations in which quotations become incorporated into, and in effect part of, the narrative. At the sentential or homiletic end of this continuum we might place the verses quoted in the account of Sultan Muhammad ibn Maḥmūd's retreat from Baghdad after his siege of that city in 550.[11] The Sultan had, with difficulty, made his way from the west side of the Tigris to the east side, where he camped half a farsang from Baghdad, preparing to return to Hamadan.

> And although (his army was) in disarray, the Baghdadi troops did not have enough strength left to pursue him. Proverb: "Wrongdoing blessings sacks; and injustice misfortunes attracts."
>
> > Verse: Injustice everywhere doth anger bring;
> > wrongdoing brings from blessings evil things.
>
> The sultan salvaged only (the effects of) his vestibule, a single rug and five pack animals. The amirs brought (him) food from their own kitchens until

they reached Hulwan. Proverb: "He who is content with little will have no
need of abundance."

> Verse: Although the world withholds its goods from me,
> let my contentment be felicity.[12]

The Persian verse, from Nizami's description of how he came to write his
poem,[13] serves (as in the preceding instance) to gloss the Arabic proverb
and to reinforce the moral (and political) lesson that contentment with little
is better than desire for the things of this world. The technique is seen frequently in the *Rāḥat al-ṣudūr,* and one suspects that many of the unidentified Persian verses used as glosses may be of Rāvandī's own composition.

The practice of quoting exemplary verses to fit specific situations was
a common one; examples are found throughout Arabic and Persian literature. Rāvandī alludes to this practice, which was termed *tamaththul/
tamassul,* in a passage early in the book that moves from a simple insertion of verses to their incorporation in the narrative, and that occurs in
the account of the rise of the Saljūqs during the latter part of the reign of
Mas'ūd of Ghazna.[14]

When Mas'ūd returned to Ghazna from India (in 429/1037) he learned
of the Saljūq's ascendancy and of their growing might. He sent a messenger to the Amir of Khurasan (telling him), "You must fight the Saljūq
s and drive them out of Khurasan." The Amir of Khurasan replied, "They
are too powerful for me and the likes of me to oppose them.

> Place no more burden on me than I can
> endure; lade me according to my strength."

The sultan said, "Either he is fleeing from his duty, or he is making his
own plans, so that if something happens, he can make the most of it." He
ordered him firmly: "You must deal with this important matter;" and he
felt it necessary to quote, by way of example [*imtisāl*]:

> "It must be thus, in being or non-being,
> that you must gain the pleasure of the king."

The Amir of Khurasan rose and mustered his army; and the battle and the defeat were one."[15]

Both verses are from Nizami's prayer to God at the beginning of *Khusraw u Shirin.*[16] The first is put into the mouth of the Amir of Khurasan as his response to Mas'ūd; the second forms part of Mas'ūd's answer. As such, it has undergone considerable alteration from Nizami's entreaty to God:

> Maintain me such that, whether live or dead,
> I will be such a one as merited
> Your pleasure.

Would the audience have recognized the change? And what, one wonders, would they have made of it? Rāvandī is clearly playing games with the conventions of *tamassul:* first, by the anachronistic placing of Nizami's verses in the mouths of the Amir of Khurasan (the general Sūbāshī) and of Mas'ūd (conventionally, it is verses by poets of the past that are quoted as examples of perennial wisdom); and second, by transforming the meaning of both verses, which originally formed part of a pious prayer for God's mercy, into an excuse for the dereliction of duty and a royal reprimand. This transformation serves to highlight the moral collapse of the Ghaznavīds, which (for Saljūq apologists) led to their inevitable replacement by the Saljūqs.[17] The episode, with its quotations, thus forms part and parcel of the legitimating enterprise which marks both Nīshāpūrī's and (to a far greater extent) Rāvandī's treatment of the Saljūqs' rise to power.

Quotations from *Khusraw u Shirin* become more frequent as the history progresses, especially from the reign of Arslān ibn Ṭughril (556-71/ 1161-76) onwards, where they also become more intimately linked with the narrative. An example is found in the account of the appointment in 582/1186 of Qizil Arslān ibn Ildegüz as Ṭughril's Atabeg, following the death of his brother Muhammad Jahān Pahlavān.[18] On his appointment,

(Qizil Arslān) came from Bardan [?] in Azarbaijan with a large army, and paid homage to the Sultan in the palace. Qarāquz-i Sulṭānī [the Sultan's *hajib*] wanted to stab him; the Sultan forbade him with a glance, so he did not dare, though the deed could have been accomplished. Verse [from the *Shahnamih*]:

> Don't leave today's work till tomorrow comes;
> who knows how, on the morrow, times may change.
> When the red rose blossoms fresh today,
> one cannot wait to pluck it the next day.

Qizil Arslān found out (about this). He trusted the Sultan, but separated his familiars and (personal) slaves from him, and had Qarāquz-i Sulṭānī's eyes put out.

> From his two beauties they have torn the veil,
> and wounded with the rod the path of kohl.
> They've robbed the world of his pearls twain;
> not on a thread, but on two needles strung.[19]

These lines appear in Nizami's account of how Khusraw learned of the blinding of his father Hurmuz.[20] They are clearly meant to arouse pity, and Rāvandī's antipathy towards Qizil Arslān (who later imprisoned Ṭughril and claimed the sultanate) is clear, as is seen from his comment, "The deed could have been accomplished [*ān ḥarakatī kardanī būd*]," followed by Firdawsi's verses enjoining not putting off till tomorrow what should be done today. Earlier Nizami presented Hurmuz as an exemplar of royal justice (an exemplar of which Rāvandī himself makes use; see further below); but after lapsing into injustice, he was blinded by his rebellious nobles.[21] This appears to be the point that Rāvandī wishes to stress here: Qarāquz-i Sulṭānī, the Sultan's *ḥājib*, could have averted the subsequent usurpation of power by Qizil Arslān, who stands in contrast to Hurmuz as an exemplar of injustice and disloyalty toward his sovereign. His act thus represents an act of treachery parallel to that of Hurmuz's nobles.[22] However, Rāvandī's treatment of Ṭughril is not uncritical, and the verses may also be seen as anticipating his own lapses later in his reign.

Panegyrics feature prominently amongst Rāvandī's "interpolations," as noted earlier. They include *qasida*s of his own composition praising Kaykhusraw ibn Qilij Arslān, and others by poets of the Saljūqs, praising the sultans or their Atabegs. (There are also, at appropriate points, elegies, invective verses, and complaints of the times.) Panegyric poetry served important functions in promoting the achievements of a ruler or a dynasty, and was routinely incorporated into dynastic histories, where it helped to preserve the name and fame of the rulers extolled, as well as establishing the formation of both contemporary and retrospective images of those rulers.

In addition to panegyric *qasida*s, Rāvandī also quotes a number of panegyric passages from *Khusraw u Shirin*. Here, however, things are not always as straightforward as might be expected. Take, for example, the passage that follows Rāvandī's account of Ṭughril Beg's "investiture," outside the gates of Hamadan, by Bābā Ṭāhir (a clearly apocryphal invention that has no parallel in Nīshāpūrī). After enjoining Ṭughril to justice, the holy man drew off a broken bit from the neck of a pitcher that he wore as a ring, and placed it on Ṭughril's finger. Rāvandī now quotes seven lines from Nizami's praise of the Atabeg Muhammad ibn Ildegüz:

> When mercy was bestowed on humankind,
> two lords were named Muhammad. One became
> Through his pure essence, Seal of Prophecy;
> the other Kingdoms' Seal, in his own days.
> One ever of the Arabs' house the Moon;
> one ever of the Persians' realm the king.
> One liberated faith from tyranny;
> one through his justice made the world to thrive ... [23]

The verses are appropriate in that Ṭughril's Islamic name was Muhammad, and the account as a whole is again linked to Rāvandī's legitimating exercise, and demonstrates that the early Saljūqs enjoyed divine sanction. But the fact that Nizami's verses were addressed to Muhammad ibn Ildegüz would not have been lost upon the audience. And here, as elsewhere, it is the Atabeg who stands as the model of royal greatness and exemplary justice.[24]

Nor would this fact have been lost upon the audience in a second instance, when, after praising Sultan Kaykhusraw for his conquest of Antalya, Rāvandī quotes more verses from the same section of Nizami's poem.[25] The numbers in brackets represent the order of the verses in the printed text:

> 1   Rum's troops, more numerous than the Turks, he's made
> his Hindu slaves, wielding his Indian blade. [22,1]

2   The black iron cross they bore with them he's chewed
     as if it were of wax with victory's tooth. [21,13][26]

3   His steed, so swiftly speeding on its course,
     has given the sphere a seven-lap advance. [20,10]

4   By his good judgement he the world has seized;
     indeed, such does it mean to be God's shade! [21,1]

5   Whatever lives within creation's bounds,
     aside from the Creator, worships him. [21,2]

6   He ne'er neglects his foe—there's vigilance!
     He never sleeps.—There is true kingliness! [21,6]

7   None with such fortune has a mother born;
     with it he's conquered from Ethiop' to Chin. [21,11]

8   His hunting-ground is Abkhāz and Darband;
     his night-raids on Khwarazm and Samarqand. [22,2]

9   The customs of his father he maintains:
     supports the faith, holds bounty in his hand.[27]

10   May from this moon's face brightness never fade;
     may the crown never fall from this king's head. [22,4]

11   That king is a true Solomon of whom
     both faith and kingdom will preserve the name.[28]

12   Solomon had a ring; you've true belief;
     Alexander had a mirror; you've right conduct. [22,16]

13   What you have seen from Time they never saw:
     Alexander from his mirror, Kaykhusraw from his cup. [22,17]

This example contrasts with the previous one, in that while in the earlier passage the verses appear in the order in which they are found in the printed text, here Rāvandī has rearranged them to convey a particular effect, beginning with the victory over the Byzantines and ending with mention of Kaykhusraw (the printed text has "Jamshid"), while the central line (7) presents the image of Kaykhusraw (a potential analogue of Jahān Pahlavān himself) as a ruler of unprecedented fortune and a world-conqueror.[29] Such rearrangement is typical of Rāvandī's use of *Shahnameh* materials, in which he combines verses from different sections of the poem into one long passage. It is less typical of his use of Nizami's verses, however, and one may imagine that the audience would not have missed the rhetorical effect that is clearly intended.

Other panegyric passages bear more specific topical relevance. For example, on Ṭughril's restoration to the throne in 588, after he had been freed from the prison in which Qizil Arslān had placed him, Rāvandī quotes Nizami's lines celebrating his succession to Arslān:[30]

1   Once more, in youthful fortune, the Sultan—
      may he long prosper with both throne and crown—[15,7]
2   In glorious rule was joined to crown and throne,
      and mounted there, in place of Arslān. [15,11]
3   The kingdom's refuge, sovereign lord, Ṭughril,
      a monarch of just rule, lord of the world; [15,9]
4   The throne-illumer of the clime of thought;
      the kingdom-taker of the realm of life. [15,8]
5   Ṭughril, who holdes existence in his hands—
      a heaven of fortune, sea of bounteousness—[15,10]
6   Exalts in conquest of the seven climes,
      and brings within his yoke the heavens nine; [16,5]
7   Binds Ethiops' dark curls to fair Tamghach;
      brings Shushtar's finest silks to far-off Chach; [16,2]
8   With the falcon of his parasol doth seize
      the Phoenix; his gold crown the Pleiades; [16,3]
9   His glory lifts his parasol to the heavens;
      his leaping stallion looses Oxus' bonds; [16,4]
10   Now sends him taxes the Khaqan of Chin;
      now infidels' tribute does the Qaysar send. [16,6]

Here again, the changes are noteworthy and made for rhetorical effect.
Where Nizami wrote,

When, graced by youthful fortune, the Sultan—
may he long prosper with both throne and crown ...[31]
In glorious rule was joined to crown and throne,
and mounted there in place of Arslān,

Rāvandī inserts the emphatic "Once more" to mark the event of Ṭughril's
restoration. Nizami follows these lines of praise (15:7-11) with a passage

describing how he had begun his poem upon Ṭughril's accession, and apologizes for the delay in its presentation:

> If on this road I tarried, 'twas that he
> might from his other occupations be
> At ease; bind Ethiops' curls to fair Tamghāch ... [32]

Rāvandī changes Nizami's optative to the past tense (e.g., in the line just quoted, he substitutes *payvast* for Nizami's *bandad*), and changes the subject in the final line from Khusraw, who "takes taxes and tributes" from the Khaqan and Qaysar, to those rulers themselves, who send the same to Ṭughril. The passage thus reads as a catalogue of Ṭughril's accomplishments, rather than of those preoccupations from which Nizami waited for him to find leisure.[33] Again, Rāvandī moves to a climax, as the passage that began with Ṭughril's restoration to the throne then moves through his virtues and achievements, and ends with the universal doublet: that he is sent taxes by Chīn and Rūm (East and West) establishes him as ruler of the world.

Other examples are somewhat less straightforward. Noting the accession of Malikshāh ibn Maḥmūd (who reigned for four months and sixteen days) in 547/1152, Rāvandī describes that ruler as "powerful, majestic, with a mighty arm, a powerful archer, generous and good-tempered, a lover of jest (*hazl*) who patronized the base, avid for sexual relations, adorner of crown and throne, with balanced movements and praiseworthy character."[34] We may note how Malikshāh's less desirable qualities are sandwiched between more admirable ones. He then quotes (again, with some reworking) verses from *Khusraw u Shirin,* in which Shapur describes Khusraw to Shirin.[35] In Rāvandī's version this passage begins, "An Alexander in his retinue; / a Darius in horsemanship"[36] and ends, "The heart bids welcome to his fortune blest; / where there is fortune, there too is success."[37] Shapur's description emphasizes, in particular, Khusraw's magnificence ("The world is straightened by his retinue; / his standard flies above the seven thrones"; 70:6), his beauty ("His beauty does illumine the 'Īd's feast; / virtue's his essence, beauty the excess"; 70:12), and his youth:

> A rose without the harm of autumn's wind;
> a fresh spring blossom on youth's supple branch ...

> No box-tree round his rose has sprouted yet;
> his cypress is still, like the lily, white.[38]

The audience, aware of Nizami's poem, would also have been aware that Khusraw spent much of his time in the pursuit of pleasure (a theme Nizami stresses throughout), and that it was his self-indulgent conduct that earned him punishment by Hurmuz (see below).

Malikshāh ibn Maḥmūd ascended the throne in Rajab 547/October 1152 and was deposed in Shawwal 547/January 1153. The cause of his deposition was this: that he was continually occupied with drinking and pleasure with two or three base persons. Proverb: "A king who inclines to excessive obscenity [*sukhf*] and to jest [*hazl*] will be connected with the base and with those lacking wits." [A *dubayti* of similar purport follows.] "A woman named Jamal was his partner (in pleasure) and dominated him." [An Arabic proverb and verses follow.] "He lived in great comfort and pomp, and passed his life in pleasure and enjoyment, boasting of kingship, and of a kingdom remote from enemies." [A *qasida* by Sayyid Ashraf [Ḥasan-i Ghaznavī] congratulating Malikshāh on his accession, which is over three pages in length, follows.]

> Sultan Malikshāh gave the amirs of the court less [than was customary?]. Khāṣbik became suspicious of him, and avoided him, (thinking that) he was plotting to summon him in private and seize him.[39]

Khāṣbik decided on a preemptive strike (both Nīshāpūrī and Rāvandī use the expression, "Before [the Sultan] could sup he [Khāṣbik] breakfasted"). He and the sultan's bodyguard (Ḥasan-i Jāndār) (and, according to Nīshāpūrī, several others), arranged to invite the Sultan to Khāṣbik's palace for three days. There,

> while the Sultan slept, he, the woman, and two or three
> servants were seized, and a messenger was sent to his
> brother Sultan Muhammad, who came from Khuzistan and
> ascended the throne in the palace of Hamadan.[40]

Khusraw, fleeing from Bahram Chubin, tarried in Armenia to dally with Shirin; later, he sought out the courtesan Shakar in Isfahan. Similarly,

Malikshāh ibn Maḥmūd spent his time enjoying wine, women, and song; his disaffected courtiers seized and deposed him. Rāvandī's moral is clear, and is pushed home by the use of proverbs and verses, amongst which the quotation from Nizami (which points to unfulfilled—or, in the case of Khusraw, only lately fulfilled—potential) anticipates the fate of kings who devote themselves to pleasure.

A similar passage occurs in connection with Ṭughril, following his seizure of the fortress of Ṭabarak in Rayy from the Khvarazmian troops in 590/1194 and his defeat of the Khvarazmians in battle outside the city, after which he returned triumphant to Hamadan. It is taken from the section in *Khusraw u Shirin* in which Shapur goes to seek Shirin for a second time.[41]

That sovereign ruler, who was the shadow of the Creator (may His name be exalted!)—the face of the earth was covered with the light of his justice and beauty, and his fortune increased each day, and good luck showed its face (to him).

1   O happy realm, that is the realm of life!
     O lovely day, that is the day of youth! [102,12]
2   No love is sweeter than the love of life,
     no time more precious than the time of youth. [102,13]
3   The king Ṭughril, who the world's master was,
     was young—and what a charming youth he was! [103,1]
4   Since Adam's time until his own, no youth
     in all the world his royal *farr* has owned.[42]
5   He drank no draught of wine without a song,
     nor merry made without the minstrel's tune. [103,2]
6   For every song the singer sang, he'd measure
     as its reward, no less than a rich treasure. [103,3]

Rāvandī goes on to describe Ṭughril's pride in his physical strength (he spent much time in martial exercise), and quotes a *dubayti* that the Sultan had composed and was fond of reciting:

I'm not a branch's fruit in shade grown ripe,
nor am I even dust in the sun's eye;
But if upon my foes' unmanly heads
I place not women's veils, no man am I.

Rāvandī concludes: "He could not prevail over his enemies [literally: "he could not put a veil over their heads"]; but his enemies exposed his delicate head on the scaffold, and upturned the standard of his fortune."[43] The quotation from Nizami is clearly meant to arouse sympathy for the young Sultan and pity for his ultimate fate. However, it suggests further that he (like Malikshāh before him, and like Nizami's Khusraw) neglected affairs of state for more self-indulgent pursuits.

A final encomiastic quotation appears in the context of Jamāl al-Dīn Ay Aba's taking over the rule of the region of Hamadan in 593.[44] The event was a recent one; the passage functions as a prayer for Ay Aba's well-being and his continued rule. It is taken from one of a series of lengthy dialogues between Khusraw and Shirin, and comes from one of her responses that typically begin with expressions of homage, and go on to reproach Khusraw.[45]

All was in the control of the possessor of the great lord, Malik al-Umarā' Jamāl al-Dīn Ay Aba, and Hamadan and the province became quiet.

> May that great king forever rule the world,
> God his support and Fortune his true friend.
> May the sphere serve his belted sword, and he
> possess the elephant's strength, the lion's awe.
> May that head which seeks separation from
> his service, not escape his sword's sharp blow.
> May his command e'er rule throughout the world,
> and God be his supporter in both worlds.

Rāvandī makes a number of alterations to Nizami's text. The first one is only logical: Nizami's line reads,

> That cypress with the tulip-cheeks replied,
> "May fortune the world's sovereign ever aid."

He changes (again logically) Shirin's address to Khusraw in the second person ("May the sphere serve *your* belted sword," etc.) to the third person, characteristic of the *du'a,* and in the third line substitutes *khidmat-ash*

("his service") for Nizami's *ṭawq-i tu* ("your yoke"). The fourth line
(which does not appear in this passage in the printed text) replaces
Nizami's fourth line, which is a prayer to avert the evil eye.

These verses precede an account of an attack by the caliphal army on
Hamadan, which they easily seized, as Malik Uzbak, the ruler of Persian
Iraq, shut himself up in the fortress. The Amir-i 'Alam, who had accom-
panied the army from Baghdad, presented the caliph's greetings to Malik
Uzbak, along with an elaborate sword-belt, saying, "The caliph sent this
to you." A quotation from *Layli u Majnun* follows, which begins:

> To those who ask for justice, do not send
> a message, unless on a truthful tongue.

Malik Uzbak was restored to his own abode and things quieted down, but
Ay Aba left Hamadan, "because he did not trust the Baghdadis' word."
Another quotation from *Layli u Majnun* follows, beginning

> Don't trust the covenant of anyone
> if in your heart you've found no place for him,[46]

and continues with warnings against underestimating one's enemies
and exhortations to avoid hypocrites and false friends. One such "false
friend" was the former *mamlūk* Miyājuq, who drove the Amir-i 'Alam
from Hamadan. Another was Malik Uzbak himself, who reinstalled Nūr
al-Dīn Kukja (see further below). While the verses from *Khusraw u
Shirin* stand as a prayer for Ay Aba's continued good fortune, those from
Layli u Majnun point to his wisdom in not putting his trust in unreliable
allies.

Rāvandī is not noteworthy for his use of elaborate descriptive passages, in contrast to his older contemporary Afẓal al-Dīn Kirmanī, whose
'Iqd al-ūlā abounds with descriptions that are rhetorical *tours de force*.
Two lengthy quotations are notable exceptions. The first is a description
of Mazandaran, quoted from the *Shahnameh,* which precedes Rāvandī's
account of his ill-fated journey there in 585/1189.[47] The second is a

battle scene taken from Nizami's description of Khusraw's battle with Bahram Chubin, inserted into an account of Sultan Arslān's battle with the ruler of Abkhāz in 556/1161, where it merges into the narrative.[48]

Rāvandī greatly embellishes Nīshāpūrī's rather terse account of these events,[49] which simply states that during the Atabeg Ildegüz's extended absence from Arran (while he was suppressing Muhammad ibn Maḥmūd's attempt to seize the sultanate), the "King of Abkhāz" became covetous of "the border regions of the lands of Islam" and mounted an invasion, but was defeated by a Muslim coalition led by Arslān and Ildegüz. Rāvandī employs the usual proverbs and brief verses, and indulges in a rhetorical heightening of Nīshāpūrī's somewhat telegraphic prose, but the centerpiece of the account is the lengthy quotation from Nizami, which begins:

> So many armies flocked to the Sultan
> like rows of hills they marched across the plains …

Twenty lines from Nizami's description follow, describing a bloody and violent battle. In *Khusraw u Shirin* (as in history), Khusraw had obtained troops from the Byzantine emperor to help him fight Bahram, who was supported largely by Turks. Here the roles are reversed: whereas in Nizami's poem the Turks were the defeated foe, in Rāvandī they represent the victorious Saljūq troops. Nizami's description of Khusraw's battle takes the place of a "historically accurate" description of what actually happened. The entire episode is constructed as a tribute to the wisdom and expertise of Shams al-Dīn Ildegüz, as Rāvandī concludes:

> And had it not been for the foresight and prudence of the Great Atabeg, which prevented the army of Islam from falling upon them [the Christians], not a single one would have survived, and the King of Abkhāz would have been captured. Notwithstanding, they pillaged all those white banners, the golden cross and silver chalice, and most of the effects of the treasury and *sharābkhāna;* and he, with his last breath, and without boots, mounted up and fled.[50]

One of the most interesting features of Rāvandī's use of quotations, which has already been anticipated in some of the examples quoted above, is his incorporation of them into his narrative. While his use of this technique varies, its frequency increases as the narrative moves to more recent events. Moreover, this narrative interpolation of Nizami's verses seems not without irony, as was seen in the exchange quoted above between Mas'ūd of Ghazna and Sūbāshī. An early example is seen in Rāvandī's description of the caliph al-Qa'im's welcome of Ṭughril Beg into Baghdad.[51] When Ṭughril entered Baghdad he went to the gates of the caliphal *haram* and paid homage; on his return to camp the caliph sent his respects, along with many precious gifts. Thus far, Rāvandī follows Nīshāpūrī;[52] but at this point he inserts a passage from Nizami's description of Khusraw's arrival at the court of the Armenian queen Mahīn Bānū.[53]

1   When the caliph of his arrival learned,
    he sped in royal fashion to attend. [93,8]

2   He ordered that they fly the king to meet;
    arrayed an army with well-weaponed might. [93,9]

3   Precious and kingly tributes he dispatched,
    to the treasury, as manners did prescribe. [94,1]

4   Brocades and slaves, treasures and precious gems:
    to write them all exhausted the scribes' pens. [94,2]

5   They placed a seat in the caliph's *haram;*
    while all the others stood, he sat thereon. [94,4]

6   "How do you fare?" the caliph asked of him,
    "may your life e'er be fresh, and increase gain! [94,5]

7   I've summoned you to be my guest; be sure
    I wish this visit may not burden you. [94,6]

8   This region boasts a warm and pleasant air;
    there is abundant grass and water here." [95,3]

9   He sought a pleasant region; they set down
    their baggage, there took royal throne and crown. [95,6]

10 The caliph, for that ruler of the world,
    did not fail to perform all service due. [95,8]

Rāvandī's liberties with this passage are substantial. In the opening line, his substitution of "the caliph" for Nizami's "Mahīn Bānū" is clearly required by the context. But whereas Mahīn Bānū went out to meet Khusraw ("She sprouted wings to go and meet the king"), the caliph commands that Ṭughril be met and escorted into his presence. Where Mahīn Bānū set a seat for Khusraw "beneath [her] throne," the caliph does the same for Ṭughril "in [his] *haram*"; where Khusraw asked after Mahīn Bānū's health and apologized for any inconvenience to her ("Upon your hospitality I've placed / a heavy weight; may it not cause you pain"), the caliph inquires after Ṭughril's health and hopes he will not find the reception tiring. Rāvandī omits a long passage describing how Mahīn Bānū entertained Khusraw for a week in the plain of Muqan (KS 94:3-16, 95:1-2), at the end of which she invited him to return to her capital, Barda', to winter there in its warm climate. Here Rāvandī picks up Nizami's passage, but it is Baghdad which boasts the warm climate, and instead of Nizami's description of Barda' ("It was a pleasant region"), Rāvandī has the caliph search for a suitable place for Ṭughril and his troops. In the end, like Mahīn Bānū, the caliph falls short of no service to his "guest."

The fact that this account is devoid of historical accuracy is somewhat beside the point: historical accuracy, in particular with regard to the early Saljūqs, is not one of Rāvandī's chief priorities. Legitimation is, as we saw earlier; and that the caliph should receive Ṭughril and entertain him, provide him with gifts and accommodation, and act, in every way, subservient to him, on his *first* entrance into Baghdad (rather than delaying the interview for some thirteen months; see n. 50) sets the caliphal seal of approval on the Saljūq house. But it is not without irony to see the caliph "playing hostess" to his Turkish "guest." A few pages later we learn that the caliph himself was obliged to request an allowance from the Sultan for his own living expenses.[54]

The beginning of Arslān's reign (556/1161) is marked by a passage (from "Shirin's Accession") celebrating Arslān's own accession, quoted almost verbatim except for the substitution of "the Sultan" for "Shirin" in the first line.[55]

> When on the sultan kingship was confirmed,
> his kingdom's glory reached from Fish to Moon.

The passage is encomiastic, and its usage appears unexceptional, except for the change in gender. Another passage, describing Khusraw's hunt, is used a propos of Arslān's return to Hamadan in 560/1165 following a successful campaign against the Nizari Isma'ilis in the region of Qazvin:[56]

> With an auspicious portent, and a day
> of royal fortune, the king sought the plain.

(In the original the opening line reads, "With a fortune auspicious as Shirin's face.") Omissions and the rearrangement of some lines transform a depiction of Khusraw with his retinue departing for the hunt into that of a triumphal army on parade. A final brief quotation, from "Khusraw's Accession," concludes the account of Arslān's conquest of Ray and his defeat of the rebel Inanj in 564/1169.[57]

Atabeg Ildegüz and Sultan Arslān died within a few months of each other, in 571/1176, the latter after a protracted illness. The young Ṭughril ibn Arslān, then seven years old, was placed on the throne, and his Atabeg, Muhammad ibn Ildegüz Jahān Pahlavān, quickly defeated two rival claimants to the sultanate and pacified the realm. The account of these events (which follows Nīshāpūrī, whose *Saljūq nama* ends at this point) is followed by verses from *Khusraw u Shirin* drawn (unusually) from two separate sections of the poem.[58] One describes Khusraw feasting, with all the rulers of the world subservient to him, and introduces a scene in which he asks his companions where the world's most beddable women are to be found;[59] the other describes Khusraw's restoration after his defeat of Bahrām Chūbīn.[60] A few pages later, we learn that it was the Atabeg who was the real ruler: "(The Sultan) was occupied with feasting and pleasure, the Atabeg with battle and toil."[61]

Symptoms of decline soon set in, as the Atabeg exploited the province of Fars, and divided control of Iraq amongst his own *mamlūks*.[62] When Muhammad ibn Ildegüz died in 582/1186, his brother Qizil Arslān was appointed in his stead. Fearing Qizil Arslān's rapidly increasing power, Ṭughril fled from Hamadan; meanwhile, the Atabeg began plotting to seize Ṭughril and depose him. In 583/1187, while the sultan was campaigning against the Nizārīs, Qizil Arslān, tired of waiting to see what might happen, went to Hamadan, preparing to return to his own domains in Azarbaijan.

> It was autumn. One night Amir Sayyid Fakhr al-Dīn ʾAlaʾ al-Dawla ʾArabshah [the *ra'īs* of Hamadan] lit a large fire on the roof of his house.

The Atabeg thought that the Sultan had returned to Hamadan, and had with him experienced troops. (Qizil Arslān) left by night, and took the road to Azarbaijan. Verse [from the *Shahnameh*]:

> With one's head still in place, a timely flight
> is better than for fame to seek a fight.
> He who unjustly seeks a battle will
> come out of that affair heart-sore and pale …[63]

Ten lines of similar purport follow.

Shortly after Ṭughril did indeed return to Hamadan, where he was welcomed by its officials. Lines from Nizami follow, from the scene in which Khusraw and Shirin finally meet.[64]

[The officials] paid homage (to the Sultan), and the other amirs waited on him.

> From every side new armies ever came,
> and ranged themselves in lines around the king.
> When they about the mountainside were massed,
> beneath their weight the earth groaned to the Ox.[65]

The people of Hamadan gave thanks from the depths of their hearts, and rejoiced. A heavy snow was falling; the sultan turned towards the city, and Amir Sayyid Fakhr al-Dīn 'Ala' al-Dawla paid him homage and offered him the palace of the *riyasat* to alight in.

> "O king, O lord," to the sultan he said,
> "I, and a thousand like me, are your slaves.
> The sky gains its felicity from your crown;
> the earth nobility beneath your throne.
> If the king honors me with his presence,
> this slave will proudly gird himself to serve.
> If the elephant on the ant's carpet treads,
> that lowly one in robes of joy is garbed."
> The king said, "If you will accept a guest,
> I'll come with all my soul, if you'll accept
> My soul."[66] He lodged the Sultan in a palace—
> nay, Paradise, and Tuba but a branch
> Of it—which to the heavens soared,
> boasting two courtyards vast, both long and broad.

Then, with apologies, he sent to him
such repasts as are customary for kings,
And from his coffers offered such rich treasure
that its abundance scarcely could be measured.[67]

Once again, as in the account of Ṭughril Beg's reception by the caliph, roles are reversed: where Shirin played hostess to Khusraw and lodged him in a fine palace, and Mahīn Bānū sent him fine foods and gifts, it is Ālā' al-Dawla who performs these services for Ṭughril. Ṭughril repaid the *ra'īs*'s service not long after: in 584/1189, he had Fakhr al-Dīn Ālā' al-Dawla strangled with a bowstring, after the latter was accused of having ordered the poisoning of Sultan Arslān.[68]

We may recall that when Khusraw finally met Shirin, he was fleeing from Bahrām Chūbīn, who had seized the throne, and had taken refuge in Armenia for a second time. Is this quotation, which nicely balances that on Ṭughril Beg's triumphal entrance into Baghdad, meant to anticipate Ṭughril's later imprisonment by Qizil Arslān, who claimed the sultanate for himself, and, indeed, his ultimate fate?

A similar anticipation of disaster is found in a seemingly innocuous quotation cited toward the end of Ṭughril's reign. Faced, on the one hand, by a revolt led by Qutlugh Inanch (one of Qizil Arslān's four sons), and on the other by the Khwārazmshāh (who, despite the setback at Ray, had not abandoned his designs on Iraq),

the Sultan was busy with sport and pleasure, and ignored (matters in) the outlying regions. The Khwārazmshāh violated his obligations to his lord [the Sultan]—a heritage from [his father] Atsiz, who had rebelled against Sultan Sanjar. [Verses] ... (Now) he too violated the obligations of servitude, raised the parasol, called himself "sultan," and at the invitation of a few of the (local) rulers [one of whom was Qutlugh Inanch] set out for Iraq. The Sultan was in Ray, boasting of his strength, and not one of the amirs was in concord with him or loyal to him. They continually wrote secret messages to Qutlugh Inanch and the notables in his service (saying), "When we reach the gates of Ray, we will deliver the sultan to you ..."

When they combed out the black locks of the night,
and turned into a moth day's candle bright,
Beneath the ebony backgammon board
the two sandarac dice became concealed.[69]

The lines are from a passage in *Khusraw u Shirin* describing nightfall, as Shapur makes his way to Shirin's abode in Armenia. Here, their effect is to signal the growing darkness that would soon overtake Ṭughril; and indeed, on the next page we learn of the Sultan's death in battle outside Ray, abandoned by his troops to the enemy. There is irony in the fact that in *Khusraw u Shirin,* the line immediately following these two states:

> Jupiter rose, bearing a writ: "The king's
> escaped his bonds, and Shapur's freed from pain."

While the "bonds" and "pain" represent Khusraw's preoccupation with Shirin, and Shapur's search for her, we may recall that Jupiter (Mushtarī) is the royal planet. In this context, while Khusraw is drawing closer to his goal—union with Shirin—Ṭughril's separation from his sultanate, and from his life, is drawing nearer still.

Following the Saljūq defeat, Iraq was exposed to the depredations of Khwarazmians, rebel amirs, rival ex-*mamlūks,* and caliphal troops. Qutlugh Inanch determined to join the Khvarazmshah in Ray; Jamāl al-Dīn Ay Aba disagreed, reproached him and told him:

> "This is a time of catastrophe; there is no profit in stirring up trouble. Until these days of misery and misfortune pass it is best to creep into a corner and stay there." That was his judgement; Qutlugh Inanch did not heed it, and went to Ray.

> Good judgement is the key to victory;
> for iron judgement is a golden key.
> Strong will is better than a hundred swords;
> a king's crown better than a hundred forms.[70]
> With judgement you can break an army's back;
> a sword will kill one man or ten at most.[71]

These lines are taken from Nizami's description of Khusraw's second flight from Bahram Chubin.[72] Nizami's first line reads, "The key to victory smiles as if to say"; that is, it is the personified "key" that enunciates the principle that strong judgment is the key to victory. (Rāvandī substitutes *padīd-ast,* "it is clear," to rhyme with *kilīd-ast* in the second half-line.) In Nizami's poem these lines refer to Bahrām Chūbīn, whose strong judgment enabled him to seize Khusraw's throne. Rāvandī transforms this statement into a gnomic admonition aimed at Qutlugh Inanch, whose lack of judgment led ultimately to his seizure by the Khwarazmian troops, who "cut off his head, like a sheep."[73]

Rāvandī gives a detailed account of the former Pahlavāni *mamlūk* Nūr al-Dīn Kukja, who was given control of the region of Hamadan by the Atabeg Abu Bakr, "and committed wrongs that cannot be grasped by the perception or approached by the understanding."[74] The Hamadanis wanted to depose him but Kukja declared, "I hold it (Hamadan) by the sword, and will not let it go." The Atabeg was angered but could do little about it. Meanwhile Kukja made an unprovoked attack against the ruler of Avah, who complained to Malik Uzbak, the ruler of Persian Iraq, and was given permission to repel him.

> Kukja knew that he would have to fight; he made a few raids, then came to Hamadan.

> > He bade a crier proclaim throughout the land,
> > "Woe unto those who'd raise a violent hand
> > 'Gainst others. Should a horse invade a field
> > or someone fruit from the fruit-grower steal;
> > Or look upon the face of one forbidden;
> > install a Turkish slave for acts of sin:
> > I will mete out that punishment that's fit."
> > He swore a mighty oath to this effect.[75]

> He caught the people napping, and in this way acquired much wealth ...[76]

In *Khusraw u Shirin* these lines precede the story of Hurmuz's punishment of Khusraw and exemplify his even-handed justice. Their use with respect to Kukja, whose abuses are excoriated not only by Rāvandī but by his contemporary Jarbādhqānī, constitutes the height of irony.

These verses also lead us to a final example of Rāvandī's use of quotations from Nizami: his insertion of the lengthy episode that relates how Khusraw took his pleasure in the meadow, abused the villagers, was punished, repented, and, finally, dreamed of his grandfather Anūshīrvān, who promised that the possessions taken from him in punishment would be replaced by even better ones,[77] at the end of the excursus on justice, which concludes the lengthy exordium of the *Rāḥat al-ṣudūr*. The episode functions as an exemplary tale.[78] It is followed by an exhortation to Sultan Kaykhusraw, "heir to the rule of the Saljūqs," to "revive these customs," suppress the conflict between Hanafis and Shafiʿis that is so detrimental to Islam, and restore the pious foundations and endowments (*awqāf*) of his ancestors.[79] This is the only instance in which a quotation from *Khusraw u Shirin* relates explicitly to an event in the past. In the examples seen above, by contrast, the poem seems to represent for Rāvandī not past but living history. The integration of quotations into Rāvandī's own narrative further highlights the contemporary relevance of Nizami's poem.

Nizami wrote *Khusraw u Shirin* in Rāvandī's own time. It contains dedications to Nizami's patron Ṭughril, to Ṭughril's Atabeg Muhammad ibn Eldiguz, and to Qizil Arslān. The poet was still alive; indeed, he had recently completed the *Haft Paykar* (dedicated to the Atabeg of Maragha, Alaʾ al-Dīn Korp-Arslān, whose relations with the Saljūqs and, in particular, with the Ildegüzids, were strained, to say the least), and his *Iskandarnama* contains a dedication to the Atabeg Abu Bakr, of whose misgovernment Rāvandī is openly and scathingly critical.[80] We have no way of knowing what Nizami might have thought of Rāvandī's use of his verses (or even whether he knew of it) and of the liberties he often took with them.[81]

These liberties raise a number of questions, most of which must remain unanswered, as we know nothing about the reception of the *Rāḥat al-ṣudūr* itself. Apart from such stylistic strategies as rearranging verses to form what is essentially a new composition, or of integrating verses into the narrative in the ways that we have seen above,[82] several other issues bear further consideration. But before exploring these issues, let me return briefly to Luther's comments on Rāvandī.

Luther stressed that Rāvandī was writing for a highly sophisticated audience, an audience of his peers, skilled in the intricacies and the subtleties of the secretarial or chancery style.[83] We should perhaps extend the characterization of Rāvandī's "ideal reader(s)" to include not merely rhetorical but literary competence. Such readers would be familiar with the sources of Rāvandī's quotations: Firdawsi, or the version of Firdawsi Rāvandī may have used;[84] contemporary or recent court poetry; and the works of Nizami. While it is possible that such readers might not always have recalled the precise context of a given quotation, especially if it was a brief one, they would most likely have known where long passages were taken from. More importantly, we must assume that Rāvandī himself knew precisely where in Nizami's text his quotations came from and might well have expected his audience—his peers—to do the same.

This leads to a second point. Luther, discussing manuals for secretaries written in the Saljūq period, asserted that they laid down the "rules of the game" of composition, which were then assiduously, if not religiously, followed by writers from the secretarial cadre—among them "historians" like Rāvandī—who, anxious for preferment, sought to conform to the aforesaid "rules."[85] This raises two other questions: first, to what extent were such rules *descriptive* rather than merely *prescriptive;* and second, is not setting out the "rules of the game" an invitation to play the greater game—that is, to manipulate them, to bend, if not actually to break them? I have indicated above that Rāvandī plays games with the conventions of *tamassul;* I hope also to show, or at least to suggest, that in his use of quotations from Nizami he also bends the "rules," often to ironic effect.

We may perhaps class this use of quotations into two overlapping, interrelated categories: the general or universal, and the contingent. These categories are by no means mutually exclusive. In the case of any given quotation, both are usually present, and contingency must be extended to encompass the specific loci from which the quotations are drawn, as well as the specific situations to which they are applied. On what might be called the "general" level, Rāvandī is concerned (like other writers, both contemporary and earlier, not least among them Nizami) with presenting an ideal of kingship. Not incidentally, he also wishes to legitimate Saljūq rule both in the past and, it is to be hoped, when revived and restored by Sultan Kaykhusraw. In the equation of ideal kingship three figures are prominent: Hurmuz, Ṭughril Beg, and Muhammad Jahān Pahlavān, although the latter verges on "contingency." These three figures may be seen as virtual analogues. For example, when praising Ṭughril Beg Rāvandī quotes Nizami's praise of Muhammad Jahān Pahlavān, while in the exordium he relates the long story of Hurmuz's punishment of Khusraw. The three are thus linked as exemplars of kingship.

"Contingency" surfaces in passages relating both to Ṭughril III and to Sultan Kaykhusraw, the envisioned restorer of the Saljūq *dawlat.* With respect to the former, Rāvandī quotes Nizami's lines celebrating his accession in the context of his later restoration. There is a suggestion (with all due regard for panegyric hyperbole) that the accomplishments listed were not really within Ṭughril's grasp, either past or present. As for Sultan Kaykhusraw, the exemplar who is the actual subject of praise in Nizami is, of course, Muhammad Jahān Pahlavān, the model of ideal rule.

When we extend this notion of contingency to textual contexts, as well as to the situations in respect of which certain verses are quotes, things become more complicated and, as Sherlock Holmes was wont to say, "The game's afoot!" We noted, for example, Rāvandī's quotation of

Shapur's description of the youthful prince Khusraw in connection with the rapidly deposed Malikshāh ibn Maḥmūd and, perhaps more significantly, of a description of Khusraw's youthful merrymaking that follows Ṭughril III's defeat of the Khwarazmians outside of Ray in 590/1194, a defeat that inspired in that ruler what might be called a false sense of security. The depiction of the triumphant Sultan devoting himself to the pursuit of pleasure does not augur well for the future.

Perhaps the most perplexing—and interesting—aspect of Rāvandī's use of Nizami is the question of role and/or gender reversal, of which there are several conspicuous examples. The first, chronologically speaking, is the description of Ṭughril Beg's supposed reception by the caliph on the occasion of his first entry into Baghdad in 447/1055. Not only is this historically inaccurate, it is also a major example of both role and gender reversal, as the positive role played by the Armenian queen Mahīn Bānū in welcoming Khusraw in her domains, providing him refuge, and accommodating him in princely fashion, is translated by Rāvandī into the caliph's subservient welcoming of the Saljūq into his capital of Baghdad. (This is even more ironic when we recall that the caliph was obliged to seek an allowance from Ṭughril.) The second conspicuous example is that of Fakhr al-Dīn ʿAlāʾ al-Dawla's similar welcoming of Ṭughril III on his return to Hamadan in 583/1187. Here the words and actions of Shirin and Mahīn Bānū in receiving Khusraw, on his second flight to Armenia, are performed by the *ra'is* of Hamadan, who was ultimately rewarded for his "hospitality" by losing his life on Ṭughril's order. (So much, we might say, for hospitality.)

Could Rāvandī's ideal audience/reader(s) have been impervious to such manipulations, such subtleties, such ironies? Or did Rāvandī choose his verses simply because he found them most apt to the particular context or more rhetorically persuasive than others, without concern for context and without imagining that his audience would not have registered either what sections of Nizami's poem his quotations were drawn from or how, on occasion, they were reworked? Despite repeated complaints by contemporary writers on the decline of learning in Saljūq times, the existence of such sophisticated and complex writers as Rāvandī, Kirmanī, Jarbādhqānī, and Nizami (to name only those directly relevant to this discussion) demonstrates that there would have been others like them who would have been appreciative of their highly rhetorical styles, although perhaps contemporary rulers might not have been amongst them.[86] Whatever the case, the *Rāḥat al-ṣudūr* is a work of remarkable sophistication (as well as of considerable passion, in its accounts of contemporary events), as is seen not least in Rāvandī's use of quotations by his contemporary Nizami.

Notes

1. Julie Scott Meisami, "Rāvandī's *Rāḥat al-ṣudūr:* History or Hybrid?," *Edebiyat* 5 (1994): 181-215.

2. Julie Scott Meisami, "The *Shah-name* as Mirror for Princes: A Study in Reception," in *Pand-o Sokhan: Melanges Offerts A Charles-Henri de Fouchecour,* eds. Christophe Balay, Claire Kappler, and Ziva Vesel (Tehran: Institut Francais de Recherche en Iran, 1995), 265-73.

3. Julie Scott Meisami, *Persian Historiography to the End of the Twelfth Century,* chapter 3 (Edinburgh: Edinburgh University Press, forthcoming).

4. Muhammad ibn ʿAlī Rāvandī, *The Rāḥat us-ṣudur wa Ayat as-Surur,* ed. Muhammad Iqbal (Leiden and London: E. J. Brill, 1921), 39-44.

5. K. Allin Luther, "Islamic Rhetoric and the Persian Historians, 1000-1300 A.D." In *Studies in Near Eastern Culture and History in Memory of Ernest T. Abdel-Massih* (Ann Arbor: University of Michigan, Center for Near Eastern and North African Studies, 1990), 95.

6. It seems clear that Rāvandī began his work during Ṭughril's reign. Later, mentioning a pupil whom he tutored around 593-4/1197-8 (Shihab al-Dīn Aḥmad al-Qasani), Rāvandī states: "At that time this composition was in my mind; and I agreed to include his noble name in the book ... and leave a memorial to him on this earth and express my gratitude for his patronage" (1921: 49). Rāvandī's tutelage of Shihab al-Dīn Aḥmad was preceded by that of the ʾAlaviyyan brothers, which lasted about six years, and presumably began some time after his return from Mazandaran in 586/1190 (see ibid., 45-46; see also xvii-xviii). The work breaks off around 595/1199; the latest events in the historical section concern the career of the *mamlūk* Kukja and the misrule of the Atabeg Abu Bakr ibn Qizil Arslān. As these events are described as current, and as Rāvandī does not mention Kukja's murder in 600/1203, this seems a likely date for the completion of this section. The exordium and the *khatima* were probably composed later, with Rāvandī's dedicatee in mind (on the problem of the original dedicatee see ibid., xvii-xix), as were the sections praising Sultan Kaykhusraw.

7. Rāvandī, 44.

8. Ibid., 394.

9. Ibid., xxii.

10. Ibid., 234. Compare Zahir al-Dīn Nīshāpūrī (1953). *Saljūq nama,* ed. Isma'il Afshar. Tehran: Gulala Khavar, 58-59; al-Bundari (1886). *Histoire Des Seldjoucides de L'Iraq ... D'après Imad Ad-din Al-Katib Al-Isfahani,* ed. M. Th. Houtsma. *Recueil de texts relatifs a l'histoire des Seldjoucides,* vol. 1. Leiden: E. J. Brill, 192-93. The quotation replaces that with which Nīshāpūrī concludes this episode (and that I have not attempted to trace), which consists of two lines of praise of such heroic qualities as horsemanship, strength, boldness, and so on.

11. Ibid., 267-69, and see Nīshāpūrī, 70-72.

12. Rāvandī, 269.
13. Nizami Ganjavi (1954). *Khusraw u Shirin,* ed. Vahid Dastgirdī. 2d ed. Tehran: Ibn Sina, 15:6; hereafter KS; the references are to page and line number(s). The translations are my own, from a verse translation of the poem currently in progress; they have often required modification, however, due to Rāvandī's frequent "rewriting" of Nizami's verses, as discussed infra.
14. Ibid., 96-97.
15. The account refers to Mas‘ūd's campaign against the Indian fort of Hansi in 428/1037 and the occupation of Khurasan by the Saljūqs, and to their defeat of the Amir of Khurasan, Sūbāshī, at Sarakhs in 429/1038.
16. KS 10:6,4.
17. Compare Nīshāpūrī, 17; al-Bundari, 3.
18. In 581/1185 Jahān Pahlavān had denied Salah al-Din's (Saladin) request to pass through Iraq on his way to campaign against the Nizaris, sensing that the Ayyubid had designs on Saljūq territory. This effort, says Rāvandī, resulted in the attack of dysentery from which he died. The amirs concealed his death for several months, hoping to retain rule for themselves; but seeing the impossibility of this, a group of Qizil Arslān's supporters prevailed upon Ṭughril to appoint him. Ṭughril, fearing a rebellion, acquiesced; and Qizil Arslān's power and ambition soon reached the point where the Sultan was powerless to oppose him (Rāvandī, 337-39; see also Nīshāpūrī, 86 [Abu Hamid's continuation]).
19. Rāvandī, 338-39.
20. KS 108:5,4.
21. In the *Shahnameh,* as in other historical sources, it was Hurmuz's injustice and ill-treatment of his nobles which aroused their fear and disaffection and led to his deposition and to the usurpation of the throne by the rebel Bahram Chubin. The latter is the villain of Nizami's poem (as of Firdawsi's); and it is tempting to see a parallel between Qizil Arslān's designs on the sultanate and Bahram's on the throne of Persia. Rāvandī omits the line that, in Nizami, follows these two (whose order in Rāvandī is reversed): "When Joseph from his justice's *divan* / was lost, Time placed upon him Jacob's brand" (KS 108:6; "Jacob's brand" refers to the blindness that resulted from Jacob's copious weeping over the lost Joseph), and which constitutes a brief allusion to Hurmuz's lapse.
22. This brutal act of vengeance at the beginning of Qizil Arslān's atabegate foreshadows subsequent actions that will lead ultimately to his murder and to the collapse of the Great Saljūqs. It thus parallels Rāvandī's account of the murder of the former vizier 'Amid al-Mulk al-Kunduri at the beginning of Alp Arslān's reign, at the instigation of the latter's vizier Nizam al-Mulk, another act of injustice which anticipates the ultimate fall of the dynasty. The technique is also used by Nizami in *Khusraw u Shirin,* as well as by other writers. See further Meisami 1994: 193-95, 210-11 (for a translation of Rāvandī's account); and see also Meisami 1989: 63-67 and notes.
23. Rāvandī, 99; KS 19:2-8. The last three lines, which I have not quoted here, contain a number of orthographic puns based on the fact that the name "Muhammad" has two *mim*s. For explanatory notes see KS, 19; nn. 2-3.

24. This might be considered an instance of typological parallelism: Ṭughril Beg is presented as the type of the just ruler at the beginning of the Saljūqs' reign; Muhammad ibn Ildegüz repeats that type toward the end of it. That Muhammad was an atabeg and not a sultan reflects the shift in the exercise of actual power during the course of the Saljūq period. Moreover, it was the consensus of most historians that his death marked the beginning of the end for the Saljūqs (compare, for example, Abu Sharaf Nasih ibn Zafar Jarbadhqani (1966)). *Tarjuma-i Tarikh-i Yamini,* ed. Jafar Shi'ar (Tehran: Bungah-i Tarjuma va-Nashr-i Kitab), 421-23.

25. Rāvandī, 138; KS 20-22.

26. The printed edition has *salib-i sang-ra bar taruk-i Rumi;* Dastgirdi glosses this as referring to the iron crosses the Byzantines bore into battle with them (KS 21; n. 6). Rāvandī's text has *sarir-i sang-ra bar taruk-i Rum,* which does not make much sense and is perhaps a scribal error. It is customary in both Arabic and Persian texts (prose and poetry) to refer to the crosses that the Byzantines carried into battle; I take the printed text to be the preferred reading.

27. This line comes, not from Nizami's praise of Muhammad ibn Ildegüz, but from the beginning of the narrative, and his description of Hurmuz (KS 40: 4). The lines which follow tell of Hurmuz's desire for an heir; is it significant that Muhammad ibn Ildegüz left no son, and that Sultan Kaykhusraw is frequently addressed as "heir to the Saljūq *dawlat*"?

28. This line is not part of the passage quoted. I have not been able to locate it in Nizami's poem.

29. Other variations include the interpolation of two lines (9,11) from other sections of Nizami's poem. Rāvandī's l. 12 has *zin,* for Nizami's *din,* and his l. 13 *bi-didand* for *na-didand;* these are most likely scribal errors, and I have preferred the readings in the printed edition. All this, of course, raises problems with respect to textual reliability. But while in some cases we may have to do with variant readings, Rāvandī's procedure of rearranging verses to rhetorical effect is well-attested in his use of verses by Firdawsi (see Meisami 1995:268-69), though it is less frequent with respect to Nizami.

30. Rāvandī, 364; KS 15-16.

31. The ellipsis represents KS 15:8,10, Rāvandī's lines 3-4.

32. KS 16:1-2.

33. In point of fact, it was Muhammad Jahān Pahlavān who pacified the kingdom for the seven-year-old Sultan; see further infra.

34. Rāvandī, 249-50. Compare Nīshāpūrī, 66: "Sultan Malikshāh was powerful, majestic, with a mighty arm, a powerful archer, generous, openhanded and liberal; but he was a lover of jest who patronized the base, avid for wine, the hunt, and sexual relations." In what follows the text has "a black [*zangi*] named Jamal" for Rāvandī's "a woman [*zani*] named Jamal" as the sultan's partner in pleasure; since Nīshāpūrī's editor is notoriously careless, Rāvandī's version is to be preferred.

35. Rāvandī, 250; KS 67-70.

36. KS 67:8.

37. Ibid., 70:13.

38. Ibid., 69:10-11.
39. Nīshāpūrī notes (but Rāvandī omits to state) that Khāṣbik was the organizer of Malikshāh's "entertainments," 66.
40. Rāvandī, 250-55.
41. 1921:368; KS 102-103.
42. Dastgirdi considers this verse an interpolation (*ilhāqi*); in his edition the second hemistich reads, "In all the world no one was more content."
43. Rāvandī, 369.
44. Jamāl al-Dīn Ay Aba Ulugh Barbak (whose vizier in Kashan encouraged Jarbadhqani to make his translation of ʿUtbi's *Ta'rikh al-Yamini*) had been a *mamlūk* of Muhammad Jahān Pahlavān, and was the leader of the Iraqi armies. Rāvandī terms him "the peerless one of the age," and praises him for his justice and leadership. Hamadan had been oppressed by the misgovernment and abuses of Nūr al-Dīn Kukja (see infra). Ay Aba was made Atabeg by Malik Uzbak, who ruled Persian Iraq, and took control of the region of Hamadan (see Rāvandī, 388-89).
45. Rāvandī, 389; KS 307:2-4.
46. Iqbal states (1921:390; n. 2) that the last line of this quotation (*hich-ast bali ki hich bar zist / an-kas ki darun-i u du darzist*) is not found in the *Khamsa* and that its meaning is unclear. As the preceding line warns against frequenting those who are "now soft, now sharp," it would seem to continue the meaning of avoiding the hypocritical or duplicitous.
47. In 585/1189 Rāvandī accompanied his uncle Zayn al-Dīn Maḥmūd on a diplomatic mission to the ruler of Mazandaran, where he fell ill, and was forced to remain for some time. Shortly after his return (in 586/1190) to his home town of Ravand, where he continued to suffer from his illness for some months, he learned that Sultan Ṭughril had been seized and imprisoned by the Atabeg Qizil Arslān (see 1921:362-63).
48. Rāvandī, 287-88; KS 160:14, 161:1,6-8,10, 162:1-6,8-11, 163:1-3; for a partial translation see Meisami 1987:114-16.
49. Nīshāpūrī, 77.
50. Rāvandī, 288-89.
51. According to Rāvandī, this was on Ṭughril's first entrance into Baghdad, in 447/1055; but other sources state that the audience did not take place until 449, thirteen months later (see George Makdisi (1963)). *Ibn 'Aqil et la résurgence de l'Islam traditionaliste au XIe siècle (Ve siècle de l'Hegire).* Damascus: Institut Français de Damas, 88; Makdisi discusses at length the strained relations between the caliph and Ṭughril.
52. Nīshāpūrī, 19.
53. Rāvandī, 106; KS 93-95.
54. Ibid., 110-11.
55. Ibid., 283; KS 181:1-11.
56. Ibid., 290-91; KS 296-98.
57. Ibid., 297; KS 110-11.
58. Ibid., 332-33.
59. KS 277:13-16.

60. Ibid., 166:4-7,9. I have not been able to trace the last line of this passage ("By him both crown and throne were blessed; / the world rejoiced in him, he in success") in *Khusraw u Shirin;* Iqbal notes a variant (Rāvandī, 333; n. 2).

61. Rāvandī, 335.

62. Luther (1971b) described this move as an "administrative reform." Both Rāvandī and Jarbādhqāni clearly saw it as a misguided policy, which backfired disastrously and led to the increasing fragmentation of the Saljūq territories in Iraq, endless military conflicts between various rival factions, and widespread fiscal abuse and corruption, all of which resulted in the devastation of the region and the destitution of its inhabitants (see Rāvandī, 336; Jarbādhqāni, 421-23).

63. Ibid., 342.

64. Rāvandī, 343; KS 117-18.

65. KS 117:9-10.

66. Four lines are omitted here, in which Shirin takes Khusraw to her palace, and Mahīn Bānū, learning of his arrival there, comes to welcome him.

67. KS 117:11-12,15-17, 118:1,6-9.

68. See Rāvandī, 349.

69. Ibid., 370; KS 58:7-8.

70. By "forms," according to Dastgirdi, is meant hat-forms.

71. Rāvandī, 380.

72. KS 113:1-3.

73. Rāvandī, 381.

74. Ibid.

75. KS 43:1-4.

76. Ibid., 391-92.

77. Ibid., 81-84; KS 43-48.

78. Rāvandī, like Nizami, makes the point that if, in the "*Jāhiliyyat,*" the "unbelievers" practiced such justice, how shameful it would be for Muslim rulers to commit injustice.

79. Rāvandī, 84.

80. Political reasons may explain why Rāvandī quotes from neither of the latter two works, nor from Nizami's praise of Qizil Arslān. For criticism of Abu Bakr see Rāvandī, 401-402; on the rulers of Maragha see EI$_2$, art. "Aḥmad il"; on Abu Bakr see EI$_2$, art. "Ildenizids." The precise date of completion of the *Iskandarnama* is not known, as it contains a variety of dedications, and may in fact have been presented to various dedicatees in sections over a period of time; see EI$_2$, art. "Nizami Gandjawi."

81. We do, however, have Nizami's imprecation, in *Khusraw u Shirin,* against anyone who might alter a word of his poem (KS 35:4-5; Dastgirdi glosses the last line as referring to the *Muzd-i Kitabat,* the fee paid the copyist):

> May no base man e'er have a share in it;
> only who sweetly sings, and fairly writes.

> I made this well; should it be copied ill,
> he his own sins has added to my bill.

The lines seem remarkably prescient.

82. Among contemporary historians Rāvandī seems unique in recombining verses (often from different parts of a poem) into a new composition. This is especially true in the case of verses from the *Shahnameh,* but also occurs in a few instances with respect to Nizami, as we have seen. Nor do other writers, in general, quote such extensive passages (except in the case of panegyrics) as does Rāvandī. While contemporary writers often use interpolations copiously, they do not, as a rule, integrate them into the narrative (for example, Rāvandī's contemporary Afzal al-Dīn Kirmanī, whose *'Iqd al-ūlā* was completed in 584/1188-9, uses abundant interpolations, much as Rāvandī uses Koranic verses, *hadith*s, proverbs, and sentential poetic verses, but does not incorporate them into the narrative). Somewhat later, however, the Mongol historian Juvayni, who completed (or rather discontinued the writing of) his *Tarikh-i Jahāngusha* around 1260 (see 1958, 1:xxv-xxvii), approaches Rāvandī's technique of combining (brief) verse quotations and narrative. One example will suffice by way of illustration: the description of the feast celebrating the election of Guyuk Khan as successor to Mengu Qa'an (ibid., 1:252-53; the verses are all drawn from the *Shahnameh*):

> And in this manner till midnight of that day the wine
> cups were filled to the brim, and the princes in the
> presence of the peerless King
>> To the tune of the strings and the melody of the
>> flute, with jessamine-cheeked beauties at the feet
>> of the Chosroes,
>> Drank wine till midnight, and the minstrels opened
>> their lips in song.
> When they had grown drunk, after uniting in praising
> and belauding the Monarch of the Face of the Earth,
> they departed to their sleeping quarters; and on the
> next day ... the princes, *noyans* and common people
>> Came strutting to the king's court, open-hearted and
>> well-wishing they came.
> And when the bright banner of the sun was unfurled on
> the roof of the azure vault, the mighty king and puissant
> monarch, preparing to leave his chamber,
>> Donned imperial brocade, placed on his head the crown of
>> greatness,

> and with the arrogance of greatness and the haughtiness of pride
> Came strutting from the pavilion, a shining banner standing behind
>   him,
> and sat down in his audience-hall upon the throne of pomp and
>   magnificence ...

83. *Kitabat al-insha';* see Luther, 1990:93-94.
84. This was most likely a compilation—perhaps that known as the *Ikhtiyarat-i Shahnameh,* made for Malikshāh (see Meisami 1994:187; 1995:268).
85. See especially Luther (1977), "Chancery Writing as a Source of Constraints on History Writing in the Sixth and Seventh Centuries of the Hijra," Unpublished Paper. University of Michigan.
86. On the question of the extent to which Saljūq amirs, atabegs, and *mamlūks* possessed a literary education, see K. Allin Luther (1971a), "Bayhaqi and the Later Seljuq Historians: Some Comparative Remarks." In *Yadnama-i Abu Al-Fazl Bayhaqi* (English Section). Mashhad: Danishgah-i Mashhad, 30-31 and 1971b: 398.

Chapter 6

Occult Sciences in The *Iskandarnameh* of Nizami[1]

J. Christoph Bürgel

In his last and largest epos, the *Iskandarnameh*,[2] Nizami develops the image of an ideal statesman following the concept of Farabi in his political philosophy.[3] His hero is Alexander the Great, whom he portrays with this idealized vision in mind, freely deviating from what he found in the sources whenever his vision told him to do so. Besides his military and political faculties, an ideal statesman should incorporate, so the Farabian concept requires, the qualities of a philosopher and ultimately those of a prophet. Nizami's Sikandar develops according to this concept.[4] In the first part, the so-called *Sharafnameh* or "Book of Honor," we are told all about Sikandar's conquests; in the second part, the *Iqbalnameh* or "Book of Blessings," the poet tackles Sikandar's experiences as a philosopher and then those of his final stage, that of a prophet.[5] As a philosopher, Sikandar visits Socrates and has a talk with the Greek sages, but he is also confronted with a number of sciences, including astrology, alchemy and magic, and music and medicine—in other words, the three major branches of the so-called occult sciences, which stand above philosophy according to the Brethren of Purity, and two other sciences, whose effects gave them an aura of magic power as well.[6] These sciences are not dealt with in an abstract theoretical essay however, but in the form of entertaining stories that throw light on their sometimes wholesome, sometimes dangerous power. The total of these stories is seven, seven being an important number not only in the fourth epos of our poet, the *Haft Paikar* or "Seven Beauties," but also in his last poem, where it appears a number of times with an important function: seven battles are fought against the Rus, the number of philosophers gathered around Sikandar is seven et cetera.[7] Let us now have a somewhat closer look at these seven tales.[8]

1. The Tale of Archimedes and his Chinese Slave-girl[9]

Archimedes, here introduced as the favorite disciple of Aristotle, falls in love with the slave-girl whom the emperor of China presented to Sikandar.[10] (This is one of the devices used by the poet to link these stories with the main hero.) Obsessed by love, he abandons his studies. Aristotle, annoyed by this negligence, brews a potion and has the girl drink it, which draws the humor of beauty out of her body. He calls in the lover and shows him the bowl with the humor and the girl, who is now as ugly as a scarecrow. "This is the lady you are in love with, and this is her beauty!" he remarks ironically, whereupon the young man turns back to science.

2. Mary the Copt[11]

Mary, the daughter of a Syrian prince, sought the help of Aristotle when she felt threatened by enemies. He taught her the science of alchemy, by which knowledge she succeeded in making gold and solving all her problems.[12] When some philosophers visited her to be initiated into the great art, she spoke to them in a cryptic language, which only a few of them were able to grasp. When Sikandar is warned that the powerful Coptic queen is going to attack him, Aristotle contradicts them and vouches for her integrity.

Mary the Copt is a well-known figure in the history of alchemy. Jews identified her with the sister of Moses, Christians with the mother of Christ, Muslims with that slave-girl whom the Muqawqis (Christian ruler) of Alexandria sent as a present to the Prophet Muhammad. In Arabic sources, however, she also appears either as a Coptic scholar who lived at the time of the caliph al-Ma'mun, or as the daughter of an unknown king of Sheba. A number of Arabic treatises on alchemy are attributed to her.[13] Nizami follows neither of these identifications but places Mary within the circle of personages surrounding Sikandar. In this story, alchemy appears as a serious science taught by Aristotle. The next story, however, is about a swindler who only shams knowledge of the great art.

3. The Story of the Man from Khorasan, Who Cheated the Caliph[14]

This story is a burlesque about the danger of being cheated, which is always implicit in some one's pretending to possess alchemical knowledge.

A man from Khorasan came to Baghdad and introduced himself as an alchemist. He ground up the 100 dinars he possessed, mixed them with rose-leaves, and made them into small balls that he then sold to a druggist, saying the name of this stuff was *tabaryak* and announcing that he would come and buy it back for ten times the price he had sold it for. Whereupon he betook himself to the caliph and introduced himself as an alchemist. Should the caliph harbor any doubt, he might have him watched as he performed an experiment, but he would need 100 dinars. The caliph named a few inspectors and sent them in town to buy *tabaryak*. Meanwhile, the swindler erected an alchemist's stove, and when the caliph's men returned with the stuff, he threw it into the stove. The rose-leaves evaporated, while molten gold dripped from its bung. Now the caliph trusted the man, and gave him 10,000 dinars as recompense and to finance his further work. The Khorasani took the money and disappeared. When the caliph finally realized that he had been cheated, the only means he had of identifying the swindler was the name of the stuff. But now it turned out that *tabaryak* was a play on *nayrang,* "conjuring trick," achieved by changing some diacritical marks. A further point, not expressly mentioned by the poet, lies in the fact that the meaningless *tabaryak* (this reading being required by the meter) would normally be read as *tabrik,* which means "blessing," a subtle hint to the frequent fusion of pious speech and impious intentions.

This story belongs in the context of treatises opposed to alchemy, the most famous of which stems from the well-known Egyptian scholar ʿAbd al-Latif al-Baghdadi, and is entitled "Dispute between the two philosophers, the theoretician and the alchemist." It contains some hair-raising reports about cheats, but even more about the follies and atrocities committed by adepts of the art who were obsessed with and blinded by their avidity. They will not refrain from committing the most outrageous acts in order to get hold of things they consider necessary for the production of an elixir, such as human gall-bladders or even human eyeballs—an aspect or their work that is normally overlooked in the idealizing presentations of Arabic alchemy of our day.[15]

4. The Story of the Breadless Baker, Who Gained a Fortune through the Horoscope of his Son[16]

As mentioned in the title, this story deals with astrology. It is about a stranger who first appeared in the Islamic empire at the border of Byzantium, where, after a vain attempt to earn his living as a baker, he became rich virtually overnight. When people in his neighborhood became aware of this, they grew suspicious and reported the affair to the king, Sikandar. He had the baker brought before him to tell his story, which was the following. On the night when his wife was in labor he left the house to get her barley water. Since the shops were closed, he ran on until he came to the ruins of a palace, where he met a black person busy boiling a broth. They ate and drank together until the black man, having become intoxicated, revealed a secret to him. He and a companion of his had discovered a treasure, but he had decided to kill his companion, which he did a little later before the eyes of the terrified baker. When he left to remove the dead body, the baker availed himself of the occasion, took the bag with the jewels and the pot with the broth, and ran away. When he arrived home, his wife had delivered a healthy son. Having listened to the story, Sikandar inquired as to the position of the stars at the time of conception and birth and gave these dates to his chief astrologer Walis—that is, Thales—for his examination, and Thales cast a horoscope that confirmed the events related in all essential points.[17]

Astrology plays an important part in all of Nizami's works. For the most part he limits himself to reporting birth horoscopes, for example that of Khusraw Parviz in *Khusraw and Shirin,* but also that of Alexander. It has been shown that these are artificial horoscopes in which a wealth of fortunate constellations have been brought together.[18]

5. *Seventy Sages Deny the Doctrines of Hermes and Perish*[19]

The baker's tale is followed by a strange story dealing with a spiritual power struggle. It tells of a group of 70 philosophers who refuse to accept the doctrines of Hermes as truth. Having made three vain efforts to convince them, the mighty sage punishes them by casting a lethal paralysis over them. Once he has done this, Sikandar appears and approves of Hermes' action. It is clear that here we are dealing with Hermes Trismegistos, a mythical figure who embodies everything magical and occult in late antiquity. Islamic culture came to know him under the name of *Hirmis al-muthallath,* the threefold or trinitarian Hermes, who passed for the author of treatises on alchemy, astrology, and magic, among them the famous *Istamakhis,* which Nizami mentions at the beginning of the *Iqbalnameh* as one of his sources along with the *Almagest* of Ptolemy.[20]

However, the Hermes of Nizami is not the representative of occult sciences but appears as a teacher of truth and in possessor of that *himmat* or psychic energy, which became a mark of true mystics.[21] In a way, this Hermes appears as an intensified echo of that ascetic mentioned in the first part of the *Iskandarnameh,* who by dint of a mere sigh conquered a castle inhabited by robbers that had withstood the attacks of Sikandar's armies for several weeks.[22] It also may be that Nizami is here influenced by those gnostic and sufi concepts that saw in Hermes the supernatural being possessing and bestowing upon man the so-called perfect nature, or even "the prophet of the perfect nature."[23] The meaning of the story would thus be, that philosophers, who do not care about how to achieve this perfect nature will end up in a sort of spiritual paralysis.

6. Plato Composes Songs to Put Aristotle to Shame[24]

With this story we remain still somewhat in the sphere of the previous one, paralysis being its main motif. But the paralysis here is not brought about by *himmat,* but through music. Moreover, it is not a punishment and it is not permanent, so the story does not have a gloomy ending. Given the fact that our story is reminiscent of another contest between two sages, told in Nizami's first epos, the *Makhzan al-asrar* or "Treasury of Secrets," which ends with the death of one of the two protagonists, this might even be intended by the author as a conscious self-correction.[25] At any rate, it is one of those cases, not infrequent in the *Iskandarnameh,* where Nizami echoes, modifies, or alludes to stories told in one of his earlier poems in an apparent endeavor to give a global structure to his work. The story about Plato and Aristotle also echoes the story about the contest of the two painters, the Greek and the Chinese, which Nizami told at a previous juncture of his Sikandar novel, making use of a parable told in Ghazzali's *Ihya' 'ulum al-dīn* that was also taken up in Rumi's *Mathnawi.*[26]

The focus of the present story is on the extraordinary power of music, its quasi-magical influence. The topic, already known in Greek antiquity, where it crystallized in the myth of Orpheus, found its way into the Islamic world via translated texts, and was then promulgated—mainly through the *Treatises* of the Brethren of Purity, but certainly also through musical writing. The basic assumption is that the various modes of music (in Arabic *maqam;* in Persian *pardah*) affect the human psyche and through it the body in different ways, the doctrine of the so-called musical ethos.[27] In the present story, however, a musical mode does not affect a person's character or mood but puts a person (or an animal) into a deathlike sleep, from which only another mode or *pardah* can resuscitate the victim.

In an assembly of philosophers, gathered at the court of Sikandar, Aristotle is acclaimed as the greatest philosopher. All agree except one,

Plato, who leaves the room in silent protest. In order to prove his superiority, he develops, by listening to the music of the spheres, the two mighty modes (*pardah*) and demonstrates their power on a few animals. When Aristotle hears of this, he does not want to stay behind. He indeed succeeds in finding the first mode and puts a few persons to sleep. But only when he wants to wake them up does he realize that he does not know the second mode, and so he has to call upon Plato for help.[28]

The story is thus not only about the power of music, it is also about the superiority of Plato over Aristotle. This is not so by chance. The *Iskandarnameh* was written only a few years after the death of Ibn Rushd/Averroes, the last great representative of Aristotelian thought in the Arabic-speaking world.[29] After him the Peripatetic school was to be superseded by Neoplatonic movements—by Ibn 'Arabi's monism in the West, and, in particular, by the so-called Wisdom of Illumination (*Hikmat al-ishraq*), founded by the Persian Suhrawardi (with some precursors such as Ibn Sina).[30] Neoplatonism has merged with Islamic mysticism, and the latter is often closely linked with occult practices. In fact, it is difficult to find a mystic's vita in hagiographic writings in which the tale of at least one miracle is not related. On the other hand, already in late Greek antiquity Plato, and even Aristotle, had been endowed with an ever-growing aura of occult knowledge, and writings on magic, alchemy, and similar subjects were attributed to them. So we must not be astonished that in the present story Plato's procedures are clearly depicted as magical. For instance, before he begins his work he draws a circle around himself. Now, magic is in fact the main issue in the last of these seven stories. In this way the present story skillfully links the fifth story to the final one.

7. The Story of the Shepherd and the Ring[31]

Before entering upon this tale, let me note the following: the appearance of magic in the *Iskandarnameh* is not restricted to this story and, perhaps, the preceding one. Actually, Sikandar possesses an instrument enabling him to foresee whether or not he will be victorious in an impending battle, in other words warning or encouraging him to embark upon it.[32] Furthermore, he is accompanied during his conquests by a certain Balinas, whose name is the Arabic version of Appolonius (of Tyana), a well-known sage and magician of the first century and the author of a number of handbooks on magic translated into Arabic. In the Islamic Middle Ages he became known as the *sahib al-tilismat* or "Master of the Talismans."[33] During his conquest of Persia and the destruction of Zoroastrian temples—something for which the historical Alexander is not responsible!—Sikandar arrives at a fire-shrine dominated by a witch as beautiful as she is powerful. She has control of a dragon, which she unleashes against the aggressors. For Balinas, however, this is an easy challenge. He defeats the phantom, but he also marries the witch with the permission of Sikandar, and learns many magical procedures from her so that, according to Nizami, it was because of her that he became a famous magician.[34]

Here, Nizami presents us with a story that deals with the power of magic and the dangers involved in it, particularly if it is misused. Of all the seven stories about occult sciences, this is the only one traceable to an Arabic and, ultimately, a Greek source, as we will presently see. But let us first summarize the story.

During an earthquake a cleft in a rock is opened, and in it a shepherd discovers a brazen horse with a gaping flank in which lies a dead man wearing a signet ring. The shepherd removes the ring, and soon realizes that when he turns it on his finger he becomes invisible. He now uses the power of the ring to procure all kinds of privileges for himself. At last he penetrates into the castle of the king, whom he threatens with a sword. When asked who he is, he gives the following answer, "I am a prophet. Quickly! Follow me and be grateful to your fate! If I wish, nobody can see me. This is my miracle (*mu'jiz*), this is my mission (*da'wa*)!"

The story closes by saying that out of fear the king became a follower of the shepherd, as did the people of the town, an enormous number. The shepherd became so powerful that the whole kingdom submitted to him. "Look," Nizami exclaims in conclusion, "how a gem may enable one to become a prophet!"

As I have already mentioned, there can be little doubt about the sources of this story. Nizami follows the Arabic version contained in the fifty-second of the famous *Epistles* of the Brethren of Purity, in which magic is being tackled.[35] But there is more to it. In the description of the cleft in the rock, Nizami uses the Arabic term *khasf,* which was more or less unknown to Persian readers. Even in Arabic, this is a rare expression, but it does appear in the version of the story in the *Epistles.* Nizami apparently took it from there unchanged, because he too did not know what exactly it meant. So we may be almost certain that he used this version as his source for the present story. The Brethren, for their part, do mention their source: the second *maqala* of Plato's *Republic.* The story is known to Western readers under the name of "The Ring of Gyges."[36] A comparison shows that the Brethren's text constitutes a generally accurate rendering of the Greek original.

Remarkably enough, the story underwent one change when it passed into the text of Nizami. In Plato's version, the shepherd mingles among the messengers of the king and kills him. The Arabic version renders messengers with *rusul,* a term that also means prophet(s). This is the source of Nizami's making the shepherd pretend to be a prophet and represent his invisibility as the miracle (*mu'jiz*) attesting his prophetic mission (*da'wa*).

The old story thus has been invested with a new meaning. It is no longer just about magic power and the danger involved in its being misused by an irresponsible person; it is about false prophets and their unscrupulous use of power and violence.

Conclusion

Let me summarize the preceding discussion as follows. Nizami does not reject the three great occult sciences. Rather he accepts them, like the Brethren of Purity, as a part of philosophy. He was not keen on creating the weird, uncanny atmosphere of fairy tales, as we find it in so many other Persian romances and in the Greek Alexander novel by Pseudo-Callisthenes, which is the main source of all later Alexander novels including the Arabic and Persian ones. What he took a particular interest in was their power, not as it related to these three sciences only, but also to medicine, music, and painting. Of course, this power varied in degree in all of them, as did their legitimacy and their social utility. In other words, he wanted to show that to deal with such sciences appropriately required not only skill but a high degree of responsibility. The correct use of the power of the occult sciences, and also of music and medicine, is thus a topic that is rightly included in a work that deals with the development of a prince, which is, after all, the overall subject of Nizami's epics.[37]

Aristotle uses medicine to help his disciple achieve mental maturity. Plato uses music to make Aristotle aware of his limits. Furthermore, it is noteworthy that Plato finds the two modes by listening to the music of the spheres and imitating their proportions (*nisab*), a clear hint to the correspondences between macro- and microcosm as a source of magic power.[38] Responsible use of an occult power is also the subject of the stories about Mary the Copt and, even though it is less persuasive for a modern reader, the story about Hermes Trismegistos. On the other hand, the stories about the Khorasani and about the shepherd illustrate the dangers of the irresponsible use of such power, which, in the one case the protagonist only pretends to possess, while in the other he has got hold of it by mere chance and uses it to devastating effect.

Nizami's humanist rationalism (or rationalist humanism), which has already been mentioned by Bertel's and highlighted by Bausani as a particular feature of the *Iskandarnameh,* is thus confirmed also by the way he tackles the problem of how to deal with the power of the occult.[39] By having his hero learn these lessons when he has reached the degree of philosopher, he makes him advance to the last and most difficult stage, that of correct commerce with prophetic power.

Notes

1. A German version of this chapter appeared in *Proceedings of the Second European Conference of Iranian Studies,* ed. B. Fragner et al. (Rome 1995), pp. 103-12.

2. The Persian text will be cited according to V. Dastgirdi's edition (Tehran 1334/1956). German translation, *Nizami: Das Alexanderbuch. Übertragung aus dem Persischen, Nachwort un Anmerkungen von J. C. Bürgel* (Zurich 1991).

3. Cf. my *Allmacht und Mächtigkeit. Religion und Welt im Islam* (Munich 1991), 131ff.

4. The form Sikandar, instead of the normal Iskandar, is required by the meter of this poem, which is *mutaqarib* (the same meter as the *Shahnameh*).

5. Cf. my, "Conquérant, philosophe, prophète. L'image d'Alexandre le Grand dans l"épopée de Nezāmi." In *Pand-o Sokhan. Mélanges offerts à Charles-Henri de Fouchécour,* ed. C. Balaÿ, C. Kappler, and Z. Vesel, pp. 65-78. Tehran: Institut Français de Recherche en Iran.

6. The Brethren of Purity counted medicine as part of magic. For the magic power of music, see my *The Feather of Simurgh: The "Licit" Magic of the Arts in Medieval Islam* (New York University Press, 1988), pp. 101ff.

7. For the role of seven in the work of Nizami, see M. Mu'in, *Tahlil-i haft paikar-i nizami. Bakhsh-i avval,* Intisharat-i Danishgah-i Tihran #596 (Tehran 1960). The seven occult stories are preceded by two simple healing stories: the story about Alexander and the shepherd, and, inserted in the former, the story about the shepherd. Both deal with the falling ill of a beloved person and the grief caused by this; they teach one not to give up hope in such a situation.

8. Summaries of tales 1, 2, 5, and 6 were given by P. Chelkowski in his article, "Nizami's Iskandarnameh," in *Colloquio sul poeta persiano Nizami e la leggenda iranica di Alessandro magno,* Roma, 25/26 Marzo 1975 (Rome 1977), pp. 211-53. I have prepared my own summaries.

9. Text in Dastgirdi's edition (henceforth D) II, 55-60. References to the German translation are given in the German version of this article. Jami's treatment of

a related theme in his *Salaman and Absal* is discussed by Kamran Talattof in his chapter in this volume.

10. Cf. D I, 413.

11. D II, 62/67; 71-72.

12. In the Islamic tradition, Aristotle does in fact appear as author of alchemical treatises, cf. M. Ullmann: *Die Natur- und Geheimwissenschaften im Islam. Handbuch der Orientalistik* I, VI, 2 (Leiden 1972), 157ff.

13. For Mary the Copt cf. Ullmann, ibid., pp. 181-83; F. Sezgin, *Geschichte des arabischen Schrifttums IV: Achimie, Chemie, Botanik Agrikultur bis ca. 430* (Leiden 1971), pp. 70-73.

14. D II, 67-71.

15. 'Abdallatif al-Baghdadi, *Mujadalat al-hakimain al-naẓari wal-kimiya'i.* cf. *The Feather of Simurgh,* p. 45ff. Typical examples of modern idealizing presentations of Arabic alchemy are the works of T. Burckhardt and H. Nasr.

16. D II, 73-82.

17. In the Islamic Middle Ages Thales apparently was known principally as an alchemist, and was cited more frequently than Jabir ibn Hayyam (cf. Sezgin: l.c., IV, 45).

18. Marianne Glünz, *Die Astrologie in Nizamis Khamse.* Lic. phil. Bern 1983.

19. D II, 82-85.

20. For Hirmis al-muthallath, cf. Ullmann, ibid. p. 368ff. For *istamakhis* see ibid. p. 374ff.

21. For *himmat* cf. F. Meier, *Die fawa'ih al-gamal wa-fawatih al-galal des Nagm ad-Din al-Kubra,* Akademie der Wissenschaften und der Literatur. Veröffentlichungen der Orientalischen Kommission 9 (Wiesbaden 1957), pp. 226-40.

22. D I, 314-23.

23. H. Corbin, *L'homme de lumiere dans le soufisme iranien* (Paris 1971), p. 35ff.

24. D II, 85-92; cf. also my "Der Wettstreit zwischen Plato und Aristoteles im Alexander-Buch des persischen Dichters Nizami" in *Die Welt des Orients* 17 (1986), pp. 95-109.

25. Cf. my, "The Contest of the Two Philosophers in Nizami's First and Last Epics," *Yadnama: In memoria di Alessandro Bausani. A cura di Biancamaria Scarcia Amoretti et Lucia Ratno.* Studi Orientali 10 (Rome 1991) I, pp. 109-17.

26. Cf. P. Soucek, "Nizami on Painters and Painting," *Islamic Art in the Metropolitan Museum* (New York 1972).

27. Cf. H. G. Farmer, "The Influence of Music from Arabic Sources," a lecture delivered before the Musical Association, London 1916; cf. also *The Feather of Simurgh,* p. 92ff.

28. This story also provides the starting point for F. Khazrai's chapter in the present volume. Cf. p. 163 [editor].

29. Cf. M. Fakhry, *A History of Islamic Philosophy* (London 1983), pp. 270-92; I. A. Bello, *The Medieval Islamic Controversy Between Philosophy and*

Orthodoxy: Ijmaʿ and taʾwil in the conflict between al-Ghazali and Ibn Rushd (Leyden 1989).

30. Cf. M. Fakhry, l.c. 293-304; H. Corbin, *Histoire de la philosophie islamique I: Des origines jusqʾa la mort dʾAverroes (1198)* (Paris 1964), pp. 284-304.

31. D II, 92-97.

32. A similar instrument is shown in the John Addis Islamic Gallery of the British Museum in London.

33. About Balinas, cf. Ullmann, ibid. p. 378ff., and M. Plessner in EI$_2$, s.v.

34. D I, 242ff.

35. *Rasaʾil Ikhwan al-Safaʾ* (Beirut 1957), IV, 287-88.

36. Plato, *Republic* II, 359.

37. Julie S. Meisami, *Medieval Persian Court Poetry,* especially chapter V, "Romance as Mirror: Allegories of Kingship and Justice" (Princeton 1987).

38. This is also one of the basic ideas of the *Epistles;* cf. my *Allmacht und Mächtigkeit* (note 3 above), pp. 153-56.

39. E. E. Bertels, *Nizami i Fuzuli* (Moscow 1962), p. 355ff; A. Bausani, "Tendenza a spiegare in modo razionale antichi miti" (cf. note 8 above), p. 157.

Chapter 7

Nizami's Poetry Versus Scientific Knowledge: The Case of the Pomegranate

Christine van Ruymbeke

It is an undisputed fact that Nizami and his fellow Western Iranian poets of the twelfth century made extensive use of vocabulary and images derived from contemporary knowledge about the exact sciences.[1] Nizami himself repeatedly declares his overwhelming interest in science, as in the following verse where he tells us that happy slumber eludes him if he has not first forced open the door of a new science:

> *na-khoftam shabī shād bar bastarī / ke nagushādam ān shab ze-dānesh darī*
>
> (*SN* 7,88)[2]
>
> I don't fall asleep—happy—at night on my bed, have I not [first] that night opened one of science's doors.

However, an analysis of the extent of knowledge about which he boasts has been lacking until now. This chapter is based on the premise that Nizami's knowledge of and interest in science—which cannot be limited to him alone but was widespread among contemporary medieval Persian poets—can be deduced by the allusions he makes.[3] This study will focus on a very limited part of this huge debate, notably on the references to arboricultural and pharmacological knowledge concerning the pomegranate tree and its fruit, *nār* and *nārbon*.[4] The starting point of this enquiry might be the following brief passage of Nizami's second *masnavi: Khusraw o Shirin*.

On hearing the false report of Shirin's death, Farhād falls from the cliff at Bisūtūn, which he was carving with perseverance. Recording the end of the builder-architect, Nizami specifically mentions an interesting phenomenon. The instrument held by Farhād, which was fashioned out of a stick of young pomegranate wood, drops with force into moist ground and eventually grows into a tree bearing a rich crop of fruit with wonderful healing powers.

> The head [of the instrument] fell on the rocks and the handle in the earth
> they say that this [happened to be] moist ground.
> Out of this handle grew the branch of a pomegranate
> it changed into a tree and bore numerous fruit.
> If now, you [should] find a pomegranate [originating] from this branch
> you [would] have found a remedy [against] the pain of any sick man.
> Though Nizami [himself] didn't see this pomegranate tree, he has read in a
> book precisely this story.[5]

The scientific allusions might at first glance be concealed by the manifestly powerful romantic value of the incident. But arboricultural knowledge (concerning the reproduction of pomegranate trees and the soil conditions in which they thrive) and pharmacological knowledge (concerning the healing qualities of the fruit) form the background of the passage and testify to its verisimilitude. In view of the records of comments on poetic works by rival poets or by professional critics that have reached us—incidents that bear witness to the intricacies of vocabulary and to the danger of a wrongly used word, or of a faulty allegation for a poet's renown[6]— it would seem likely that if the above episode hadn't matched the then-known scientific facts, the poet's false pretense to knowledge would have been exposed and the poem ripped to pieces by the critics. This, however, surprisingly, has not been the case (see below). The growing refinement in the poet's vocabulary quite early took a turn toward scientific terms and images. Although it might already be present in earlier poets, like Manūchehrī[7] (d. 1040), for example, the tendency becomes marked in the twelfth century. The verses of Anvarī (d. 1187) bear testimony to this new fashion. It is probably Khāqānī (d. 1199) who takes this movement to its peak, while his contemporary, Nizami, makes a more discreet use of this specialized lexicography.[8]

The relationship between science and poetry needs first to be briefly highlighted in order for us to understand the feat represented by the composition of a poem that should ally perfection of form, contents, beauty, and genius. Nizami's own attitude toward science, as can be glimpsed in several passages of the *Khamseh,* will confirm the central place held by learning in the poet's concerns. Next will come the analysis of the central quotation, which evokes Nizami's multiple attitudes toward science. Following this, we will examine the general use of the terms *nār* and *nārbon* in Nizami's *Khamseh.*[9] Finally, we will briefly compare his use of the plant with that of other Persian poets, thereby endeavoring to sketch a comparative study of the use of this fruit between two important periods of Persian poetry.

Nizami vs. Science

There is an obvious and long-standing tie between Persian poetry and science. This relation is manifold. To name but a few instances, the first, most obvious link is that poetics was early on stabilized into a science. Poetical rules were part of an orderly, logically built whole, the keystone of this edifice being the Holy Book itself, which had provided Arabic verse with its letters of nobility and its grammatical and logical construction. Conversely, the rules, established early on by the Arabic poets into a delicate science, provided a lexical and grammatical help to understand the Quran itself.[10] Although the Arabic poetical terminology dominates the classical Persian poetical system, the latter should not be considered as deriving from the Arabic poetical system.[11] It nevertheless can be said that for Persian and Arabic poets alike, throughout history up to modern times, there could be no poetry, no art, without mastering the rules of this science.[12] In short, poetry, this form of art that early on had been condemned in religious quarters,[13] managed to survive by metamorphosing into a skill that soon developed into a science.[14] The price to pay was that it had to submit to the critics of grammarians and lexicographers, and it had to please to stay in existence.

Another aspect of this interaction between poetry and science is the versification of scientific works, which might have encouraged memorization. Scholars in science were often poets themselves or at least were open admirers of poetry. A good example is Ibn Sīnā's Arabic *Poem of Medicine,* wherein he versified a summary of his complete medical theory. An interesting passage is the following verse of the Preface, in which he juxtaposes doctors and poets, both of whom have a beneficial effect on either psychic or somatic illnesses:

> Poets are the verb's princes; doctors rule over the body. The eloquence of
> the former rejoices the spirit; the dedication of the latter cures the ailing.[15]

Science also pervaded poetry's texture as the process of refinement of
the medieval courts advanced. The greater the number of scholars
dwelling there, the more elements of the several sciences debated at court
would be picked up by court poets and introduced into their verses. Some
poets even seem to have been scholars in their own right.[16]

The pleasure experienced on hearing good poetry is brought about
by the simultaneous and harmonious coincidence of both perfection of
form and of image, combined with fullness of meaning. If, however, we
artificially attempt to dissect the way a poem was judged, it seems that
artistic sense and pleasure would come second and be tested only once
the poem had passed several critical examinations. A first step would be
a look into the correct application of the rules of style, such as metrics
and prosody.[17] A second step would be to examine critically the correct
use of vocabulary.

Nizami, having mastered the indispensable tools of his trade, was
undoubtedly aware of the importance of instruction in the formative
years of a poet. It is thus remarkable to hear his characterisation of
Majnun's refusal to be attentive during his classes (*LM* 11, 75-79). In the
introduction to this *masnavī,* Nizami seems to allude to a certain reluctance to undertake the versification of Majnun's story.[18] Although this
assertion should be received with a duly critical spirit and caution,[19]
might it not be that Nizami's carefully chiseled art did not feel much
enthusiasm in reproducing the story of a rough and "natural" poet?[20]

Apart from his use of specific vocabulary and images, often independent of the action of the *masnavī,* Nizami has also manifested his interest
in science by his portraiture of scholars and his report of learned *séances,*
for example. From a well-known, humorous, but revealing passage of the
Haft Peykar (*HP* 28, 51-92), we can deduce *a contrario* what kind of
scholar Nizami would admire or possibly consider himself to be. The first
protagonist, the evil, stupid Malīkhā, boasts of his limitless knowledge.
He sounds remarkably like the famous barber of the *1001 Nights,*[21] (to
which collection Nizami doubtlessly and recurrently refers in his *HP*).
The effect is ridiculous and stresses Malīkhā's utter stupidity. Although
his counterpart, the consistently religion-abiding hero, Bishr, eventually
earns a brilliant reward for his blind faith, his attitude in this passage is as

caricatured as that of Malīkhā. The comic effect of their dialogue spares neither the stupidity of assumed polyvalent knowledge nor the blindly law-abiding Muslim, who sees no use in the search for knowledge and is content to rest passively in the hands of Supreme Providence. From this interplay, we may safely enough deduce that Nizami's own position toward science is different.

From numerous other passages,[22] it becomes evident that Nizami has alluded to many elements regarding science. This forms an important part of any consideration on Nizami's learned vocabulary and expressions. However the subject of this chapter is limited to Nizami's use of specific "botanical"[23] allusions in the *Khamseh*.

The general principle on which this study is based is that an image used by the poet concerning trees or their fruit is considered as an example of scientific knowledge, provided a similar indication has been found in learned treatises on the subject. The number of treatises considered in this research is necessarily limited, whereby important works of undisputed value were cast aside in favor of other, possibly lesser works, but belonging to another tradition or another branch of knowledge and therefore shedding a different and useful light on the question. The choice was governed by two irreconcilable wishes: to remain as close as possible to Nizami's time and yet to cover as complete a spectrum of traditions as possible. Persian as well as Arabic works were used, most of which date back to the medieval period. More recent works were considered as well, which, by their importance, their sources, or their rarity, were indispensable to completing the contents of given branches of science. The works themselves belong to several categories: pharmacology, arboriculture, descriptive geography, encyclopaedias, and lexicons.[24] The results obtained are provisional and likely to alter after consulting additional sources.

The anār-e Farhād

The quotation on the strange fate of Farhād's wooden implement (see above) raises three questions. As stated above, there is first of all the issue of arboricultural knowledge regarding the specific pomegranate plant. We must inquire whether it is indeed possible to multiply the pomegranate tree by means of cuttings. And more particularly, whether it is imaginable that a cutting that is no longer fresh—having been used as a handle for a sculptor's instrument—may still produce shoots and blossoms, even after several months' sojourn in clement soil conditions. These conditions also need to be examined and proven hospitable to the culture of pomegranate trees. Secondly, considering the pharmacological aspect of his statement, we must examine Nizami's assertion that there existed in his time a given pomegranate tree, identified as having grown near Bisūtūn, possibly named after this mythical incident and bearing fruit possessing universal healing qualities. Finally, as Nizami clearly mentions the existence of trustworthy sources in which he has found this information, we might try to identify these sources.

When one inquires into the first question, it appears that it is indeed possible to reproduce *nārbon* by means of cuttings. Writing about a century after Nizami's death, Rashīd al-Dīn Fazl-Allah Hamadānī (d. 1318)[25] has shown his interest in plants in his agricultural work entitled *Athār wa ahyā'*, written in Persian. There, he reports an occurrence in which people:

> brought a pomegranate twig from a faraway country and planted it in moist sand (*rīg-e namnāk*) and it so happened that it remained three or four months in that sand. In the spring, they saw that it had brought forth pomegranate blossoms.[26]

This is noticeably similar to the words of the poet. The fact that the twig originates from a faraway country indicates that it would not be a freshly cut branch. Other elements are the moist sand and the interval necessary for the cutting to produce roots and finally blossoms, which one may suppose will eventually turn into fruit. There is an obvious inference, namely that Rashīd al-Dīn is a younger writer and that he might have been influenced by Nizami's story. However, this particular treatise seems as a rule to be based on sources of a scientific nature. The writer's aim was certainly not to compose a collection of alleged truths mentioned by poets. Furthermore, another, earlier agricultural work written in the western parts of the Muslim world (and thus quite free of any possible influence by a contemporary Oriental writer), the *Book of Agriculture* of Ibn al ʿAwām, contains similar indications on the reproduction of the pomegranate by means of cuttings. The author makes a point of particularly mentioning the pomegranate trees as allowing an easier treatment for reproduction than most other trees:[27]

> All the masters in agriculture, Castos and Junius, say that the planting of trees should always be done before the blossoms open and the leaves

appear, except for the pomegranate tree which one may plant when its leaves have appeared (lit. after the opening). This [is due] to a special disposition of its nature.

Furthermore, it is doubly interesting to note that the poet is especially careful to indicate the fitting nature of the soil into which Farhād's pomegranate stick falls: though Rashīd al-Dīn mentions sand (*rīg*) and Nizami earth (*khāk*), the latter is careful to emphasize that this was moist earth (*namnak*). It might be that the poet is knowledgeable about the necessity for humidity if one desires any cuttings to produce roots, but on the other hand, this allows us to conjecture that he might have consulted a treatise that might be germane to Rashīd al-Dīn's source.

It seems thus that in this passage Nizami has kept fully abreast of arboricultural facts concerning the pomegranate tree's reproduction. Facts on soil conditions, age of the cuttings, and ease of the reproduction process have been checked out and found correct. Allowing for some poetical freedom (concerning the obvious lack of freshness of the cutting, or the lack of careful planting), we may still consider that this part of Nizami's verses refers to actual medieval scientific knowledge.

The second set of questions raised by this passage concern the pharmacological aspect: do we find traces of a special variety of pomegranate bearing an actual reminiscence to Farhād's drama and producing powerfully healing fruit? Research concerning the first part of the problem draws a blank: none of the medieval sources on geography, pharmacology, or arboriculture we have consulted contain information on any such variety. However, later sources mention it. We find for instance in the *Borhān-e Qat'e*,[28] a rather obscure statement that the heart of these pomegranates (that is, the *anār-e farhād*) is burned to the likeness of ash. Though it remains a mystery to what influence this charred state of the *anār-e farhād* is due or to what possible symbol this might allude, we may however conclude that five centuries after Nizami's *Khamseh*, lexicographers knew about an *anār-e farhād*. Considering the lateness of these testimonies, the wide variety of sources consulted by their authors and the importance of poetical citations in these works, and in view of the somewhat diverse information they give on the tree, we must question their exactness. The spirit in which these authors composed their lexicographic works is very different from that animating an author like Rashīd al-Dīn. If in his case we rejected the idea of an influence exerted by the poet on the scientific treatise, here the situation is reversed. It cannot be excluded, and indeed it is even probable, that the authors of these later lexicographic works simply gave an account of a well-known and widely circulating legend, possibly originating in Nizami's famous verses. At this stage, the verification of the existence of the actual variety of fruit is thus not possible. However, owing to the nonexhaustive character of our research, our conclusion needs to be prudent: although we found no mention of the *anār-e farhād* in the medieval treatises we consulted, this leads to a presumption, but not a proof, of Nizami's fantasy.

Pharmacological treatises list the virtues of pomegranates. Though variations occur between the different pharmacological authorities, they all indicate that the fruit has healing action in numerous, well-defined cases (see below where we will consider other references to the healing action of the pomegranate).[29] There is no question, however, of an "all-healing" pomegranate. Pharmacological knowledge is held aloof from legendary universal panaceas and magical practices. The medieval authors approached the classification of the healing powers of plants with due seriousness and a critical mind. Thus this part of the story, namely that the fruit of the tree heals all ills, appears to be an incorrect generalization and one opposed to the then-prevailing rigorous attitude to scientific research.

The final question raised by the above citation is Nizami's indication of written and trustworthy sources, specifically applied to what we have exposed as a fantastic element. Such mention of sources in the middle of his story is a rare enough occurrence to deserve attention. The poet usually sets these general references to the numerous consulted sources (which he does not identify), in the introductory chapters to his *masnavīs*.[30] It is a fact that placed as it is in the middle of this story, the addition lends verisimilitude to his words. The poet paraphrases the honest scientist,[31] who admits he is dealing with a phenomenon he knows from hearsay only. He has no direct knowledge about it, nor has he verified the facts himself. Nizami nevertheless reports it, in view of the value of his sources, which, as is his usual practice, he does not name. Taking the poet at his word, we could not, however, discover what these sources were.

Several possible motives for this insertion by Nizami come to mind. By thus calling attention to the (alleged) scientific exactitude of his words, Nizami might mischievously have intended to make us aware of just the opposite, namely that they were a fabrication. Alternatively, he might in all honesty have found this indication in one of his sources and have wished to defend himself against just such an accusation of fabrication, which would then indicate that the poet was possibly aware of the improbability of these all-healing pomegranates. His words might also refer to a then well-known story about this tree. Finally, Nizami may have intended this as a pun on someone he and his readers knew or as a reference to a well-known literary character, whose idiosyncrasy is thus called to mind. This would have enlivened his story at the time but is naturally lost on us.

The examination of the above passage thus yields a mixed picture of Nizami's scientific allusions, but it seems to be a good synthesis of the author's varied attitudes to science. We have discovered real references to the knowledge of the learned, albeit limited here to arboricultural facts, coupled with a possible voluntary fabrication concerning pharmacological knowledge and with a lively account of the attitudes and habits of learned people.

The Use of nār in the Khamseh

An examination of all the trees and fruits mentioned in the *Khamseh* shows that Nizami generally displays sound, if apparently not very detailed, knowledge about the pharmacological and agricultural potential of trees and fruit.[32] The rare occasions when he refers to the geographical provenance of plants show his information to be correct, though of a general character. The pomegranate tree is one of 58 different trees mentioned by the poet. Though some tree varieties are rare, some even appearing only once throughout the five *masnavi*s, 17 plants are mentioned more than 20 times each. The pomegranate is amongst them, *nār* appearing 49 times and *nārbon* 4 times.[33] It is worth noting that *nārbon*, the pomegranate tree, is thus of far lesser use to the poet than its fruit and consequently, it yields less interest as it appears three times in the *Khamseh* simply as a fruit-bearing tree. As with other trees and most frequently with the *sarv* (see below), its stature, comparable to that of a person, is once used to personify someone (*SN* 29, 5). In view of the fact that the pomegranate tree is described in our modern flora[34] as a bush, a shrub, or a small tree, which may attain 5 (16.4 ft.) or 7 (23 ft.) meters in height, while the *sarv* reaches up to 30 meters (98.4 ft.), it is perhaps useful to add that this *nārbon* refers to a *botī* (beauty) appearing in the previous verse (*SN* 29, 4), not to any of the real heroes of the epic.

The pomegranate itself, *nār* (fruit of the *Punica granatum*), is among Nizami's favorite trees and fruit. The majority of the occurrences of such "star" fruits and trees are metaphorical—for example, *sarv* (*Cupressus sempervirens*) occurs 172 times; of these the term is used as a metaphor for the hero, for the heroine, or for their lofty stature 109 times.[35] Although most of the metaphorical uses originate in the figurative value of the plants (and are thus related to either their color or their form), it is possible also to find pharmacological links for some particular metaphorical uses. Thus *shemshād* (*Buxus sempervirens*) might be used to refer to hair.[36] This has readily been explained by the appearance of the branches of box, covered as they are with small, round, and tough dark green leaves. By somewhat stretching the imagination, it can be interpreted as having some visual resemblance to curly masses of dark hair. However, it is also true that there is a preparation based on *shemshād* leaves that is recommended to strengthen the hair.[37]

Nizami's poetic use of *nār* is dominated by the metaphor for breasts (20 occurrences). These pomegranate-breasts are repeatedly described as "silver" (six occurrences). Another frequent metaphor is that of the pomegranate as a heart bursting through excess of love (ten occurrences). The red color of the fruit explains its use in comparisons with that color (nine occurrences). These metaphorical uses are based on the outward form, the structure and the color of the fruit, and seem straightforward enough. No specific references to a pharmaceutical use of *nār* in the context of breasts were found in the consulted treatises; such references would have placed these verses in the above-mentioned category of metaphors (see *shemshād*). However, it is possible that the image of the bursting heart might have such a pharmacological origin. The pomegranate possesses the virtue to clot blood (see below). There might be a possible link between the healing quality of *nār* and the injured organ. But this phenomenon needs to be further analyzed as a whole before any reliable conclusion can be reached. There is certainly a ready analogy between the condition of the overripe fruit bursting open and liberating its juice, and the image of a heart so filled with emotion that it can no longer contain its feelings and overflows with the excess of love.

Other poetic uses of the pomegranate occur when the plant as such appears in the course of the story: as wood out of which the handle of an instrument is fashioned, as a plant multiplied by cuttings, as a fruit with pharmacological value, as a fruit mentioned in company of other fruits like apples (*sīb*), jujube (*senjed*), et cetera, and growing in tended gardens.

A number of these uses may be pinpointed in our study of learned knowledge of the plant. The pharmacological and medical images are important, as is the arboricultural information. It is interesting to notice that the latter mostly appears in what might be termed involuntary information given by the poet (*a priori* knowledge), while the former images are expressly included (explicit references).

The *a priori* knowledge concerning the pomegranate is difficult to gauge, as this fruit is so well known and few questions are raised about it. For the sake of the demonstration, however, let us shortly examine whether Nizami presents the pomegranate tree as growing in a correct environment and whether the fruit is described as it is in reality. These *a priori* allusions are part of the elementary tools required by any poet writing about pomegranates. Although the example of the *nār* is too straightforward to yield any contradiction, a study of the poetic use of other trees, however (such as those belonging to the *bīd* family), has shown that some terms, understood by our dictionaries as designating, for example, the *Salix* family, might be identified as different trees according to the period and the place.[38]

In the present case, Nizami knows what the pomegranate looks like. Several times he uses the image of the thousand grains forming the heart of the burst pomegranate (for example, *HP* 22, 50). He also compares the unripe pomegranate grains to pearls, although they look like rubies once they ripen (*HP* 27, 159). The comparisons and metaphors using the red color of the fruit (for example, *SN* 11, 12) also derive from a correct identification. Apart from these observations, we also discover that Nizami knows that the pomegranate tree needs attention and grows in gardens, not in the wilderness (*HP* 32, 240; *SN* 58, 161). He names it in the company of roses (*LM* 11, 27), or cypresses, as planted close to a stream (*HP* 32, 131).

Far more interesting is the second part of our investigation, the search for explicit scientific allusions. Nizami gives no geographical information about the types of places or countries where the *nār* grows. In fact, the *Punica granatum* is cultivated all around the Mediterranean and in warm or temperate countries. Even in the time of Nizami, it must have been so familiar to the poet and to his readers that mention of its habitat might have seemed boring and commonplace. In the passage analyzed above, concerning Farhād's instrument, traces of sound arboricultural knowledge have been identified. In this passage, Nizami's pharmacological knowledge however, was very unsatisfactory and seemed akin to blatant falsification or, at the very least, the pointed reporting of a totally fantastic allegation. Fortunately, other passages show that he was perfectly aware of the real curative potential contained in the juice and skin of the pomegranate.

In the following example, taken from Nizami's third *masnavī*, he uses a medical image in which the pharmacological virtue of the fruit cures the fruit itself. This is a complex variant of the more frequently encountered image of plants and fruit helping and curing one another in the garden. The poet describes the effect of autumn's arrival on the fruits in the garden, which coincides with Leylā's swift agony:

nār az jegar-e kafideh-ye khuīsh / khūnābeh chekandeh bar del-e rīsh.
(*LM* 44, 14)[39]

The *nār* exudes bloody water from its own burst liver onto its wounded heart.

Under the surface image of an overripe fruit dripping juice through its burst skin, there also might be hidden a possible reminder of the fruit's pharmacological use. Indeed, several authors recommend the use of pomegranates—especially pomegranate skin—as a remedy for bleeding.[40] The complex image becomes that of the wounded side of the fruit, occurring through overripeness (excess of love) that has made the fruit burst. The juice it exudes is compared to blood. To quench the hemorrhage, a fitting remedy is the application of pomegranate juice. The fruit is curing itself thanks to the red juice that flows from its inside. The rather messy picture that this calls to mind is naturally not a very pleasant image to be found in a description of the arrival of autumn in the garden. The study of the use of medical imagery by poets like Khāqānī and Nizami—sometimes so explicit as to embarrass our aesthetic sense—is additionally rewarding as it gives insight into the sensibilities, fashions, and interests then current.[41] This particular image might thus show a knowledge of the fruit's virtues, though according to the majority of the pharmacological sources consulted, the poet's allusion is exact only to a point. It is mostly the pomegranate skin that is recommended to stop hemorrhages.

Our second example comes from the *Haft Paykar,* where the pomegranate is described as "the sweets of drunken people" (*HP* 32, 17):

> *begozar az nār noql-e mastān būd / khod hameh khāneh nār-pestān būd*[42]

To say nought of the drinker's sweet, the pomegranate; for those pomegranate breasts filled the house.

Wine and drunkenness, its pleasures and grief, have as a rule fascinated and delighted Persian poets.[43] Nizami is no exception and was evidently well-read on the subject. He displays inside knowledge on the effects and simultaneously on the best cures recommended to dispel the fumes of alcohol. The above *beyt* is no exception, as *nār* is well-known to be beneficial against drunkenness, as in Ibn al-Baytār's words:

It dispels the accidents of drunkenness and calms the indigestion.[44]

A study such as this presents several dangers into which it might be worthwhile to look briefly. A first surprising occurrence is that according to the treatises consulted, the pharmacological value of a plant might vary to a sometimes considerable extent. This is the consequence of the fact that medieval science was anything but static. It is important to remember that the poet might have used genuine scientific information, which other treatises will present as blatant mistakes. Any conclusion reached here must thus be considered provisional. Another danger is provided by the vagueness of the designations given by Nizami. His verses contain no precise information on the subspecies of fruits and trees, or on the degree of ripeness of the fruit, while pharmacologists sharply distinguish the use of, for example, the sweet pomegranate from that of the acid pomegranate; their effects differ or might even be opposed.[45] In such cases, it must be conjectured which subspecies Nizami might have meant, and the natural reaction is to incline toward the species answering best to his description, while this actually may be too farfetched. Finally, the important caveat against forcing a scientific interpretation on every possible passage must be constantly present to the mind.

Though the interpretation of the earlier passages are relatively safe, the following passage might well illustrate these just mentioned difficulties. It is tempting to look for a pharmaceutical explanation of the following difficult verse, as it contains an indication to a "sick person" (*LM* 36, 56):[46]

āb az del-e bāghbān khorad nār / bāshad ke khorad chū noql bīmār

the pomegranate which originates [*āb khordan az*] from the heart of the gardener, [this], the sick person must eat as if [it were] a sweet.

The pomegranate is to be eaten by the ailing as a sweet (*noql*). Sugar and sweets in general are recommended to fight cold humors, as they produce warmth.[47] Nizami has explicitly referred to this in his previous *masnavī* (*KH* 77, 29).[48] In the present example, the sick man who is recommended to eat *nār* as if it were a sweet may thus be supposed to suffer from a cold illness that can be cured by warm remedies. It is a simple enough matter to verify whether the pomegranate can be used in this case. However Heravī informs us that *nār* is "cold and dry in the first degree"[49] and Rhazes, more detailed in his exposition, indicates that the acid pomegranate "is absolutely counter-indicated for subjects with a cold temperament: it cools the liver ... Nothing is more salutary for subjects with a warm liver."[50]

We cannot, however conclude that this is an obvious error by Nizami. A first possibility is that no scientific intention is to be found in this passage. Considering that these verses are presented as the words of Majnun, who is a "natural" poet, there is a good chance that this is indeed the case. Another possibility is that Nizami, aware of the "cold and dry" nature of the pomegranate, might have meant to indicate that the sick man mistakes the effects of the pomegranate on his health, though the context doesn't help us much in understanding the verse. A third possibility could be that Nizami didn't distinguish clearly between stages of ripeness or subspecies and meant not the acid but the sweet pomegranate. Indeed, it is no surprise to find that Ibn Sīnā is reported to have said that:

the sweet pomegranate is tempered. It is beneficial by its goodness and its sweetness to the constitution of the vital spirit, especially the liver.[51]

In this case, any generally sick man, whose illness is not further defined, might do well to partake of these generally tempered fruits as if they were sweets.[52]

Comparison

There is a further difficulty in gauging the extent of Nizami's scientific knowledge, caused by the placing of the border between common knowledge—often derived from exact sciences but so widespread that the man in the street was informed about it—on the one hand, and specialized knowledge, which was restricted to a circle of a few well-read members of the intelligentsia, on the other. In order to discern the extent of refinement of Nizami's knowledge, a comparative study of the vocabulary of several poets would be necessary. This study—still lacking up to now— might bring an element of answer, albeit an answer limited to the poetical arena, and would shed light on the common elements known to several poets of different times and areas, which might then be considered as widespread knowledge. The last section of this chapter presents the embryo of such a comparison in a very limited domain.

It does not seem possible to reduce this difference to a simple equation: common knowledge equals legends and myths, while restricted knowledge equals truth and science. The study of Qazvīnī's *Book of Marvels* has yielded too many elements that were found, with nearly the same wording, in "scientific" pharmacological treatises.[53] We need another criterion to verify the originality and personal learning of Nizami. The following brief comparative study of the use by several poets of images containing the pomegranate tree and fruit might provide the first element of an answer. A recurring image or expression might then be considered as having less value in our attempt to classify knowledge. To this end, we have chosen 'Onsorī (d. 1039), Farrokhī (d. ca. 1037), and Manūchehrī (d. ca. 1040) as contradictory examples to Nizami and we shall now compare their use of the pomegranate, fruit and tree (*nār, nārbon*). The vocabulary of nature used by these poets has been fully itemized,[54] and we are thus working with reliable material.

In the case of the pomegranate, 6 references were found in 'Onsorī's *dīvān;* 2 references to the tree and 16 to the fruit in Farrokhī's; and 26 to the fruit in Manūchehrī's *divān*. Nizami, on the other hand, refers to this fruit 49 times in the *Khamseh*. The length of their respective works must naturally not be overlooked if these figures are to be used to gauge the relative frequency of images among these four poets.

The following allusions—attesting *a priori* knowledge concerning the pomegranate by the Ghaznavīd poets—are also found in Nizami's verse (I have cited only one reference for Nizami's verse, though several instances might occur in the *Khamseh*):

HP 27, 159: the unripe pomegranate grains are likened to pearls ('Onsorī 9:12; Farrokhī 50:2135; Manūchehrī 58:1912), once ripe, they resemble rubies ('Onsorī, 9:12; Manūchehrī 58:1911);

LM 12, 5: the unhappy heart is like a burst pomegranate (Farrokhī 78:3235);

SN 11, 12: lips look like pomegranates (Farrokhī 201:7751);

SN 38, 92: a ruby-encrusted gold cup resembles the pomegranate (a possible variant by 'Onsorī: the warrior's belt, of gold encrusted with rubies, resembles half a pomegranate, 9:12);

SN 58, 161: *nār* grows in gardens (Manūchehrī 31:976);

SN 34, 59: *nār* appears with *nāranj* (Manūchehrī 38:1441).

The metaphor for breasts, as seen above, is of very frequent occurrence in the *Khamseh* but is unknown in these Ghaznavīd poems.

Ghaznavīd poetry might contain possible scientific allusions, but these must be examined carefully. For example, 'Onsorī notes that both pomegranate and cypress keep their leaves all the year round (53:32). In the case of the cypress, this has become a *lieu commun* that really cannot be considered as partaking of any precise arboricultural knowledge of the said cypress. The habits of the pomegranate tree, although it is a very frequently encountered tree in Persian poetry, are not as commonly described as those of the cypress. Unfortunately for 'Onsorī, the *Punica granatum* is a deciduous tree.[55] The poet appears to be mistaken here. It must be said in his favor, however, that the pomegranate leaves are not described in any of the treatises we have examined. Again, it might also be important to remark that as is the case with Nizami's mistaken pharmacological assumption on the all-healing fruit, the verses have passed the obstacle of the critical readers. Is it possible that the idea prevailed at the time that the pomegranate tree is deciduous?

A possible pharmacological allusion might also be contained in Farrokhī's verse, namely when he repeatedly compares the burst pomegranate to crying eyes (Farrokhī 79:3290, 196:7566). Pomegranate juice is used as a collyrium to protect and disinfect the eyes,[56] and a possible pharmacological link might thus tentatively be recognized in this metaphorical use.

It is interesting to note that Farrokhī mentions that the *nār* will never grow on a *nārvan* (162:6420), thus taking a firm stand against this wrong identification of the elm with the pomegranate tree, a mistake due to the resemblance of their names. Manūchehrī, on the contrary, insists that pomegranates grow both on the *nārbon* and on the *nārvan* (38:1445, 67:2440). This is also attested in the *Khamseh* (*KH* 71, 9), although other references to the *nārvan* tend to prove that Nizami knew the difference between these trees and was simply attracted by the word-play. Another word-play is that based on the analogy between the terms *nār* and *nāranj*. As mentioned above, both Manūchehrī (38:1441) and Nizami (*SN* 34, 59) make use of it. We have also seen that the awareness that pomegranate grains change from white to red as they ripen is a long-standing poetical image and is not the result of Nizami's personal power of observation.

These sketchy results have little value on their own. They are not an indication of a direct loan by Nizami—indeed, too many possible poetical intermediaries crowd the time gap between them—nor are they a proof of an interest by the Ghaznavīd poets in learned allusions. 'Onsorī gives proof of mistaken arboricultural knowledge, while the possible pharmacological knowledge attributed here to Farrokhī is naturally dependent on further investigations into the work of the poet and on the formation of metaphors.

In concluding this short analysis both of Nizami's allusions to science in a general way and of his particular references to pomegranate trees and fruit, we may thus deduce that his interest in the world of science is obvious. By the humorous stance he takes towards both assumed universal knowledge and unquestioning reliance on a higher omniscient power, he seems to imply a third position, namely that of real, moderate knowledge and inquisitiveness; and this can be conjectured as being his own. Regarding his use of plants in the *Khamseh,* three kinds of allusions have been identified. First, the plants occur in overwhelming majority in metaphors, which, however, might sometimes be linked with knowledge of their pharmaceutical value. A second kind of allusions are those requiring only *a priori* knowledge of the plants. This is a more straightforward type of knowledge about the habits, color, form, and structure of fruits and trees. Finally, the most interesting, but also most delicate, analysis concerns explicit scientific allusions. The poet gives glimpses of interest in and knowledge of learned treatises or traditions regarding the virtues of the fruit in question. However, he is not always completely in accord with the information we have found in our sources. Details might differ. We have caught him red-handed, too, when he gives his alleged pharmacological information an improbable and magical content. It is interesting to remark here that later traditions have adopted just this improbable element and unblushingly report on the existing of "Farhād's pomegranate," the origin of which seems to be Nizami's story. We may wonder at the way the critic seems to have meekly adopted his allegation. Nizami's assertation that he has "read precisely this story" (Verse *KH* 59, 103) seems to have acted as the potent buffer it was probably meant to be, or this could also be put at the door of the poet's powerful reputation, which might have placed him in a position high above any critic.

A real danger is the inclination to force a scientific meaning into each and every mention of a given plant. Another difficulty not to be overlooked is the confusing wealth of sometimes contradictory information found in the learned treatises themselves. Finally, it is almost impossible to gauge Nizami's intentions: his verses are often obscure, and even if the meaning seems to be straightforward, how can one be sure that he really means what he says, or that he is not mischievously teasing the reader?

However incomplete, the results of this research demonstrate the interest of comparing the learned allusions found in Persian poetry with the contents of the branches of medieval science. An important question concerning the introduction of this knowledge in Nizami's poetic works is whether in any way the aim of the author could have been the scientific education of his readers. It has been argued successfully[57] that most of his works have a "Mirror for Princes" element. But this concerns the ethical content of the stories. So far as the vocabulary of the poet is concerned, we cannot consider that this was the case. Nowhere do we find an attempt to explain a given phenomenon in a scientific way or to "instruct while diverting" as is the aim of Qazvīnī's *Book of Marvels*. At most may we safely conjecture that the reader, faced with an incomprehensible scientific allusion, would be encouraged to look it up in a learned volume and so augment his knowledge.

Finally, the rather sketchy outline of a comparative study of the images, metaphors, and allusions used by different poets from different periods of Persian poetry is meant as a foretaste of a full-scale study, yet to be undertaken. This will, we are convinced, yield the most interesting results for our knowledge of image filiations, plagiarism, transformation, and originality in Persian poetry.

Notes

1. See C. van Ruymbeke, *Recherches sur les connaissances scientifiques dans la poésie persane classique.* Unpublished doctoral thesis, 1997, Université Libre de Bruxelles, pp. 9-10. The present paper is based on the results obtained in this thesis and further develops one of its elements.

2. I have used the edition by Vahīd Dastgirdī: *Kolliyyat-e Khamseh-ye Nizami,* Tehrān, 1372 H. I have abbreviated the titles of the *masnavī (MA* for *Makhzan al-asrār; KH* for *Khusraww o Shirin;* LM for *Leylā o Majnun,* HP for *Haft Peykar,* SN for *Sharaf Nāmeh,* and *EN* for *Eqbāl Nāmeh),* followed by the number of the chapter (given by the editor), followed by the number of the *beyt.*

3. An important remark here concerns the obvious problem of finding a fitting definition for scientific knowledge in the medieval period. It is evident that the margin between the modern understanding and the medieval concept of scientific knowledge is wide, but it would lead us too far from the subject of this paper to identify the common points and the differences. As it is, it might be sufficient indication to say that we can discern a common aim in medieval and modern sciences alike to arrive at undisputed truth, by means of a logical thought process and the search for an orderly classification of its elements.

4. The problem of the identification of the term *golnār,* in particular whether it simply means "pomegranate flower" or refers to the "flower of the wild pomegranate", is not yet solved, and for this reason, *golnār* was not considered in this study.

5. *Senan dar sang rafteh va dasteh dar khāk / chonīn gūyand ke khākī būd namnāk*
   az ān dasteh bar āmad shūsheh-ye nār / derakhtī gasht va bār āvard besyār
   az ān shūsheh ke-nūn gar nār yābī / da'vā-ye dard-e har bīmār yābī
   nizami gar nadīd ān nārbon-rā / be-daftar dar chonīn khānad īn sokhan-rā

6. See, for example, M. E. Subtelny, "Literary Life of Timurid Heart," in *Logos Islamikos,* Toronto, 1984, p. 147 and J. W. Clinton, "Shams-i Qays on the Nature of poetry" in *Edebiyat* 1/2, 1989, p. 125.

7. A. L. F. A. Beelaert, *A Cure for the Grieving, Studies on the Poetry of the Twelfth-Century Persian Court Poet Khāqānī Shirwānī,* Proefschrift ter verkrijging van de graad van Doctor aan de Rijksuniversiteit te Leiden, op 7 februari 1996, does not specifically mention Manūchehrī as using typically scientific imagery (though see p. 194). A similar study as that to which Nizami was submitted is being conducted on Manūchehrī. No conclusions have been reached as yet, but there are indications in this direction.

8. According to A. L. F. A. Beelaert, op. cit., p. 170, Nizami has borrowed many an image and idea from Khāqānī's verse.

9. Nizami's *divān* has not been considered here.

10. J. E. Bencheikkh, *Poétique arabe,* Paris, 1975, p. ii.

11. L. P. Ellwell-Sutton, *The Persian Metres,* Cambridge, London, New York, Melbourne, 1976, p. vii.

12. J. E. Bencheikkh, op. cit., p. 83.

13. See, for example D. Urvoy, *Les Penseurs libres dans l'Islam classique,* Paris, 1995, pp. 163-65.

14. Poetry is mentioned in the classifications of sciences. It even holds an enviable position, as it appears amongst the sciences derived from the Quran. See J. E. Urvoy, op. cit., Préface, p. vi.

15. Avicenne, *Urjūza fi 't-tibb.* Cantica Avicennae. My translation after the French translation by H. Jahier and A. Noureddine, Paris 1956, Préface, no. 13 and 14.

16. A well-known example would be Anvarī (d. 1187), who studied science before turning to poetry, apparently because it provided him with a better livelihood. See *E.Ir. s.v.* "Anvarī" and *s.v.* "Court Poetry."

17. The meter is the poetic rhythm, its kind being determined by the character and number of feet or groups of syllables of which it consists. Prosody is the science of versification, that part of the study of language which deals with the forms of metrical composition (*Oxford English Dictionary,* vol. XII, Oxford, 1989, p. 666).

18. As in *LM* 4, 57-59.

19. As shown by J. S. Meisami, *Medieval Persian Court Poetry,* Princeton, 1987, p. 158.

20. As far as I am aware, no specific study of Nizami's rendering of Majnun's verses has been made up to now. It might well be worthwhile, however, to examine how Nizami's refined verse managed to convey Majnun's natural outbursts of poetry.

21. G. Anawati, "Islam. Les expressions de l'Islam. F. Les mathématiques et les autres sciences," in *Encyclopaedia Universalis,* pp. 705-706.

22. To cite but the most obvious ones: the learned *séances* between Khusraw and his wise counselor, Bozorg-Omīd, come naturally to mind; the *Iskandar Nāmeh* also features repeated learned discussions, and it is evident that the symbolism and imagery used in the *Haft Paykar* are derived from a wide variety of scientific branches.

23. The term "botanical" is used but this once, and reluctantly at that, in the course of this study, for we have not found a fully formed, united botanical science in medieval times. Information on plants is mainly to be gathered from pharmacological, agricultural and geographical treatises. Works on magic have not been considered here. See M. Ullmann, *Die Natur- und Geheimwissenschaften im Islam,* Handbuch der Orientalistik, I, VI, 2, Leiden, 1972, p. 62.

24. The sources considered in this study are: (1) Pharmacological treatises: Ibn Māsawaih, *Ketāb javāher al-tīb al-mufrada;* Abū Mansūr Movaffaq Heravī, *Ketāb al-abnīa 'an haqā'eq al-advīa;* Abū Rayhān Bīrūnī, *Ketāb al-saydana fi'l tibb;* Abū Hamayd al-Samarqandī, *Ketāb al-Qarābādīn 'ala tartib al-ilal;* Ibn al-Baytār, *Al-Jāmi' li mufradāt al-advīa va al-agdīa;* Moh. Mo'men Tonokabonī, *Tohfat-e Hakīm Mo'men;* (2) Encyclopaedia and Book of Marvels: Fakhr al-Dīn Rāzī, *Jāme' al-'Olum;* Abū Yahyā Zakariyā al-Qazvīnī, *'Ajāā'eb al-Makhluqāt va qarāā'eb al-mowjūdāt;* (3) Agricultural Works: Ibn al-'Awām, *Ketāb al-Felāha;* Rashīd al-Dīn Fazl-Allah Hamedānī, *Athār va Ahyāā';* Qāsem b. Yusof Abū Nasri Heravī, *Ershād al-Zerā'a;* (4) Descriptive geographical works: Anon., *al-Ketāb al-tāmī min akhbār al-Sīn wa' l-Hind;* Mas'ūdī, *Al-Ketāb murūj al-zahab wa-ma'ādīn al-jawhar;* Anon. *Hudūd al-'alam;* Nāser-e Khusraww, *Safar Nāma;* Yāqūt, *Mo'jam al-Buldan;* (5) Lexicographies: Asadī Tūsī, *Loghāt-e Fors;* Muh. b. Hendūshāh-e Nakhjavānī, *Sahāh al-Fors;* Mah. Qāsem b. Hājī Mah. Kāshānī, *Majma' al-Fors;* Moh. Hosayn b. Khalaf Tabrīzī, *Borhān-e Qat'e.* For a brief presentation on their authors and their contents, as well as the editions used, see C. van Ruymbeke, op. cit., chapter 3, Les sources consultées, pp. 100-26.

25. Rashid Al-Dīn started his career by training as a doctor under the supervision of his father, who was an apothecary himself. He chanced to become vizier to the Ilkhans Ghazān Khān and Öldjaytü and wrote for them the famous *History of the World.*

26. Rashid Al-Dīn Fazl-Allah Hamedanī, *Athār va Ahyā',* edited by M. Sotūdeh and I. Afshar, Tehrān 1989, pp. 9-11, dar ma'arefat-e derakht-e anār, esp. p. 11.

27. Ibnn Al-'Awam, *Ketāb al-Felāha, Le Livre de l'Agriculture,* trans. J. J. Clement-Mullet, 3 vols., Paris, 1864-67, vol. 2, pp. 253-54 (my English translation after the French translation of Clement-Mullet).

28. The author, Mohammad Hoseyn b. Khalaf-e Tabrizi Motekhalles b. Borhan, compiled this lexicographical work in Golconda, in 1651-52: *Borhān-e Qat'e,* ed. M. Mo'īn, 5 vols., Tehrān, 1357 sh, I, p. 162. See also Mahmūd Qāsem Kashani, *Majma' al-Fors,* ed. Dabīrsīyāāqī, 3 vols., Tehrān, 1338 H., I, p. 33.

29. Ibn Al-Baytar, *Le Traité des Simples,* trans. Lucien Leclerc, 3 vols., Paris 1877, repr. Institut du monde arabe, Paris, s.d., A 417 pp. 311-13; Qazvini, *Ajā'eb al-makhluqāt,* be-tasbih va maqābeleh-ye Nasrollah Sabūhī, Tehrān, 1361 H., 2nd ed., p. 220; Kashani, *Majma' al-Furs* be kūshesh-e M. Dabīrsīyāqī, 3 vols., Tehran, 1338 H., p. 91; Heravi, *Ershād-e Zerā'a,* Tehrān, 1134 H., M. Mushīrī, ed., pp. 25-26; Hakim Momen, *Tohfat-e Hakīm Mo'men,* Mir Seyyed Ahmad Rūzātī, Ketābforūshī-ye Mahmūdī, s.l., s.d.,

pp. 213-14; A-Samarqandī, *Ketāb al-qarābādhīn 'ala tartīb al-ilal. The Medical Formulary of al-Samarqandi,* trans. with commentary, critical notes, and comparisons by M. Levey and N. Al-Khaledy, London, Bombay, 1967, pp. 92 and 160.

30. See, for example, *HP* 4, 26-32. In this passage, however, Nizami apparently names Bokhārī and Tabarī as two of his sources, though opinions diverge on this point. See J. S. Meisami, *Nizami. Haft Paykar. A medieval Persian Romance,* Oxford, 1995, note 4:28, p. 276.

31. See, for example, Ibn Al-Baytar, op. cit., p. 2 (my translation from the French translation by L. Leclerc): "I will constantly attach citations to the name of their authors, and will make known the way through which this information have reached me. I will especially indicate what I have learned by myself, and which I can guarantee as to the exactness and authenticity."

32. C. van Ruymbeke, op. cit., pp. 278-79.

33. *Nārvan,* the elm, occasionally appears as *nārbon:* C. van Ruymbeke, op. cit., pp. 200-201 and 246.

34. *Flora Europaea,* Cambridge University Press, 1968, vol. I, p. 37 and vol. II, p. 305.

35. The remaining 63 occurrences either present *sarv* as one of the trees in the garden, companion to the rose and refuge for numerous birds, projecting a cool, dark green shadow. Six verses mention that *sarv* grows along watercourses; 5 verses that it is sometimes trimmed; 6 others that it produces no fruit, except in miraculous cases (Ibid., pp. 181-85).

36. Ibid., pp. 192-93.

37. Ibn Al Baytar, op. cit., A no. 315, pp. 245-6 and Hakim Mo'men, op. cit., p. 171. These links are tenuous and, as far as we are aware, have not yet been studied in Persian poetry; but their recurrence awoke our interest.

38. C. van Ruymbeke, op. cit., pp. 164-75.

39. "The *nār* exudes bloody water from its own burst liver onto its wounded heart."

40. Ibn Al Baytar, op. cit., no. 1058, p. 182, Al Samarqandi, op. cit., p. 130. This use is still testified in contemporary Iran, see A. Parsa, "Medicinal Plants and Drugs of Plant Origin in Iran" in *Qualitas Plantarum et Materiae vegetabilis,* 1960, vol. VII-1, p. 103.

41. A. L. F. A. Beelaert, op. cit., pp. 170-71. This author's capital analysis of examples of Khāqānī's and Nizami's medical imagery with reference to the garden has provided an illuminating cue for our study.

42. J. S. Meisami, op. cit., p. 217, translates this difficult verse: "To say nought of the drinker's sweet, the pomegranate; for those breasts with pomegranates filled the house."

43. See, for example, C. van Ruymbeke, "Le vin. Interdiction et licence dans la poésie persane," in *Acta Orientalia Belgica,* Bruxelles and Leuven, 1997, pp. 173-86. See also D. S. Feins, recent doctoral thesis on wine-drinking in Islam, presented in Edinburgh, 1997. My heartiest thanks to Professor R. Hillenbrand for making me aware of this reference.

44. Ibn Al Baytar, op. cit., B no. 1058, pp. 180-81.

45. For example, Nizami mentions the *nār* in general, while we discover there is a capital difference between the acid, the sweet-and-acid, and the sweet *nār.* See the very long entry in Ibid., B no. 1058, pp. 180-84. This difference is well illustrated when dealing with the date in its different stages of ripeness (see C. van Ruymbeke, op. cit., pp. 228-35).

46. Though this verse's signification remains obscure, a possible translation could be: "the pomegranate which originates [*āb khordan az*] from the heart of the gardener, [this], the sick person must eat as if [it were] a sweet."

47. Medieval pharmacology holds its basic postulates from the famous theory of the four humors explained by Galen. For an explanation of this well-known theory, see, for example, H. Elkhadem, *Le Taqwīm al-Sihha (Tacuini Sanitatis) d'Ibn Butlān,* Histoire du Texte, Edition critique, Traduction, Commentaire, Louvain, 1990, pp. 29-32; see also M. Levey and N. Al-Khaledy, op. cit., pp. 30-35.

48. *maranj az garmī-ye Shirin-e ranjūr / ke shirinī be garmī hast mashhūr,* with a pun on Shirin/*Shirinī* and *garmī* (fierceness/hot quality).

49. Heravi, op. cit., p. 162.

50. Cited by Ibn Al Baytar, op. cit., B no. 1058, pp. 180-81.

51. Ibid.

52. This should not be taken as an example *a contrario* of what is stated above (point 2.) concerning fruit that would heal all ills. The pomegranate is said to be only temperate and generally beneficial, not a universal panacea.

53. See C. van Ruymbeke, op. cit., p. 113.

54. See C.-H. de Fouchécour, *La description de la nature dans la poésie lyrique persane du XIè siècle. Inventaire et analyse des thèmes,* Paris, 1969, pp. 60-61.

55. *Flora Europaea,* op. cit., vol. 2, p. 305.

56. Ibn Al Baytar, op. cit., B no. 1058, p. 181, citing Ibn Sīnā.

57. See, for example, J. S. Meisami, op. cit., chapter V.

Chapter 8

Music in *Khusraw Va Shirin*[1]

Firoozeh Khazrai

There is an episode in the *Iqbāl-nāmah,* the first part of *Iskandar-nāmah,* that raises the question of the role of music and musicians in Nizami's poetry. In the section entitled "Plato's Music Making," the philosophers of Alexander's court are vying for superiority, and the competition intensifies between Aristotle and Plato. Plato becomes so indignant at Aristotle's claim to superiority over all the other philosophers that he leaves the court in search of the music of the universe. In doing so he invents the organun (*arghanon*) with which he is able to make other beings, human or animal, sleepy or alert, or induce whatever mood in them that he desires. When Aristotle hears of Plato's invention he strives to match his creativeness, and although he is able to induce sleep in his subjects, he is unable to wake them up. Aristotle feels humiliated. He confesses his own shortcomings, apologizes to Plato for his arrogance, and seeks his guidance on the science of music.[2] In this episode Nizami demonstrates the supernatural potency of music and its superiority to logic—a quality that might be extended to include Nizami's own art, that is, poetry, since it, too, is often characterized as appealing to the emotions rather than to reason.

This story prompted me to think about Nizami's musical allusions. What sources did he have at his disposal to draw upon, and how did he use them? More important, what was his purpose in weaving these musical images, metaphors and allegories into the web of his poetry? I would like to locate my answers to these questions in two specific episodes from Nizami's *Khusraw va Shirin,* both of which involve Barbad, the renowned poet-musician of Khusraw Parviz's (590-628 A.D.) court. The first of these is the famous passage concerning Barbad's *sī laḥn* (thirty tunes or songs), in which Nizami claims that though Barbad knew hundreds of *dastān* (tunes), Nizami has chosen only thirty of them, and he lists them as in a catalogue, each in an individual line of poetry.[3] The second passage is the lengthy musical duel between Barbad and Nakisa, who are acting as spokesmen for Khusraw and Shirin.[4] This episode, which comprises 263 couplets, is virtually unique in the corpus of Persian poetry.

The technique of incorporating music (a ghazal with instrumental accompaniment) into a poem in order to convey the emotions of the main characters has almost no precedents or parallels in Islamic Persian. There is a passage comprising eight lines in the *Vīs va Rāmīn* of Fakhr al-dīn As'ad Gurgānī[5] in which the *gūsān* or *khunyāgar* (minstrel) sings a song that symbolically represents the relationship between Mūbad, Vīs, and Rāmīn.[6] However, Gurgānī's use of interpolated music (in the form of a song) is fundamentally different from Nizami's. In *Vīs va Rāmīn,* the *gūsān* himself chooses to comment on the relationship between the characters and events. In *Khusraw va Shirin,* it is Shirin who appeals to the minstrel Nakisa to sing of her passionate love, and instructs him to employ the appropriate *dastān* or *pardeh* to express her feelings. In return, another minstrel, Barbad, sings as if from Khusraw's heart. This episode occurs at a crucial juncture in the story. The two lovers both feel hopeless and hurt, and unable to express their true feelings toward each other. At the same time they also know that they can no longer continue living without each other. Nizami confers the important role of uniting the lovers on music and musicians. Apparently music and minstrelsy must have been very important elements for Nizami to have devoted the entire climax of the story to it. He must have felt a special kinship or affinity with the Iranian minstrels of the pre-Islamic era, who were conversant with the art of music as well as that of the poetry.

Mary Boyce has an excellent survey of the relevant sources pertinent to the minstrel tradition in Iran with an emphasis on the Sassanid period in her article, "The Parthian Gūsān and the Iranian Minstrel Tradition."[7] This tradition, in my opinion, plays an influential role in the psyche of the subsequent Persian poets,[8] and therefore it is important to highlight some of its features. Boyce concludes that the Parthian minstrel (*gūsān*) "played a considerable part in the life of the Parthians and their neighbors down to late in the Sassanid epoch: entertainer of king and commoner, privileged at court and popular with the people; present at the graveside and at the feast; eulogist, satirist, storyteller, musician; recorder of past achievements, and commentator of his own times."[9] From the extant sources she deduces that minstrelsy flourished under both the Achaemenians and the Sassanians in Persia proper, while the *gūsān* tradition continued in the north.[10] She believes that in the early Islamic period the poet/minstrel (*khunyāgar*), "like the *gūsān*, clearly inherited a body of traditional material, on which he could extemporize as called upon; and he also contributed poems of his own invention, of varied character, sung to an instrumental accompaniment."[11] Jerome W. Clinton discusses the relationship of the poet and the musician in his *Dīvān of Manūchehrī Dāmghānī*, and provides a brief survey of the sources on their status in the early Islamic era. He concludes that poets and musicians were in the process of diverging in the ninth through the eleventh centuries, while there still existed an abundant overlap between the two groups.[12] It is this particular admixture of a poet/musician that I would like to draw upon as a background for my discussions of Nizami's musical references.

With the foregoing in mind, and before setting out to discuss these episodes, I would like to give a short survey of the sources that tell us something about Barbad or his compositions and then return to Nizami's treatment of Barbad and his music. The sources that inform us about Barbad are mostly of two types: historical works of various kinds, including some musical tracts, and literary texts, mostly poetry.

Historical Sources on Barbad

There are many iconographical representations of musicians and musical instruments in the rock reliefs of Tāq-i Bustān and artifacts of the period that signify the exalted status of music and musicians at the Sassanid court but we do not have any written documents that inform us about the actual nature of Sassanid music.[13] From all the most famous Pahlavi texts that have so far reached us, only the so-called *Khusraw qubādān va rīdak* (Khusraw Qubādān and his Page), contains a short passage that mentions music.[14] The *rīdak* describes the most sublime of *khunyagarān* (poet-minstrels), and, in response to the inquiries of the king, singles out the *kanīz-e chang-sarāy* (a slave-girl who plays a kind of harp) with a clear, beautiful voice as the most exalted of them. This same story is recounted in the *Ghurar al-sayar* of al-Tha'ālibī (d. 1037 or 1038) where he names the *rīdak* as one of the unique elements of the court of Khusraw Parviz (d. 628) along with Barbad and Shirin.[15] These two stories display some divergences that show that Tha'ālibī might have had access to a different version of the story from the one that has reached us, or else his understanding of the Pahlavi text differed from our contemporary interpretation.

None of the surviving Pahlavi sources mention Barbad or any of his work. All our knowledge about Barbad has come down to us through the scanty information in Persian and Arabic sources that are mostly of a literary nature rather than a musical one.[16] The first Islamic source that mentions Barbad is an Arabic poem by Khaled ibn Fayyaz, a poet of the late seventh through eighth centuries,[17] that I will discuss more below in the section on literary sources. Here I will only point out that in Fayyaz's poem for the first time, the famous story of the death of Shabdīz, Khusraw Parviz's favorite horse, is narrated. Since this story becomes the focal point in many sources on Barbad, I will include it here. The story goes that Shabdīz had died but nobody dared to inform Parviz of his death because the king had declared that he would execute anybody who ventured to bring him the news of his beloved horse's death. After much hesitation the responsibility of informing Parviz fell on Barbad, who in a rueful song, sang "Shabdiz does not eat, Shabdiz does not breathe..." whereupon Parviz cried out, "Then my horse Shabdīz is dead!" and all the attendants said, "It is the King who said this" and thereby saved themselves.[18] Fayyaz praises Barbad for the power of his music that could soften even a despotic king's heart and soul.

The next source that informs us about Barbad is *Kitāb al-lahw wa al-malāhī* by Ibn Khurdādhbih (d. ca. 910), which is one of the earliest sources on music in the Arabic language, dating from the ninth century.[19] It recounts some of the tales about Barbad and mentions that he is from Marv. Ibn Khurdādhbih is the only source that cites three hemistichs of one of Barbad's songs, but unfortunately without any musical notation. One of Ibn Khurdādhbih's stories about Barbad and his student Sharkas, whom he poisons out of jealousy, is recounted in many variants in later Arabic sources. Ibn Khurdādhbih's version, for example, differs from Tha'ālibi's.[20] In Ibn Khurdādhbih it is Barbad who is condemned to death and Khusraw tells him, "I took delight in both of you and now you have destroyed half of my joy," and orders Barbad's execution, but Barbad saves his own life by responding, "If I spoiled half of the Shah's joy why do you want to spoil his whole joy by killing me." Parviz spares him by saying that such an eloquent man must be forgiven.[21] In Tha'ālibi's, it is Sarkash who poisons Barbad out of jealousy.[22]

Ibn Khurdādhbih also mentions eight modes in connection with the Persians: *bandastān, bahār, ibrīn, ibrīneh, madārūsnān, shīsam, al-ghabih, isbirās*. Unfortunately all these names are approximates because the original manuscript has not been easily accessible and the only printed version is abridged and relies heavily on the interpretation of the reader of the old manuscript. Ibn Khurdādhbih calls these modes *Turuq al-mulūkīyya* or "royal modes," but he does not attribute the invention of any of these modes to Barbad.[23]

Ibn Qutayba (d. 889) in his *'Uyūn al-akhbār* narrates the same story of the poisoning but this time Barbad is poisoned by a musician called

Yūsht.[24] In the same century, al-Jāḥiz recounts this story in his *Kitāb al-ḥayawān,* with Yūsht changed to Zivasht.[25] In his *'Iqd al-Farīd,* Ibn 'Abd Rabbih (d. 940) relates the story in the same words as Ibn Qutayba.[26] Zamakhsharī (early twelfth century) also retells Shabdiz's story in his *Rabī' al-abrār wa nuṣūṣ al-akhbār.*

Al-Iṣfahānī in his *Kitāb al-āghānī* relates a new story about Barbad that he attributes to Isḥaq Muṣalī (776-856), who was one of the most famous minstrels and *nadīm*s who served Harūn al-Rashīd, and subsequent Abbasid caliphs. Isḥaq had heard a story about Barbad that he narrates for his friends. At one of Parviz's parties Barbad had performed well as usual. One of the guests present, envious of Barbad, alters the tuning of his instrument when Barbad goes out of the room on an errand. When he returns he finds the tuning of his instrument altered, but he proceeds with the performance as though the instrument was still tuned as before. No one suspects anything till the end when Barbad informs Khusraw Parviz of what has happened, and Parviz praises him to the skies. Isḥaq Muṣali claims that he had heard the story retold by different people and was impressed by Barbad's mastery. He had decided to practice in this way so that he could equal Barbad.[27]

According to al-Hamdhānī (d. 903) in his *Kitāb al-buldān,* Barbad's music was so influential and powerful that Shirin asked him to use his music to remind Parviz to fulfill his promise to build a castle for her. Shirin bestowed an estate near Iṣfahān on Barbad for this favor.[28] In his *Ghurar al-sayar,* Tha'ālibī, the contemporary of Firdawsī, has a more extensive section on Barbad. He recounts the same story of the rivalry between Sargas (apparently the same as Sarkash) and Barbad, and the latter's hiding in a tree in order to charm Khusraw.[29] I will discuss Tha'ālibī's comments below in the next section in relation to Firdawsī's account of Barbad.

From the sources and nature of the things attributed to Barbad, we can conclude that Barbad survived in an oral popular culture that immortalized him by continually retelling old stories about him, and the legendary power of his music, and by spinning out new ones. While all these stories mythologize Barbad without telling us any solid information about the actual nature of his music, they underscore the unparalleled authority of the minstrel and the powerful grip he and his music continued to exercise on the imagination of the people in the post-Sassanid era.

Literary Sources on Barbad

As I mentioned above, the earliest source that informs us about Barbad is literary—Khālid ibn Fayyāz's poem on the death of Shabdiz. From this early poem, which is in Arabic rather than in Barbad's native tongue, we can surmise that Barbad's myth had far-reaching effects on the imagination of poets in the surrounding countries even a hundred years after his death. Ibn Fayyāz relates Shabdiz's story to reveal the mythical power of Barbad and his art and in turn, by invoking the perpetuity of Barbad's fame, implies that his own poetry will endure as well:

> And Khusraw, King of Kings, him too an arrow
> Plumed from the wings of Death did sorely smite,
> E'en as he slept in Shirin's soft embraces
> Amidst brocades and perfumes, through the night
> > Dreaming of Shabdīz, whom he used to ride,
> > His noble steed, his glory and his pride.
>
> He with an oath solemn and most binding,
> Not to be loosed, had sworn upon the Fire
> That who so first should say, "Shabdīz hath perished,"
> Should die upon the cross in torments dire;
> Until one morn that horse lay low in death
> Like whom no horse hath been since man drew breath
>
> Four strings wailed o'er him, while the minstrel kindled
> Pity and passion by the witchery
> Of his left hand, and while the strings vibrated,
> Chanted a wailing Persian threnody,
> > Till the King cried, "My horse Shabdīz is dead!"
> > "It is the King that sayeth it," they said.[30]

This poem is a reminder of another early Persian poet-musician, Rudaki (middle third to early fourth centuries A.D.) about the power of whose music similar stories circulated. Nizami ʾAruzi in his *Chahār maqālah* narrates that one year Amīr Naṣr-e Sāmānī had gone to Herāt for the summer and he enjoyed the weather and fruits of that region so much that he and his retinue remained there for four years. The courtiers, who had lost any hope of returning and who longed for their dear ones and their homes, sought Rudaki's help. He composed the famous *qaṣidah* of "*Būy-e jūy-e mūliyān āyad hamī*" and accompanied it with his *chang* (harp). Upon hearing the song, the amīr mounted his horse without putting on his boots and rode non-stop toward Bukhārā.[31] Firdawsī narrates a similar tale in the beginning of the story of Kay Kāvus, when he is newly installed on the Iranian throne. A *rāmeshgar* (minstrel) from Māzandarān requests an audience with the Shāh and when his wish is granted, he sings the praises of Māzandarān—its nature, its climate, and its creatures—to the accompaniment of his *barbaṭ* (Sassanid short-necked lute). Kay Kāvus, moved and mesmerized by his music, calls his lieutenants and commands them to prepare the troops for the invasion of Māzandarān.[32] His courtiers are so dismayed at this sudden impulse to invade Māzandarān that they attribute it to the teachings of *ahreman,* the representative of evil in the Zoroastrian religion.[33] In other words, there is a clear implication that the *rāmeshgar* is an instrument of a supernatural force rather than an ordinary person practicing his art, thus attributing a metaphysical power to the music and the musician who could compel the king to undertake such a perilous campaign. The significance of these stories lies in their emphasis on the persuasive power of the poetry/music and the influential role played by the poet/musicians in the Persian courts even after the advent of Islam, in an obvious continuation of the Barbad tradition.

The most renowned source for Barbad in Persian literature is the *Shāhnāmeh* of Firdawsī (950-1032), in which he narrates the famous story of the first encounter of Barbad with Khusraw Parviz in his account of that Shāh's reign. Barbad had tried unsuccessfully to get an audience with Khusraw, but Khusraw's chief minstrel, Sarkash, blocked all his attempts. Finally Barbad charmed Khusraw by hiding in a tree and singing three *sorūds* (songs) to the accompaniment of his *barbaṭ.* Firdawsī gives the names of these songs as *dād-afarīd, peykār-e gurd,* and *sabz dar sabz.* After hearing Barbad's performance Parviz made him his chief minstrel.[34] In his *Ghurar al-sayar,* Tha'ālibī, Firdawsī's contemporary, recounts the same story with slight differences in the names of the songs.[35] Of all these songs Nizami only mentions *sabz dar sabz* among his "thirty songs" in *Khusraw va Shirin.*[36] Tha'ālibī then goes on to enumerate and describe some of the wonders of Parviz's court among which he names *takht-e ṭāqdīs* (the throne of *ṭāqdīs*), *ganj-e bād-āvard* (the wind-borne treasure), *gāv-e ganj* (the bull's treasure), *shabdīz* (the name of Khusraw's beloved horse) and of course *Shirin* (Khusraw's beloved wife).[37] These five wonders appear with the same names among the "thirty songs" attributed to Barbad by Nizami, and Nizami might have conjectured from Tha'ālibi's history that Barbad also composed some songs praising and glorifying Khusraw's favorite objects, like *takht-e ṭāqdīs.* Firdawsī also makes a reference to the *ganj-e bād-āvard* and *ganj-e sūkhteh* though he does not refer to them as songs of Barbad.[38] Tha'ālibī further attributes the composition of *khosravānī-hā* or "royal modes" to Barbad and points out that these have survived to his day and are still performed by contemporary musicians.[39] These "royal modes" might be the same as *ṭuruq al-mulūkīya*[40] mentioned earlier by Ibn Khurdādhbih, but we cannot verify this, because Tha'ālibī fails to mention their names.

Both Christensen in his *L'Iran sous les Sassanides*[41] and Browne in his 1899 article[42] attribute 360 songs to Barbad (without mentioning any names) that he composed, one for each day of the year. These are in addition to the "Thirty Songs" and the *khusravānī-hā* already mentioned. Both Christensen and Browne rely on Mustawfī's *Tārikh-e guzideh*[43] (fourteenth century) for their attribution, which is the only source that supports the attribution to Barbad of a year-long daily cycle of songs. Since it was written at least 700 years after Barbad's time, we should probably regard its assertions with respect to Barbad as bordering on the legendary until a new source that supports them comes to light.

Ascription of "Thirty Songs"

To return to the "Thirty songs" attributed by Nizami to Barbad, the poet names these as: *ganj-e bād-āvard, ganj-e gāv, ganj-e sūkhteh, shādurvān murvārīd, takht-e ṭāqdīsī, naqūsī, awrang, ḥuqqeh kālūs (kāvūs), māh bar kūhān, mushk dāneh, ārāyesh-e khūrshīd, nīmrūz, sabz dar sabz, qufl-e rūmī, sarvestān, sarv-e sahī, nūshīn bādeh, rāmesh-e jān, nowrūz, mushk-mālī, mehregānī, marvāy-e nīk, shabdīz, shab-e farrukh, farrukh-rūz, ghuncheh-e kabk-darī, nakhjīrgān, khūn-e sīyavūsh, kīn-e Īraj, bāgh-e Shirin.*[44]

In his *Dīvān,* Manūchehrī (d. 1040) mentions twelve songs whose titles are either exactly the same as these or differ from them only slightly: *bāgh-e sīyavashān, sarv-e setāh, nūsh-labīneh, takht-e ardeshir, ganj-e bād-āvard, ganj-e gāv, nāqūsī, sabzeh Bahār, sarvestān, sarv-e sahī, bādeh, mehregān-khurdak.*[45] He does not attribute these songs to Barbad, nor does he allude to any of the stories about him,[46] although he mentions his name several times.[47] Thus there are no sources earlier than Nizami (1155-1223) that refer to these songs as belonging to Barbad. All later sources like the *Burhān-e qāṭi'* of the seventeenth century[48] refer to Nīzāmī as the source for the attribution of these songs.[49] We can infer from this that Nizami was alone in attributing these thirty songs to Barbad, and did so as a kind of poetic license.[50]

To summarize briefly, it appears from our sources that an exceptionally gifted musician called Barbad existed at some point during Khusraw Parviz's reign (ca. 591-628), and that his name and reputation survived in the oral culture of Iran down into the Islamic era. From our earliest source, Khālid Fayyāz's poem, we learn that Barbad's myth was well-established as a vehicle for the imagination of poets. During the course of time various anecdotes became attached to his name as well as the names of many extant compositions. Until a new independent source on the subject comes to light, many of these attributions should be regarded as authorial inventions. The point to emphasize here is that we may reasonably assume both that there was a historical Barbad and that the names of the songs that Nizami attributes to him are authentic, but that Nizami's assertion that these songs belong to Barbad is doubtful. Certainly, there is no surviving precedent for this attribution that antedates Nizami's. The question that arises here is, "What poetic purpose of Nizami's was served by this attribution?" I will try to address this question below, after I consider Barbad's placement in the corpus of Nizami's famous predecessor, Firdawsī.

When Firdawsī relates the story of Barbad and Sarkash, he is close to the end of the *Shāhnāmeh*. He may well have employed it there as an allegory of his own difficulties with enemies at Sulṭan Maḥmūd's court.[51] Immediately following Barbad's story he goes on to write the most famous lines regarding the permanence of his work:

> sar āmad kunūn qeṣṣeh-i barbad / mabādā keh bāshad turā yār-e bad,
> jahān bar mihān u kihān bogzarad / kheradmand mardum cherā gham khurad,
> basī mihtar u kihtar az man guzasht / nakhvāham man az khāb bīdār gasht,
> hamānā ke shud sāl bar shaṣt u shesh / na nīkū buvad mardum-e pīr-kesh,
> chu in nāmvar nāmeh āyad bi-bun / ze man rūye kishvar shavad pur sakhun,
> az ān pas namīram kih man zindih-am / pih tukhm-i sukhan man parakandih-am,
> har ānkas kih dārad hush u rāy u dīn / pas az marg bar man kunad āfarīn.[52]

which literally means,

> Barbad's story has come to an end. / May you never have a bad companion.
> [since] Time will pass for the lofty and the humble, / Why should the wise be disheartened?
> I have been through many ups and downs, / But I do not wish to wake from my [pleasant] dream.

Now that I have reached the age of sixty-six years, / It is not pleasant to be old and wise.

When this renowned story comes to an end / Everyone in the country will talk about me.

Hence I will not die but live (forever), / Because I have spread the seeds of eloquence.

Whoever is wise, thoughtful and faithful / Will praise me after my death.

Firdawsī apparently identifies with Barbad and his mythical struggle with Sarkash, and sees in it a parallel with his own situation in Maḥmūd's court, where he has to confront jealous enemies. As Barbad's name and fame, despite enmities and the passage of time, has remained immortal up to Firdawsī's time, he naturally wishes the same for himself. This is reinforced by the fact that he is pondering his own mortality when he refers to his age of sixty-six in the fourth line cited above. The last three lines are so integral to Firdawsī's hopes of permanence that he reiterates them as the final lines of his monumental work[53] not only to remind himself and his readers once again of the timelessness of his *magnum opus,* but also to employ them as a fitting closure and a last prayer for his work.

Nizami employs Barbad in two different contexts, one historical and the other artistic. When Nizami cites Barbad and his "Thirty Songs," it seems that he wants to locate Barbad in the history of Khusraw Parviz's reign. He reinforces this by naming songs that he might have composed for the wonders of Parviz's court, blending them with some of the contemporary songs that might have survived to his time, and attributes them all to Barbad.[54] Of these thirty songs, seven of them, *ganj-e bād-āvard* ("wind-borne treasure"), *ganj-e gāv* ("the bull's treasure"), *ganj-e sūkhteh* ("the burnt treasure"), *shādurvān-murvārīd* ("tapestry of pearls"), *takht-e ṭāghdīs* ("throne of *tāqdis*"), *shabdīz,* and *bagh-e Shirin* ("the garden of shirin") are given names of the wonders of Parviz's court that are enumerated both by Thaʿālibī[55] and Firdawsī.[56] As I indicated above, Manūchehrī mentions two of these, *ganj-e bād-āvard* and *ganj-e gāv,* in his *Dīvān* without any attribution to Barbad.[57] So along with another ten songs or variants of their names that he mentions in his poetry, and *sabz dar sabz* ("green on green") that is mentioned in both Firdawsī and Thaʿālibī and is the only song that they refer to in relation to Barbad, it appears that only thirteen of these songs were known previously in written culture. Whether Nizami picked up the rest of these songs from the oral culture around him or thought them up with the intention of having a section on Barbad comparable to Firdawsī's, must remain a matter of speculation.

Like Firdawsī, Nizami also wished to employ Barbad as a representation of an artist who had survived the test of time, and wanted to identify with him. After enumerating Barbad's "Thirty Songs", Nizami relates how Khusraw Parviz bestowed gold on Barbad each time he performed a song that was pleasing to him, and contrasts Khusraw's behavior with that of his own patrons:[58]

> bih har pardih kih ū bar zad navāyī / malik dādash pur az guhar qabāyī
>
> darīn dowran garat bih zīn pasandand / zihī pashmīn bih gardan va nabandand
>
> zi 'ālī hemmatī gardan barafrāz / tanāb-e zuhreh ra dar gardan andāz
>
> bih khorsandī ṭama' rāā dīdih bar dūz / ze chūn man qaṭrih-ī daryāyī āmūz
>
> ki chandīn ganj bakhshīdam bih shāhī / va zān kharman najustam barg-e kāhī
>
> bih bī-bargī sukhan rā rāst kardam / na ū dād o na man darkhvāst kardam
>
> marā ān bas kih pur kardam jahān rā / valī ne'mat shudam daryā va kān rā
>
> nizami gar zih-i zarrīn basī hast / zih-i tu zuhd shud magzārash az dast
>
> bih īn zih gar garīban rā ṭarāzī / kunī bar gardanān gardanfarāzī.

Which literally means:

> With each song that he performed / Khusraw gave him a jeweled robe,
>
> Nowadays even if they like you better [than Barbad] / They will not even hang woolen rags around your neck
>
> Hold up your head with your strong will, / and become the slave of Venus
>
> By contentment do away with ambition. / From me (who is) like a drop learn a sea (of knowledge).
>
> I, who bestowed many a treasure upon a king, / did not enjoy even a blade of hay from that pile (of treasure).
>
> Without any reward, I composed my poem. / He neither gave it, nor did I seek it.
>
> It is enough for me that I filled the world (with my work), / and (thus) became the master of the earth and sea.
>
> Nizami there are many golden ties (in the world), / but your shackle is abstinence so do not let go off it.
>
> If I adorn my neck with this shackle (tie), / I will be superior to all the others.

This line, *marā ān bas keh pur kardam jahān rā / valī ne'mat shudam daryā va kān rā* (It is enough for me that I filled the world with my own work), / (and (thus) became the master of the earth and sea.), may be considered a parallel to Firdawsī's lines cited above on how his work will immortalize him, and as a response to them. Thus Barbad is, for both poets, a means to reflect on their mortality versus the immortality of their work. Nizami goes even further than Firdawsī and associates himself also with Barbad the *khunyāgar* as well when he writes that he should become a slave of Zuhrah (Venus) who is the symbol of *khunyāgarī* in Persian literature.[59]

When Nizami employs Barbad and Nakisa to speak for Khusraw and Shirin, he combines various strands of historical and contemporary features in a novel artistic way. He singles out the mythical-historical rivalry of Barbad and Nakisa, but instead of degrading them to poisoning each other, he positions them as representing the eternal opposites and complements of our human universe—man and woman. The musical vehicle he employs for this confrontation are not the historical songs of Barbad[60] but the contemporary *maqāms* of his own time.[61] Nizami employs the maqāms of *rāst, 'ushāq, ḥeṣārī, 'iraq, nowruz, sepāhān, rāhawī,* and *zīrafkand,* which, according to our information on the music of his age, were the current *maqāmāt.* In a sense, by the juxtaposition of the music from the two eras he bridges 600 years to connect his time with the time of Barbad and Khusraw Parviz, thus assuring the continuity of an ancient tradition, that is, the tradition of poet-musicians, in his own poetry.

In conclusion, I would like to emphasize my original hypothesis that Nizami exercises poetic license in his musical references and executes this with such authority that all the later sources refer to him as the source for the musical attributions to Barbad. But as the juxtaposition of the legendary musicians of Sassanid court with the contemporary musical usage of his time shows, Nizami is willing to profit from everything in his environment to fertilize his poetic imagination and to create new relationships between people and eras for the sake of artistic creation. Besides, the indebtedness to his great predecessor Firdawsī in evoking Barbad and his art should not be ignored, and this is apparent when he follows the same line of thought as Firdawsī in celebrating the immortality of the work of art beyond the mortality of its creator. With the musical duel between Barbad and Nakisa he goes even further than his predecessor in employing music to enrich his poetic language, simultaneously displaying his command of the contemporary musical usage, which was the mark of a skilled *khunyāgar* of the traditional Sassanid court, and conveying the torments of love between the two great lovers of the Persian literature through the medium of music.

Notes

1. The inspiration for this chapter came when I was attending one of the weekly sessions reading Nizami at Prof. K. Allin Luther's house in 1994 in Ann Arbor.

2. Nizami Ganjavī, *Iskandar-Nameh,* ed. V. Dastgirdī (Tehran, 1954), 85-92. J. E. Bügel discusses this story as well in chapter 6 of the present work. C.f. p. 129 [editors].

3. Nizami Ganjavī, *Khusraw va Shīrīn,* ed. Bihraz Sarvatyiān (Tehran, 1987), 339-344.

4. Ibid., 585-617.

5. Fakhr al-Dīn As'ad Gurgānī, *Vīs u Rāmīn,* ed. Muḥammad Ja'far Maḥjub (Tehran, 1959), 220.

6. V. Minorsky in his article on *Vīs u Rāmīn* has shown that this eleventh-century poem is of Parthian origins. See V. Minorsky, "Vīs u Rāmīn: A Parthian Romance," *Bulletin of the School of Oriental and African Studies,* 1946, XI, 4, 745.

7. Mary Boyce, "The Parthian Gosān and Iranian Minstrel Tradition," *Journal of the Royal Asiatic Society,* XVIII (1957), 10-45.

8. Jerome W. Clinton has a brief survey of the tradition of court poetry in Iran in the first chapter of his book, *The Dīvān of Manūchihrī Dāmghānī: A Critical Study* (Minneapolis, 1972), pp. 1-21.

9. Boyce, op. cit., 17-18.

10. Ibid., 20.

11. Ibid., 27.

12. Clinton, op. cit., 1-21.

13. On the iconographical evidences of Sassanid court, see Klaus-Peter Koch, "Persia," in *The New Grove Dictionary of Music and Musicians,* ed. Stanley Sadie (London, 1995), 550.

14. In *Tarjumah-i chand matn-e pahlavī,* trans. Malik al-Shu'ārā' Bahār, ed. Muḥammad Gulbun (Tehran, 1968), 98-104.

15. Abd al-Malik b. Muḥammad Tha'ālibi, *Shāhnāmah' kuhan: parsī-I tarīkh-i ghurar al-siyar,* trans. Muḥammad Ruḥani (Mashhad, 1994), 395.

16. For a partial list of sources that mention Barbad, see E. G. Browne, *A Literary History of Persia,* vol. I (London, 1909), 14-15. A more exhaustive list is to be found in A. Tafazzolī, "Barbad," *Encyclopedia Iranica,* ed. E. Yārshāṭer, vol. III (New York), 757-58.

17. Ibid., 17-18.

18. Ibid.

19. Ibn Khurdādhbih, *Kitāb al-lahw wa al-malāhī,* ed. I. A. Khalifa (Beirūt, 1964), and see the following note.

20. For published selections from Ibn Khurdādhbih's treatise, see "Mukhtār min kitāb al-lahw wa al-malāhī," *Al-Mashriq,* vol. 54, no. 2 (Summer 1960), 134-67. For his citation of Barbad's song, see p. 139.

21. Ibid., 138.

22. Tha'ālibi, op. cit., 392.

23. Ibn Khurdādhbih, *Al-Mashriq,* 137.

24. Ibī Muḥammad 'Abdullah b. Muslim b. Qutayba al-Dīnavarī, *Kitāb 'uyūn al-akhbār* (Qāhira, 1925), vol. I, 98.

25. Abī Uthman 'Amr b. Baḥr al-Jāḥiz, *Kitāb al-ḥayawān,* ed. 'Abd al-Salām Muḥammad Hārun (Qāhirah, 1945), vol. I, part IV, 113.

26. Muḥammad b. 'Abd Rabbih, *Al-'iqd al-farīd,* ed. A. Amīn, A. Zayn, and I. Al-Abiyārī (Qāhira, 1956), vol. II, 182.

27. Abī al-Faraj al-Iṣfahānī, *Kitāb al-aghanī* (Qāhira, 1932), vol. V, 280-81.

28. Ibn al-Faqīh al-Hamadhānī, *Kitāb al-buldān,* ed. M. J. De Goeje (Leiden, 1967), 2nd ed., 158-59.

29. Tha'ālibi, op. cit., 388-89.

30. Browne, op. cit., 17-18. For the original Arabic version see M. Murād ibn 'Abdu al-Raḥmān, *Āthar al-bilād wa akhbār al-'ibād* (Tehrān, 1994), ed. Sayyid M. Shāhmuradī, 88.

31. Browne also mentions this story on pp. 16-17 of his book, but I draw attention to it, because it is relevant to the ultimate conclusions of my paper about poet-musicians in Persian literature. For the story, refer to Nizami 'Arūzī Samarqandī, *Chahār maqālah,* corrected by Allameh M. Qazvīnī, ed. M. Mo'in (Tehran, 1996), 49-54.

32. Abu'l-Qāsem Firdawsī, *The Shāhnāmeh,* ed. Jalāl Khāleqī-Moṭlaq, 6 vols. (Costa Mesa, 1987), vol. II, 4-12.

33. Ibid., 6.

34. Abu al-Qāsīm Firdowsī Ṭūsī, *Shāhnāmeh,* ed. by Ye. E. Bertel's et al., 9 vol. (Moscow, 1960-1971), vol. IX, 226-29.

35. Tha'ālibi, op. cit., 388-89.

36. Nizami, *Khusraw va Shīrīn,* 340.

37. Tha'ālibī, op. cit., 389-96.

38. Firdowsi, Bertel's, 165.

39. Tha'ālibi, op. cit., 389.

40. Mas'ūdī in his *Murūj al-dhahab* refers to the *Ṭurūq al-mulūkiyya* in Ibn Khurdādhbih and says that there are seven of them but their names seem to be corrupted either through transmission or by way of copying. Of these only two names coincide with those of Ibn Khurdādhbih: *mādārūsnan* and *sīsum.* Mas'ūdī does not attribute any of these to Barbad. Refer to al-Mas'ūdī, *Murūj al-dhahab wa ma'ādin al-jawhar* (Beirūt, 1973), vol. IV, 132.

41. See A. Christensen, *L'Iran sous les Sassanides* (Copenhague, 1936), 478-79.

42. Refer to E. G. Browne, "The Sources of Dawlatshāh; with some remarks on the Materials available for a Literary History of Persia, and an Excursus on Barbad and Rūdagī," *JRAS,* 1899, p. 54.

43. See Ḥamdullah Mustawfī Qazvīnī, *Tārikh-e guzidah,* ed. A. Navā'ī (Tehran, 1960), 123.

44. Nizami, *Khusraw va Shīrīn,* 339-342.

45. See *Dīvān-e manūchehrī dāmghanī,* ed. Muḥammad Dabīr Sīyaqī (Tehran, 1977), 4th ed. These songs can be found (in the order I have mentioned) on

the following pages: 186-87, 88, 186, 34, and 87; 19 and 72, 19 and 69, and 87, 4, 32 and 113, 87, 88 and 127, 1, 209.

46. See also H. Mallāh's *Manūcherī dāmghanī va mūsīqī* (Tehran, 1984), 83, and Manūcherī's *Dīvān*, 18 and 159.

47. For example, *Bulbul-e bāghi be bāgh, dūsh nava'i bezad / khūbtar az barbad, khūbtar az bāmshād*, (Last night, the garden nightingale sang a song in the garden / better than Barbad, better than Bāmshād (*Dīvan-e manūchehrī dāmghānī,* 19).

48. See Muḥammad Ḥusayn ibn Khalaf Tabrīzī famous as Burhān, *Burhān-e qāṭi'*, ed. M. Mo'īn (Tehran, 1963), vol. II, 2nd ed. 1207-8, here I have to mention that I have some misgivings about the enumeration of these "Thirty Songs." Because there are discrepancies between the editions of Sarvatyiān and V. Dastgirdī's edition of *Khusraw va Shīrīn* (Tehran, 1954). For the most part, these are not major differences, but there is one variant that affects the total number of the songs. Dastgirdī's reading of the sixth and seventh song is: *chu nāghūsī va avrangī zadī sāz / shudī avrang chun nāghūs az āvaz* (p. 191). This reading makes *naghūsī* and *avrangī* two separate songs, while Sarvatyiān's reading is more ambiguous: *chu nāghūsī bar avrang āmadī bāz / shudī avrang chun nāghūs az āvāz* (p. 340). Sarvatyiān's reading connects the two words of *nāghūs* and *avrang* in a way that makes it difficult to read them as denoting two separate songs, thus making Nizami's "Thirty Songs" into twenty-nine songs. Sarvatyiān himself also alludes to this discrepancy (see pp. 893-94) but finds the fault with the reading of songs in other lines.

49. As though Nizami's goal was to give his readers a knowledge of Barbad's songs, whereas Nizami is following a more poetical path with a different goal in mind. I will talk more extensively about this later.

50. Another scenario of course is that he bases his ascriptions on a text that is no longer extant, and about which no earlier or later writer has informed us.

51. See, for example, Jules Mohl's biography of Firdawsī in the preface to his edition of *Shāhnāmeh,* where he explains how jealous some of Maḥmūd's courtiers were of Firdawsī's popularity with Maḥmūd and the court, *Shāhnameh-i firdawsī,* trans. J. Afkārī (Tehrān, 1984), 3rd ed., 86-96.

52. Firdawsī, Bertel's, vol. IX, 229-30.

53. Firdawsī, ibid., 382.

54. A. Christensen also relates these songs or melody-names to the wonders of Parvīz's court, but he moves from a different premise, that these "Thirty Songs" were really Barbad's and he accepts Nizami's attribution as a solid fact. See "Some Notes on Persian Melody-names of the Sassanian Period" in *The Dastur Hoshang Memorial Volume* (Bombay, 1918), 368-77.

55. Tha'ālibi, 389-93.

56. Firdawsī, 238-39.

57. Manūchehri, *Divān,* 19.

58. Nizami, *Khusraw va Shīrīn,* 343-44.

59. See Nizami, *Khusraw va Shīrīn,* 894.

60. The names of Nizami's "Thirty Songs" are almost all of Persian origin and display less Arabic influence while the "*maqāms*" assigned to the musical

duel between Barbad and Nakīsā certainly show the intermixture of these two cultures.

61. Theorists like Ibn Sina have generally divided the music after the advent of Islam into twelve primary modes or *maqām*s: *rāhawī, husaynī, rāst, būsalīk, zankūla, 'ushaq, hijāzī, 'iraq, isfahan, navā, buzurk, mukhālif.* All of these names can still be found in modern Persian art music, but how much they differ from or resemble the original modes unfortunately is unknown to us. H. Farhat and S. Blum in *The New Grove Dictionary of Music and Musicians,* ed. Stanley Sadie (London, 1995), vol. IX, 292-300; for this quotation, see p. 292.

Chapter 9

The Story of the Ascension (*Mi'raj*) in Nizami's Work

C.-H. De Fouchécour*
(*Translated by Kamran Talattof and Arjang Talattof*)

What would the course of Persian literary history look like without the impact of Nizami's work? The poetry of Nizami of Ganje (ca. 536/ 1141-605/1209) is so original that we have yet to appreciate its true value.

This originality is displayed through the use of traditional material. A scholar of high talent and scrupulousness, Nizami dealt with this material, imparting his personal genius to the tradition that had brought it to him. This is accomplished magnificently: his expression is entirely poetic; it is also difficult, and calls for numerous adaptations.

For example, here we will take several verses, among the thousands that compromise Nizami's work. These are the verses that the poet has devoted to the story of the Ascension of the Prophet of Islam (*mi'raj*). The story touched his soul, for we find he developed it in each of his five great works of poetry or *masnavis;* thus we have a subject that has been progressively dealt with five times. We shall see how, from traditional material that he knew very well, Nizami exercised his talent, affirmed his preferences, and produced an original work.

Conciseness and personal preference drive us to consider the story of the Ascension from the *Seven Beauties* (*Haft Paykar*) as the reference story. This is the story, it seems, in which Nezami's thought regarding this topic has come to fruition.

The materials that Nizami was able to dispose of for the treatment of the Ascension of the Prophet, were of immense and rich quality.[1] For what is written in Arabic, a man from Nayshapur, al-Qushayri,[2] had assembled, in an excellent treatise (*Kitab al-mi'raj*), written before 456/1072, a large number of the Islamic traditions on this subject, about which, he developed, in a scholastic manner, the arguments in favor of the physical reality of this Ascension, and seeing God. The story of the Ascension written by Nizami in his first *masnavi, Makhzan al-asrar,* seems to have been written under the influence of the great affirmations of Qushayri.

However, from the fourth to the tenth centuries, a rich literature of Persian expression had prevailed over the Iranian cultural area, and had developed with originality this story of the Ascension of the Prophet. This literature is under study;[3] we will be satisfied here by giving a few chronological[4] points of reference and by giving brief remarks that are necessary for our subject.

1. *Tafsir,* by Tabari, revised and written in Persian by Bal'ami, completed in 345/956.
2. *Mi'raj-nameh,* attributed to Avicenne (d. in 429/1037); old text.
3. (*Kitab al-mi'raj,* of al-Qushayri; see below; written before 456/ 1072).
4. *Tafsir,* by Surabadi, written before 494/1101.
5. *Tafsir,* by Maybudi, written before 520/1126.
6. *Hadiqat al-haqiqa,* by Sana'i, written before 525/1131.
7. *Tafsir,* by Abu al-Futuh Razi, written before 538/1144.
8. *Mi'raj-nameh,* by 'Ebadi Marvazi, written before 547/1152.
9. *Makhzan al-asrar,* by Nizami, written without a doubt in 570/1174.
10. *Khosraw-o Shirin,* by Nizami, written in 576/1181.
11. *Layli-o Majnun,* by Nizami, written in 584/1188.
12. *Musibat-nameh,* by 'Attar, written before 586/1190.
13. *Elāhi-nameh,* by 'Attar, written before 586/1190.
14. *Haft Paykar,* by Nizami, written in 593/1196.
15. *Sharaf-nameh,* by Nizami, written in 600/1203.

This is contrary to the tendency expressed by the texts attributed to Avicenna (n. 2) and al-Qushayri's (n. 3) treatise, which spread the idea of a spiritual ascension, as opposed to a physical one. We must wait for Abu al-Futuh Razi (n. 7) in order to have an all-encompassing synthesis in Persian of the traditions regarding the Ascension of the Prophet, a vast and carefully composed collection. However, the story from the *Tafsir* by Surabadi (n. 4) already features a structure that is striking in its orderliness, especially if we compare it to that of *Tasfir* of Tabari-Bal'ami (n. 1): the "horizontal" journey from Mecca to Jerusalem is a journey of initiation giving decisive proof on the way to Jerusalem that the Prophet has taken on the leadership of all of the preceding prophets. He then completes the Ascension across the angel-filled skies. The notion of the Prophet's intercession (*shafa'at*), in favor of his people, already greatly exploited, would be amplified after him, this time revolving around the term *bara'at,* Persian: *barāt* ("key to deliverance" given by God to the population of sinners).[5] Maybudi's text (n. 5), which is quite complex, distinguishes itself particularly by it's description of the vision of God, this great encounter, or the Prophet "having come out of himself in losing his self-conscience and having remained in amazement" (p. 493).[6]

Sana'i's story (n. 6; *Hadiqat,* pp. 195-97) does not include this sense of a mystical character, but it provides a new model. The story is reduced, devoid of all details, but is better as regards its concentration on the view of the Prophet's individual character. This new focus would mark the stories that came after him; Nizami knew Sana'i's text and he, as everyone knows, makes references to this text in the beginning of the *Makhzan al-asrar.* Following a brief description of each stage of the Ascension, traditional in the stories of the *Tafsirs* (the ladder, the Holy Mosque, the Rock, *Rafraf,* the distance of two arches) Sana'i introduced the Prophet's overtaking of the planets of each of the seven heavens. He thus indicates the transcosmic dimension of the Prophet's personality. This is a characteristic that made a strong impression and would be greatly developed after Sana'i. The Prophet also passes the "well-guarded Table," on which men's acts are inscribed: he therefore crosses and goes beyond the place where human destiny is marked.

We will have noticed (n. 9 to 15) that 'Attar and Nizami both produced their stories in the last quarter of the sixth and seventh centuries. Was Nizami familiar with the principle story of 'Attar, included in *Elāhi-nameh,*[7] certainly the last *masnavi* of that mystical poet? 'Attar's story is included in the Prophet's eulogy; it was conceived in order to exalt his person. In it we encounter many characters, in three periods, especially prophets and angels; importance is given to the theme of the "two arches" reunited into one single arch, an insistent image of *tawhid;* on the one hand, the heavenly bodies bestow their attributes upon the Prophet, on the other hand they receive his annexed lights. The notions of mediation and deliverance are absent; it is only shown that, even though he is living amongst the sinners, the Prophet is purified and possesses the spiritual knowledge that makes the ability to read almost superfluous.

At the time when Nizami undertakes in his turn the composition of a story of the Ascension of the Prophet, he finds himself facing a tradition that tends to eliminate certain episodes of the route toward the "other

world," especially the visits to Heaven and Hell, which have an apoca-
lyptic character. This elimination is the consequence of a new focus on
the prophet of Islam as itinerant and seer. From now on, the narrator is
no longer simply an exegete, traditionalist, or theologian, but a poet who
surpasses them all. The poet uses a whole palette of images to exalt the
exceptional person of the Prophet, whom God had exalted in the first
place by ascension. In this context we shall see to what degree of rich
insightfulness the vigorous thoughts of our poet Nizami are capable. The
story of the Ascension in *The Seven Beauties, (Haft Paykar)*,[8] holds our
attention at this point. We shall now show how the three earlier stories by
Nizami prepared the way for it. The initial bayt of the first 78, which are
devoted to the *mi'raj,* remarkably sums up the sense of the whole story.
The Prophet has such eminence that he cannot display his being except
outside the limits of this world through an Ascension that permits him to
be raised up to the Holy Throne.[9] This is what the account, which is
clearly organized in seven parts, will demonstrate. This one is quite
clearly organized in seven parts.

1. Bayts 2 to 22: Gabriel invites the Prophet to accomplish the noc-
    turnal journey toward the divine Throne. Riding Boraq, the celes-
    tial steed, the angel Gabriel presents himself to the Prophet and
    invites him to take his turn as the nocturnal warden of the world
    and sitting astride Boraq, to traverse the space of Heavenly bod-
    ies and angels in order to arrive where space is abolished, at the
    foot of the divine Throne. The proposal by Gabriel to the Prophet
    is like a story anticipating the Ascension, from which it dissemi-
    nates its goals. Early on, as he passes through space by the stars,
    the Prophet will revive and brighten them. This is the primary
    manner of affirming his superiority over the entire world. This
    superiority must then display itself as a domination: "Lead the
    journey, for thou art king" (bayt 7); "Take by lasso the Palace of
    Sanctity" (bayt 14); "Assume for yourself the crown, for it is you
    who has become the crowned being; rise above all, for it is you
    who has become the head" (bayt 19); "Seize the two worlds ... ,
    that your standard may fly over both celestial bodies" (bayts 20
    and 22). The third goal is the exaltation of the Prophet: the celes-
    tial bodies and angels await his arrival and the stars will become
    devoted to him (bayts 10 to 12), "Go with head held high in your
    exaltation (*sar farkhtani*)" (bayt 20), "Pitch your tent on the
    platform, at the foot of the divine Throne" (bayt 17). Finally, the
    last goal, expressed in one single bayt (n. 16), but well presented,

is the one of supplication (*do'a*): "This night is your night, this hour is one of prayer; you will receive all that you could desire."

2. Bayts 23 to 29: Predisposed to the prophecy, the Prophet perfectly welcomes the message of the angel Gabriel. Nizami's text flourishes in its expression, however, it clearly conveys what it intends to: the Prophet's ear perfectly transmits the message to his intelligence disposed to comprehend the mystery. The message goes from the confiding ear to penetrating and obedient reason. This process is nothing more than hearing and accepting: "In the darkest night, this radiant lamp (no one but the Prophet) was sealed with the imprint of his wish (*shod ze mohr-e morad naqsh-pazir*)" (bayt 28). The mark of prophecy appears to be applied at the time of the acceptance of the angel's message.

3. Bayts 30 to 39: Mounted upon Boraq, the Prophet is carried toward the heavens at great speed. Some comparisons serve to facilitate imagining that which is the carrier on the celestial climb: eagle, partridge, a quadruped with wings colored like those of a peacock arising from its feet, litter of the king Kavous abandoning his four carrier eagles, figures of the four material elements. It is not said that it has a human face. Its speed is that of imagination or lightning; and still: "(Have you seen) the speed with which the imagination travels the world? And the leap of the spirit toward the generous deed?" (bayt 36). All this is nothing, not more than the speed of the Poles spinning so fast upon themselves that we do not even see them moving. Boraq's quickness is incomparable. We know the care with which the miniaturists attended themselves to paint Nizami's Boraq.

4. Bayts 40 to 49: the Prophet traverses the seven skies, giving the heavenly bodies their own colors. Having come out of the terrestrial sphere, "He took the path leading to the gate of the world and attacked the Heavens" (bayt 41). The burst of his face gave the moon its verdancy, he colored Mercury in by his silver hand, covered Venus with the moon's veil, he set a crown of gold upon the sun by the dust of his path, left Bahram (Mars) to become red[10] of blushing, at the view of his green clothes, spills his wooden sandals[11] upon sick Jupiter. Finally, beyond Saturn, "His standard pierced the thick darkness" (bayt 49).

5. Bayts 50 to 60: The ultimate journey, above the seven heavens, until the test of the approach of God. Since this section requires a lengthy presentation, it is preferable here to give only the translation. 50: He proceeded superbly, resembling the dawn's breeze, astride a stead like a raging lion. 51: As his companion

Gabriel abandoned the course, Buraq as well desisted from its course. 52: For he had reached a stage so high where Gabriel had orders to keep away. 53: From Michael's litter he arose to the tower of Esrafil.[12] 54: He departed from that throne leaving Rafraf[13] and Sidra[14] behind. 55: He left his companions behind halfway en route, and moved on to the sea of selflessness. 56: He passed the ocean, drop by drop, and passed beyond all existence. 57: When he arrived to the divine throne he made a ladder (nardeban) from the lasso of his prayer (niaz). 58: He raised his head above the radiant Throne to the mysterious stage of prayers. 59: When he was lost in bewilderment, God's mercy came and took the reins in hand. 60: His distance from "two bow-lengths"[15] passed, and he went closer.

We see how Nizami has utilized the most simple facts of the tradition of the mi'raj to compose a small, precise text of spiritual initiation, with this gradation: desire, abyss, terror, Mercy, and elevation-proximity.

6. Bayts 61 to 71: Transcending his own self, the Prophet actually sees God beyond all dimensions. "When he tore the veil of one thousand lights, his eyes attained the unveiled Light. He took a step beyond his own self, so that he could see" (bayts 61-62). In this section, Nizami develops the notion of "absence of dimension": "That is how one can see the One who is without dimensions" (69). We are therefore at the opposite of the journey made by the Prophet of all created dimensions, to which a reference was made in sections 1 through 5.

7. Bayts 72 to 75: the fruit of ascension is the deliverance of the sinners. Being received by His honor, and having good fortune and spiritual recognition, the prophet, "next to God, received the letter[16] which ordained the deliverance" (bayt 72) of the people from their punishment. The bayts 76 to 78 form an exhortation in which Nizami addresses himself, with this Islamic notation: "If reason guards your faith, gain the everlasting realm through light of Law" of Islam (bayt 78).

It remains to test the originality of the story of the Ascension contained in Haft Paykar, in comparing this story to those which Nizami has contained in his other four masnavis. Sections 4 to 7 correspond with the whole story of the Ascension contained in *Makhzan al-Asrar* (ed. Vahid Dastgirdī, Tehran, pp. 14-19, 68 bayts). The first 23 bayts describe the nocturne Ascension. The Prophet's move in the middle of the night, awake at the time when people sleep; his soul rises from his body, and he frees himself from terrestrial dimensions; he adopts a dozen constellations of the Zodiac and adopts the attributes of these moving stars. Bayts 24 to 33: the Prophet passes, thanks to Boraq, the other prophets, angels, and the Sidra; he abandons those who were escorting him to reach the divine Throne. There (bayts 34 to 60), in estranged solidarity sunken in unconsciousness, he finds himself outside of time and space, which our imagination can not construe. He achieves the sight of God with his eye, but without remaining for a longtime in a place where God himself remains. The fruit of the Ascension (bayts 61 to 66), is God's mercy on the Prophet's community. This journey of love (*safar-e eshq*) is accomplished instantly (bayt 66).

This story of the Ascension in *Makhzan al-Asrar* lets us see how Nizami has decided to consider the *mi'raj:* which is that ultimate opening of the unique personality of the Prophet, who is given a momentary vision of God and is the octroyer of every mercy for the Muslim community. The prophetic, mystic, and Savior-like characteristics of the Prophet are not emphasized.

It is, on the contrary, the soteriological aspect that Nizami emphasizes in the version of the story of the Ascension, which he places at the end of *Khuraw va Shirin* (ed. De Baku, 1960, pp. 761-65, 43 bayts). This story opens with a description of Boraq ("coming from the light"); the well known stages of the Ascension are thereafter recounted, until the sight of God. This is consequently none but a voice (p. 765) telling the Prophet to express what he wanted, and, "on the field, he demanded the key (which allows to open) the treasury of mercy" (bayt 38). God answered his prayer for the sins of the community and he returns to the earth (having obtained the key to "the treasure of deliverance (*ba ganj-e exlas*)," taking to the people "the key to happiness (barat-e shadmani)" (bayt 42).

The story contained in *Layla and Majnun* (edited by Vahid Dastgerdi, Tehran pp. 12-16, 44 bayts) is a brief and simple text, written in the second person (addressed by Nizami to the Prophet: 1 to 6; addressed by Gabriel to the Prophet: 7-17; a description, in the second person, of the Ascension: 18 to 44). All of the essential elements of the *mi'raj* are in their place; Gabriel then appears, yet the story does not include the development of this spiritual character. The night of the Ascension is designated as the "night of destiny (*shab-e qadr*)," the time at which his prophetic destiny is realized (bayt 17).

With the last of the addresses, where Nizami tells the Prophet what he has accomplished through his Ascension, the poet insists upon the fact that his interlocutor [Mohammad] surpasses all levels and leaves behind all others along his path in order to enter that absence of all dimension (bayts 36-37). Up to bayt 44, the salvational function of the Prophet is well fixed: "You have carried the key of deliverance of the saved (*rastegaran*) for sinners like us."

Nizami's thought is, therefore, simplified as it progresses; it has left the great motifs that give the Ascension its decisive aspects within the Prophet's career. We would like to speak about the accomplishment once and for all of the nocturne moment and all that he will realize later in his life and on the Grand Day. The *mi'raj* in *The Seven Beauties,* developed in seven points, is not a retelling of the previous stories of Nizami, but a completely new manner of rendering them. The story's character, we have noticed, is more respected; he is presented with the force of a refined *poem,* which is rendered so to speak in the sense of a listener or of a lecturer, by the force of words which one hears or reads; important in this way is his adhesion towards its subjects: as *Prophet* (he attends, understands, and accomplishes perfectly the message of the angel; he intercedes for the sinners), as savior (he brings the key of deliverance to the sinners) and as a spiritual man (he surpasses his own being and sees God).

The last story of the Ascension composed by Nizami, in the beginning of the first section of his *The Story of Alexander* (*Sharafnameh,* edited by Vahid Dastgirdi, Tehran, pp. 17-25, 65 bayts) is, for one part (47 bayts), a story about the journey. This one poses anew the question of the Ascension stories with relation to the *masnavis* in which the stories are told. This relation is not clearly apparent. Of course, the *mi'raj* in *Makhzan al-Asrar* has a more doctrinal aspect, similarly, the one of *Khusraw va Shirin* displays more sensibilities (selflessness, deliverance, joy). That of *Layli va Majnun* has a direct tone (in the second person) and sketches the overtaking love, approaching what we have found in *Layli va Majnun* of Jami. The *mi'raj* of *Haft Paykar* comes from the writing of a man in full maturity, an alchemist, perhaps;[17] that of the *Sharafnameh* insists upon the journey, during which the Prophet encounters particularly Khezr (bayt 35). The *mi'raj* stories have a general tone which is not irrelevant to the *masnavis* that contain them. However, nothing more precise appears to us for the moment that should be emphasized here.

The story of the Ascension contained in *Sharafnameh* is arranged as follow. (1) It is a beautiful night (bayts 1 to 3) that the Prophet ascends to heavens (bayts 4 to 9). (2) Being Prince of the princes of the world, he goes from a very distant Mosque, to the naval of the world (in Jerusalem), to the highest of the skies; delivering in this way the bond of this world, he is favored among the servants of the Divine Throne. (3) This is evident in Boraq, rapid and radiant (description of the mount is in bayts 10–21), who brought him (Muhammad) there. (4) The Prophet transformed the sky on his voyage, endowing each moving star his own character. He was greeted by Khezr, Moses, and Jesus and reached the top of Heaven at great speed. He abandoned Gabriel en route, passed Esrafil, Rafraf, and the Sidra, transcending all heavenly and terrestrial dimensions. (5) Then, having passed beyond his own self, he found himself truly alone in front of God; he greeted Him and was warmly received. Without intermediation, he heard God and saw His face in an unimaginable way: his body was all eyes (bayts 54 to 57). (6) Then (bayts 58 to 65), having drunk at the table of consecration (*ekhlas*), he set aside our portion (*bakhsh-e khass kard,* 58b). Having learned all from God about the world, he returned, his face illuminated from a voyage that lasted no more than an instant.

At the beginning of *The Story of Alexander,* Nizami has also thought of narrating a journey, but in contrast to that of Alexander's: this journey of the Ascension of the Prophet reminded him of three privileged prophets in their relations with the beyond: Khezr, Moses, and Jesus. Oriented in this manner, the story had to be organized in a way different from the story of the *Haft Paykar:* Gabriel's message to the Prophet and his harkening the Prophet to him is not included, the constitutive characteristics of the prophetic image are no longer applied; and as regards the Ascension, the exchange between God and the Prophet evokes the image of sharing at a table, but Nizami says no more. Did he already have in mind Alexander's visit to the tomb of Kay Khosrow?

Among the five stories of the Ascension written by Nizami, the *Haft Paykar* offers the strongest expression of all that suggested to the poet the long tradition of the *mi'raj.* With this text, we find ourselves in front of the masterpiece of all of the literature of the Ascension. Because of this masterpiece, we have had to reconsider the entire tradition that preceded it.

Notes

*   This is a translation of C.-H. de Fouchécour, "Les récits d'ascension (*mi'raj*) dans l'oeuvre de Nezami" dans Ètudes Irano-Aryennes Offertes À Gilbert Lazard, Réunies par C.-H. Fouchécour et Ph. Gignoux, *Cahier de Studia Iranica,* 7. 99-108, (Paris: Association Pour L'Aèvancement des Etudes Iraniennes, 1989). We are thankful to Harry Neale for his useful comments.

1. We distinguish Isrsā (nocturnal journey) and meʿraj (journey to Heaven; see s.v. Encyclopédie de l'Islam, 1er éd.). We simplify, with the tradition of translation, by not talking about *mi'râj* (Pers.: *me'râj*), properly: "ladder" (*nardebân*). On Nizami, I allow myself, for the beginning, to refer to my *Histoire de la littérature persane,* 1. Période classique. Introduction, Paris, 1985, Universite de Paris III, Service des Publications, pp. 35-41 et bibl.

2. See "al-Kushayri," Encyclopédie de l'Islam, 2e éd., V, pp. 530-31.

3. For a work to appear in collaboration with Mrs. Claude Kappler.

4. For we recall Tafsir a commentary on the Quran. The stories of Ascension are usually found in the development of commentaries of the Quran XVII, 1. *Mi'raj*-name applies an independent rendering of the subject. For the rest, it is about the Persian works that contain a story of Ascension consisting of tens of bayts, usually after the eulogy of the Prophet.

5. This term is approached, in the Tafsir of Surabadi, by the usage of the root in the fifth form: 'tabarra', in the sense of "disengaging one's responsibility": the Prophet is separated from the sinner population, which allows for the mediation of the Prophet.

6. Hojviri (Kashf al-Majub, p. 364) had already touched upon the theme of proximity to God, who desired Mohammad to be annihilated.

7. *Elahi-name,* ed. F. Ruhani, Tehran, 1339/1960, p. 11, bayt 256 to p. 16, bayt 394. English translation by J. A. Boyle; *The Ilahi-nama,* Manchester, 1976, pp. 12-18.

8. *Haft Paykar* (*The Seven Beauties*), Persian text edited by Vahid Dastgirdi (Tehran, 1316/1937), pp. 9-14

9. *Chun nagonjid dar jahan tajash—takht bar 'arsh bast me'rarajsh*: "Because his crown could not be contained within the limits of the world, the Ascent (*mi'raj*) bore him to the divine throne." The crown symbolizes the eminent nature of the prophet. Cf. Nizami, *Haft Paykar,* p. 6, bayt 8: "He (the Prophet) is the king of prophets by sword and crown: his sword is the law, and his crown is the Ascent," *mi'raj*, which signifies by metonymy Ascension.

10. By love and by jealousy.

11. At times, remedy and gray paint, as Nizami explains, *Haft Paykar*, op.cit., p. 291.

12. The angel of death. On the function of the four angels (Jabra'il, Mika'il, Esrafil, and 'Azrafil), see the beautiful text of Mawlavi (Masnavi-e ma'navi, daftar V, bayts 1556 sq.), about the creation of Adam.

13. See Quran, LV, 76: This is the place where Esrafil is.

14. See Quran, LIII, 14: This Sidra marks the limit of all actions and creatures.

15. See Quran, LIII, 8-9. He is but a short distance.

16. Barat, letter of transfer of sovereign powers by which they arrange for example, the delivery of a prisoner.

17. It is the conclusion that is the strong-point of the article by Georg Krotkoff ("Color and Number in the *Haft Paykar*," in *Logos Islamikos,* in Honorem G. M. Wickens, R. M. Savory, and D. A. Agius, ed., Toronto, 1984, pp. 97-118). The author recalls that H. Ritter had already remarked the exceptional quality of the *mi'raj* in *HP,* in which he finds (p. 110) an essential reference to the nine spheres.

Chapter 10

International Recognition of Nizami's Work: A Bibliography

Kamran Talattof

The following bibliography includes the translations, criticisms, manuscripts, miniatures, and illustrations related to the work of Nizami Ganjavi. It includes information in Russian, Azeri, German, Persian, and a few other languages. This bibliography is by no means complete. It excludes bibliographic entries for Nizami in the remaining languages and the citation of articles is not extensive. It does, however, illustrate a few important points. The translation of Nizami's poetry into many Western and non-Western languages and the number of scholarly works on the subject published in these languages attest to his significance in the tradition of Persian poetry.

Years ago, Western scholars such as Claude Field, James Atkinson, E. G. Browne, C. E. Wilson, W. Bacher, James Kritzeck, Helmut Ritter, Clement Huart, E. E. Bertel's, and Iranians who came in contact with them, launched a formalist and systematic study of medieval Persian literature, including the works of Nizami. A recent generation of scholars has gone beyond formalism and has included all sorts of analytical approaches to this poet's works. Julie Scott Meisami, Heshmat Moayyad, Jalal Matini, and Hasan Vahid Dastgirdi have read Nizami's poems with an eye toward their aesthetic value, form, complexity, and/or historical significance, and they approach his stories in much the same way.

As mentioned in the introduction to this volume, the rise of Islam to state ideology after the Islamic Revolution of 1979 affected culture in Iran, lead to the production of a body of Islamic-oriented literary criticism. A great number of Muslim scholars began to reread Nizami's work in light of biography or theology. The biographical approach has, after a manner, revived the tradition of medieval Persian literary historiography based on anecdotes about the author's life. A number of ideologically motivated interpreters such as Muhammad Taqi Ja'fari, Abd al-Husayn Muvahhid, Barat Zanjani, Muhammad Riza Hakimi, Muhammad R. Rashid, and Bihruz Sarvatian have focused primarily on Islamic and Sufi elements in Nizami's stories. This has in turn given rise to a surge in secular reading of Nizami's work, as exemplified in the works of Jalal Satari and Ali Akbar Saidi Sirjani.

In the former Soviet Union and in the Republic of Azerbayjan, interest in Nizami has always been impressive. However, Russian and Azari scholars of Nizami have always read his work from a secular point of view. They portray Nizami as a "poet-humanist" and the first artist of the Middle East to celebrate "human individuality" and to advocate justice and humanism. According to them, Nizami's works contain moral instruction and promote brotherhood, equality, freedom, and love in society. These scholars also substantiate that he, by his advocacy, influenced his followers and heirs, including Khusraw Dihlavi, Navai, and Jami. (See *Iskender-name* [*Iskendername*], trans. and ed. E. E. Bertel's and A. K. Arends. Baku: Elm, 1983, 5.)

In 1941, Azerbaijanis began to plan the celebration of the eight hundredth anniversary of Nizami's birth, but the event was interrupted by the 1947 war. The purpose of promoting Nizami's work was to make it accessible to Russian readers in their own languages, so that it could be placed alongside the works of classical authors of world literature such as Homer, Dante, Shakespeare, Goethe, and Pushkin. The first complete translation of Nizami's work into Russian appeared in 1947 and included information about Nizami's mausoleum, near his birthplace at Kirovobad/Gandzha, and The Nizami Ganjavi Museum of Azerbaijani Literature in Baku. Also provided was a map of all of the 50 cities in which his works have appeared. In 1979, the Central Committee of the Communist Party ordered the study, publication, and popularization of Nizami's works, to enhance the "spiritual culture of the Azerbaijani people" and to disseminate the humanist ideas of this "titan of world literature" among progressive people everywhere (see *Bakinskii rabochii, The Baku Worker,* January 21, 1979). An editorial in *Pravda* (November 17, 1981) praised Nizami for drawing people to "humanism, the height of morality and good that fulfills the spiritual needs of socialist society, pushing its historical development toward new boundaries—to the communist tomorrow" and likened him to Shakespeare, Dante, Pushkin, Balzac, and Tolstoi. Certainly, the editorial continues, Nizami influenced the literature of Oriental peoples from India to the Black Sea by promoting romanticism in these various literatures. Lastly, an institute was named after the poet: Akademiia nauk Azerbaidzhanskoi SSR Institut Literatury imeni Nizami (Nizami Institute of Literature of the Azerbaijani Academy of Sciences). The following bibliography illustrates these points as well as the recognition that Nizami's artistic efforts have attained internationally. I am grateful to Bob D. Crews for his help in the preparation of this bibliography.

Russian and Azeri Sources

Abbasov, Ali. *Poema Nizami Giandzhevi "Iskendername"* (*Nizami Ganjavi's* Iskandername *Poem*). Baku: Izd-vo Akademii nauk Azerbaidzhanskoi SSR, 1966.

Agaev, A. *Nizami i Mirovaia Literatura* (*Nizami and World Literature*). Baku: Iazychy, 1983.

Alesker-zade, A. A. and Fikret Rzakuli ogly Babaev. *Nizami adyna Adabiiiat va Dil Institutu*. [*Laili i Madkhnun*]. n.p.: Shargshunaslyg Institutu (Azarbaijan SSR Elmlar Akademiiasy), 1954.

Aliev, Rustam M. *Nizami Ganjavi* (*Nizami Ganjavi*). Baku: Iazychy, 1991.

———. *Nizami: kratkii bibliograficheskii spravochnik* (*Nizami: A Short Bibliographic Guide*). Baku: Iazychy, 1982.

———. *Nizami: kratkii bibliograficheskii spravochni*. Baku: Iazychy, 1982.

———. *Nizami Giandzhevi, A.* Trans. by Husseinaga Rzayev. Ed. by Zeidulla Agayev. Baku: Yazichi, 1991.

———. *Nizami Giandzhevi: perevod* (*Nizami Ganjavi: A Translation*). Baku: Iazychy, 1991.

Aliyev, G. "The Role of Nezami's Khamse in Oriental Interliterary Relations". *Proceedings of the Fourth International Conference on the Theoretical Problems of Asian and African Literatures;* Lit. Inst. of the Slovak Acad. of Sciences, Bratislava. pp. 282-87.

Arasly, Nushaba. *Nizami va turk adabiiiaty*. Baky: Elm, 1980 [in Azerbaijani].

Azada, R. *Nizami Ganjavi. Russian Nizami Giandzhevi*. Baku: Izd-vo Elm, 1981.

———. *Nizami Ganjavi: Haiaty va Sanati*. Baky: Elm nashriiiaty, 1979.

Azarbaijan Renessansy va Nizami Ganjavi. Baky: Elm, 1984.

Babaev, Fikret Rzakuli ogly and Evgenii Eduardovich Bertel's, eds. *Nizami Ganjavi, Iqbal'namah*. Introduction in Russian. Baku: Farhangistan-i 'Ulum, Jumhuri Shuravi Susiyalisti-yi Azarbayjan, 1947.

Baladchi, Gysa. *Nizami Ganjavi Adyna Azarbaijan Adabiiiaty Muzeii*. Baky: Ishyg nashriiiaty, 19—.

Bertel's, Evgenii Eduardovich. *Nizami: Tvorcheskii put' poeta* (*Nizami: The Creative Path of the Poet*). Moscow: Izd-vo Akademii nauk SSR, 1956.

———. *Nizami i Fuzuli* (*Nizami and Fuzuli*). Vol. 4 of *Izbrannye Trudy* (*Selected Works*). Moscow: Izd-vo vostochnoi literatury, 1962.

Bertel's, Evgenii Eduardovich. *Velikii azerbaidzhanskii poet Nizami: epokha, zhizn', tvorchestvo* (*The Great Azerbaijani Poet, Nizami: Epoch, Life, and Work*). Baku: Izd-vo Az FAN, 1940.

———. *Sufizm i sufiiskaia literatura.* Persian: (Tasavvuf va adabiyat-i tasavvuf). Trans. Sirus Izadi. Tehran: Amir Kabir, 1977.

———. *Ocherk istorii persidskoi literatury.* n.p., 1928.

———. *Istoriia literatury i kul'tury Irana.* Moskva: Nauka, 1988.

Buniatova, Shirin Teirmur kyzy. *Etnograficheskie motivy v proizvedeniiakh Nizami* (*Ethnographic Motifs in the Work of Nizami*). Baku: Akademiia nauk Azerbaidzhana, In-t istorii, 1991.

———. *Nizami va etnografiia* (*Nizami and Ethnography*). [In Azeri] Baku, Elm, 1992.

Dzhafarov, G. "Rus' i tiurkskii mir v 'Iskender-Name' Nizami" *Sovetskaia Tiurkologiia* 4, (1990 July-Aug): p. 47-68, [in Russian].

Dzhafarov, M. Z. et al., *Al'manakh Nizami Giandzhevi* (*An Almanac of Nizami Ganjavi*). Baku: Izd-vo Elm, 1984.

Gadzhiev, A. A. *Renessans i poeziia Nizami Giandzhevi* (*The Renaissance and the Poetry of Nizami*). Baku: Izd-vo Elm, 1980.

Gahramanov, A. H. *Boiuk Azarbaijan shairi Nizami Ganjavi* (*The Great Azerbaijani Poet Nizami Ganjavi*). [In Azeri] Baku: Azarbaijan Dovlat Kitab Palatasy Nashriiaty, 1947.

Gahramanov, Jahangir. *Rukopisi Proizvedenii Nizami Giandzhevi v Mirovykh Khranilishchakh* / Dzh. V. Kagranamov, K. G. Allakhiarov. Baku: Elm, 1987.

Guliev, G. M. *Tvorchestvo Nizami Giandzhevi i puti epicheskogo povestvovaniia* (*The Work of Nizami Ganjavi and the Path of Epic Narrative*). Baku: Iazychy, 1989.

Guluzada, M. Iu. *Nizami Gizandzhevi: zhizn' i tvorchestvo* (*Nizami Ganjavi: Life and Work*). Baku: Izd-vo Akademii nauk Azerbaidzhanskoi SSR, 1953.

Guseinov, Geidar. *O sotsial'nykh vozzreniiakh Nizami* (*On the Social Views of Nizami*). Baku: Izd-vo Akademii nauk Azerbaidzhanskoi SSR, 1946.

Iusifov, Khalil. *Shargda Intibah va Nizami Ganjavi.* Baky: Iazychy, 1982.

Kagramanov, Dzh. V. ed., *Nizami Giandzhevi* (*Nizami Ganjavi*). Baku: Elm, 1979.

Kazymov, M. D. "*Khaft peikar* Nizami i traditsii nazire v persoiazychnoi literature XIV-XVI vv" (Nizami's *Haft Peykar* and the Tradition of the Nazir in Persian-Language Literature of the Fourteenth-Sixteenth Centuries). Baku: Elm, 1987.

———. *Posledovateli Nizami: k problemam nazire v persoiazychnoi literature XIII-XVI vv* (*The Heirs of Nizami: On the Nazir in Persian-Language Literature of the Fourteenth-Sixteenth Centuries*). Baku: Azerbaidzhanskoe gos. izd-vo, 1991.

Khalisbaili, Taghy. *Nizami Ganjavi va Azarbaijan gainaglary.* Baky: Azarbaijan Dovlat Nashriiaty, 1991.

———. *Nizami Ganjavi va Azarbaijan shifahi khalg adabiiaty: "Ieddi Peikar" Asari Uzra.* Baky: Azarbaijan Dovlat Pedagozhi Institutu, 1988.

Kiazimova, A. *Tvorchestvo Nizami v Anglii i SshA* (*Nizami's Work in England and the United States*). Baku: Iazychy, 1991.

Korogly, Kh. G. *Nizami Giandzhevi: 850 let so dnia rozhdenii* (*Nizami Ganjavi: 850-Year Anniversary*). Moscow: Izd-vo Znanie, 1991.

Krymskii, A. E. *Nizami i ego sovremenniki* (*Nizami and His Contemporaries*). Baku: Elm, 1981.

Kuli-zade, Z. *Teoreticheskie problemy istorii kul'tury Vostoka i nizamivedenie* (*Theoretical Problems of the History of Oriental Culture and Nizami Studies*). Baku: Elm, 1987.

Mamedov, S. F. *Filosofskie i obshchestvenno-politicheskie vzgliday Nizami: lektsiia* (*The Philosophical, Social and Political Views of Nizami: Lectures*). Moscow: Izd-vo Moskovskogo Univ., 1959.

Materialy nauchnoi konferentsii, posiashchennoi probleme "Nizami i mirovaia literatura" (*Proceedings of a Scholarly Conference Devoted to the Problem of "Nizami and World Literature"*). Eds. R. M. Aliev, M. Z. Dzhafarov, and A. M. Mirakhmedov. Baku: Elm, 1982.

Mustafaev, Dzhamal. *Filosofskie i eticheskie vozzreniia Nizami* (*The Philosophical and Ethical Views of Nizami*). Baku: Izd-vo Akademii nauk Azerbaidzhanskoi SSR, 1962.

Nizami Ganjavi, A., Alesker-zade, A. A. and Fikret Rzakuli ogly Babaev. Nizami adyna Adabiiiat va Dil Institutu. Shargshunasy Institutu (Azarbaijan SSR Elmlar Akademiiasy).

———. *Iskandarnamah*. Russian; perevod s farsi i kommentarii. E. E. Bertel's and A. K. Arendsa. Baku: Izd-vo Elm, 1983.

———. *Iskender-name* (*Iskendernam*). Trans. Konst Lipskerov. Moscow: Gosudarstvennoe izdatel'stvo khudozhestvennoi literatury, 1953.

———. *Iskender-name* (*Iskendername*). Trans. and ed. E. E. Bertel's and A. K. Arends. Baku: Elm, 1983.

———. *Khamsa, Miniatures,* Sostavitel', Avtor Predisloviia i Annotatsii Kerim Kerimov; Nauchnye redaktory Abdulvagab Salamzade, Dzhangir Kagramanov. Baky: Iazychy, 1983.

———. *Khosrov i Shirin* (*Khosrou and Shirin*). Trans. G. Iu. Aliev and M. N. Osmanov. Baku: Elm, 1985.

———. *Layla [Layli] va Majnun.* [In Russian] Baku: Elm, 1981.

———. *Leili i Medzhnun* (*Leila and Majnun*). Trans. Pavel Antokol'skii. Moscow: Molodaia gvardiia, 1948.

———. *Leili i Mezhnun* (*Leila and Majnun*). Trans. Tat'iana Streshneva. Moscow: Khudozh. lit-ra, 1986.

———. *Leili i Mezhnun* (*Leila and Majnun*). Baku: Elm, 1981.

———. *Lirika: Sokrovishchnitsa tain* (*Lyric Poetry: The Treasure-House of Mysteries*). Moscow: Khudozh. lit-ra, 1985.

———. *Piat' poem* (*Five Poems*). Eds. E. E. Bertel's and V. V. Gol'tsev. Moscow: Gosudarstvennoe izdatel'stvo khudozhestvennoi literatury, 1946.

———. *Poemy i stikhotvoreniia* (*Poems and Poetry*). Leningrad: Sovetskii pisatel', 1960.

Nizami Ganjavi, A., Alesker-zade, A. A. and Fikret Rzakuli ogly Babaev. *Sem' krasavits* (*Seven Beauties*). Trans. Rustam Aliev. Baku: Elm, 1983.

———. *Sem' krasavits* (*Seven Beauties*). Trans. Vladimir Derzhavin. Moscow: Khudozh. lit-ra, 1986.

———. *Sobranie sochinenii v piati tomakh* (*Collected Works in Five Volumes*). Eds. R. Aliev, et al. Moscow: Khudozhestvennaia literatura, 1985-1986.

———. *Sobranie sochinenii v trekh tomakh* (*Collected Works in Three Volumes*). Eds. R. M. Aliev et al. Baku: Azerneshr, 1991.

———. *Stikhotvoreniia i poemy* (*Poetry and Poems*). Ed. Rustam Aliev. Leningrad: Sovetskii Pisatel', 1981.

———. *Works* [in Russian] R. Aliev et al., eds. Moskva: Khudozhestvennaia literatura, 1985-1986.

Nizami Giandzhevi. *Lirika*. Baku: Iazychy, 1981.

———. A. *Al'manakh;* redaktsionnaia kollegiia M. Z. Dzhafarov (glavnyi redaktor) et al. Baku: Izd-vo Elm, 1991.

———. *Materialy Nauchnoi Konferentsii*, Zhizni i tvorchestvu poeta (3-6 iiunia 1947 g.), Mirza Ibragimov et al. Izd-vo AN Azerbaidzhanskoi SSR, 1947.

———. *Materialy nauchnoi konferentsii posviashchennoi zhizni i tvorchestvu poeta* (3-6 iiunia 1947 g.) (Nizami Ganjavi/Proceedings of a Scholarly Conference Devoted to the Life and Work of the Poet). Eds. Mirza Ibragimov, et al. Baku: Elm, 1947.

———. *Nizami Giandzhevi, almanakh* / In-t literatury im. Nizami. Baku: Elm, 1990.

———. *Nizami: sbornik* (*Nizami: A Collection*). Baku: Azarnashr, 1940-1947.

———. *Sochineniia v 5-ti tomakh* [Tajik]. Baku: Azrneshr, 1976.

———. *Materialy Nauchnoi Konferentsii, posviashchennoi zhizni i tvorchestvu poeta* (3-6 iiunia 1947 g.), Mirza Ibragimov et al. Baky: Izd-vo AN Azerbaidzhanskoi SSR, 1947.

———. *Zhizn' i Tvorchestvo*, M. IU. Gulizade: Izd-vo Akademii nauk Azerbaidzhanskoi SSR, 1953.

Rafili, Mikael. *Nizami Giandzhevi: epokha, zhizn', tvorchestvo* (*Nizami Ganjavi: Epoch, Life, and Work*). Moscow: Goslitizdat, 1941.

———. *Nizami Giandzhevi i ego tvorchestvo* (*Nizami Ganjavi and His Work*). Baku: n.p., 1947.

Rustamova, Azada. *Nizami Ganjavi, A*. Trans. G. Bayramov. Baku: Elm Publishers, 1981.

Rustamova, Azada. *Ganjavi*. Baky: Elm nashriiiaty, 1980.

Shaginian, Marietta Sergeevna. *Etiudy o Nizami* (*Studies on Nizami*). Erevan: Akademii nauk Armianskoi SSR, 1955.

———. *Etiudy o Nizami, 1947-1956* (*Studies on Nizami, 1947-1956*). Baku: Izdvo Iazychy, 1981.

Suleimanova, A. *Politicheskie i pravovye vozzreniia Nizami Giandzhevi* (*The Political and Legal Views of Nizami*). Baku: Elm, 1991.

Taghyieva, R. (Ro'ia) *Nizami obrazlary khalchalarda, Kovrovye obrazy Nizami* (*Nizami's characters on the carpets*) R. Baky: Ishyg, 1991.

Related Works from Russia, Azerbaijan, and Other Former Soviet Republics

Abullaev, M., ed. *Illiustratsii k "Khamse" Nizami: al'bom (Illustrations from Nizami's "Khamsa": An Album)*. Baku: Ishig, 1984.

Afsahzod, A lokhon. *Nizomii Ganjavi*. Dushanbe: Maorif, 1995.

Aliev, G. Iu. *Temy i siuzhety Nizami v literaturakh narodov Vostoka (Themes and Subjects of Nizami in the Literatures of the Peoples of the East)*. Moscow: Izd-vo Nauka, Glav. Red. Vostochnoi lit-ry, 1985.

Aliev, Rustam M. *Nizami Giandzhevi. Azerbaijani Nizami Ganjavi;* Rus Dilindan tarjuma edani Tehran Valiiev; redaktoru, Zahid Balaiev. Baky: "IAzychy", 1991.

Alieva, Diliara. *Nizami i gruzinskaia literatura (Nizami and Georgian Literature)*. Baku: Elm, 1989.

Arkhitektura Azerbaidzhana: epokha Nizami (The Architecture of Azerbaijan: The Epoch of Nizami). Moscow: Gos. Arkhitekturnoe Izd-vo, 1947.

Azerbaidzhanskii renessans i Nizami Giandzhevi (The Azerbaijani Renaissance and Nizami Ganjavi). Baku: Elm, 1984.

Baladchi, Gysa. *Nizami Ganjavi adyna Azarbaijan adabiiaty muzeii (The Nizami Ganjavi Museum of Azerbaijani Literature)*. Baku: Ishyg nashriiaty, 1986.

Danilov, D. K. *Simfoniia "Nizami" F. Amirova (F. Amirov's "Nizami" Symphony)*. 1966.

Dodkhudoeva, L. N. *Poemy Nizami v srednevekovoi miniatiurnoi zhivopisi (The Poems of Nizami in Medieval Miniature Painting)*. Moscow: Izd-vo Nauka, Glav. Red. Vostochnoi lit-ry, 1985.

Dzhakhani, G. *Traditsii Nizami v azerbaidzhanskoi literature (The Traditions of Nizami in Azerbaijani Literature)*. [In Azeri] Baku: Elm, 1979.

Gadzhiev, A. A., ed. *Problemy azerbaidzhanskogo Renessansa (Problems of the Azerbaijani Renaissance)*. Baku: Elm, 1984.

Irii Nikolaevich. *Khakani, Nezami, Rustaveli*. Tbilisi: Metsniereba, 1935.

Isupov, E. IU. et al. *Miniatiury k "Khamse" Nizami (Miniatures from Nizami's "Khamsa")*. Tashkent: Fan, 1985.

Kagramanov, Dzh. V. and K. G. Allakhiarov, eds. *Rukopisi proizvedenii Nizami Giandzhevi v mirovykh khranilishchakh (Manuscripts of Nizami's Works in the World's Repositories)*. Baku: Elm, 1985.

Karaev, Kara. *Sem' krasavits, balet v 4-kh deistviiakh, 12 kartinakh po motivam poem Nizami* (Seven Beauties, A Ballet in Four Acts based on Motifs from the Poetry of Nizami). Leningrad: n.p., 1956.

Kaziev, A. Iu. *Miniatury rukopisi "Khamse," Nizami, 1539-1543 gg (Miniatures from Nizami's "Khamsa," 1539-1543)*. Baku: Izd-vo Akademii nauk Azerbaidzhanskoi SSR, 1964.

Kerimov, K. *Miniatiury k poemam "Khamse" Nizami Giandzhevi: albom (Miniatures from the "Khamsa" of Nizami Ganjavi: An Album)*. Baku: Iazychy, 1983.

Khakani, Nezami, Rustaveli. [Otv.red.Iu.N.Marr]. Moskva: Izd-vo Akad. nauk SSSR, 1966.

Leont'ev, N. G. *Drevnie literatury narodov SSSR: Rustaveli, Nizami, Omar Khaiiam (The Ancient Literatures of the Peoples of the USSR)*. Leningrad: LGIK, 1973.

Mallaev, N. M. *Nizomii Ganzhavii merosi va uning ma"rifii-tarbiiavii ahamiiati*. Toshkent: Uqituvchi, 1985.

Marr, Iu. N., ed. *Khakani, Nezami, Rustaveli (Khakani, Nizami, and Rustaveli)*. 2 vols. Moscow: Izd-vo Akad. nauk SSSR, 1935-1966.

Nizami Ganjavi, A. *Leili i Medzhnun: Perevod Pavla Antokol'skogo*. Illus. A. Varnovitskoi. Moskva: Molodaia gvardiia, 1948.

Nizomii, [Nizami Ganjavi]. *"Khamsa"* siga ishlangan rasmlar al'bom muallifi F. Sulaimonova; muharrir Z. Rahimova, Miniatiury k "Khamsa" Nizami, avtor-sostavitel' F. Suleimanova; redaktor Z. Rakhimova, Miniature illuminations of Nizami's "Khamsah", [and compiler F. Suleimanova; editor Z. Rahimova]. Toshkent: Uzbekiston KP Markazii Komitetining Nashrieti, 1982.

Taghyieva, R. *Nizami obrazlary khalchalarda/Kovrovye obrazy Nizami (Nizami's Carpet Images)*. Baku: Ishyg, 1991.

Turabov, S., ed. *Russkie sovetskie pisateli o Nizami Giandzhevi (Russian Soviet Writers on Nizami Ganjavi)*. Baku: Iazychy, 1981.

Vydaiushchiesia russkie uchenye i pisateli o Nizami Giandzhevi (Leading Russian Scholars and Writers on Nizami). Baku: Iazychy, 1981.

Zhitomirskii, A. A. *V kraiu Nizami (In the Land of Nizami)*. Baku: Ishyg, 1976.

German Translations and Scholarship on Nizami

Bacher, Wilhelm. *Nizami's Leben und Werke und der zweite Theil des Nizamischen Alexanderbuches (Nizami's Life and Work and the Second Part of his Alexanderbook)*. Leipzig: Engelmann, 1871.

Bürgel, J. Christoph. "Die Frau als Person in der Epic Nizamis." *Asiatische Studien* 42 (1988): 137-55.

———. "Die Geheimwissenschaften im Iskandarname Nizamis." *Proceedings of the Second European Conference of Iranian Studies*. Eds. B. G. Fragner et al. Rome: n.p., 1995.

———. "Die Geheimwissenschaften im Iskandarname Nizamis" Fragner, Bert G. (ed.)—Fragner, Christa (ed.)—Gnoli, Gherardo (ed.)—Haag-Higuchi, Roxane (ed.)—Maggi, Mauro (ed.)—Orsatti, Paola (ed.); x, 779 pp.; *Proceedings of the Second European Conference of Iranian Studies Held in Bamberg*, September 30 to October 4 1991, by the Societas Iranologica Europaea; Istituto Italiano per il Medio ed Estremo Oriente, Rome, Italy Pagination: 103-12, 73. Istituto Italiano per il Medio ed Estremo Oriente, Rome, Italy, 1995.

———. "Die Frau als Persan in der Epik Nizamis." *Priatische Studen* 42: 137-55.

Die Abenteuer des Königs Bahram und seiner sieben Prinzessinnen (*The Adventure of King Bahram and His Seven Princesses*). Trans. and ed. J. Christoph Bürgel. Munich: C. H. Beck, 1997.

———. "Krieg und Frieden im Alexanderepos Nizamis" in Bridges, Margaret (ed.), Bürgel, J. Ch. (ed.); 236 pp.; *The Problematics of Power: Eastern and Western Representations of Alexander the Great;* Peter Lang, Bern, Switzerland Pagination: 91-107.

———. *Nizami über Sprache und Dichtung.* 1975.

———. "Nizami." *Die Grossen der Weltgeschichte.* Band III. Zurich: n.p., 1973.

———. *Nizami: Chosrou und Schirin.* Zurich: n.p., 1980.

———. *Nizami: Das Alexanderbuch.* Zurich: n.p., 1991.

———. *Nizami: Die Abenteuer des Königs Bahram und seiner sieben Prinzessinenen.* München: n.p., 1997.

Duda, Herbert Wilhelm. *Ferhad und Schirin.* Praha: Orientalni ustav: n.p., 1933.

Glünz, Marianne. *Die Astrologie in Nizamis Khamse.* Bern: n.p., 1983.

Lohse, Horst. *Epitaph für Nizami: Preludes für grosses Orchester, 1976/78* (*Epitaph for Nizami: Preludes for Full Orchestra, 1976-1978*). Bad Schwalbach: Edition Gravis, 1995.

Nizami Ganjavi, A. *Alexanders zug zum lebensquell im land der finsterniss; eine episode aus Nizamis Iskendername, ubersetzt, commentirt und besonders seinem mystischen inhalt nach genauer beleuchtet.* Sitzungsberichte der Bayerischen Akademie der Wissenschaften. Philosophisch-Historische Abteilung Series, Hermann Ethe 1871, Vol. II.

———. *Alexanders zug zum lebensquell im land der finsterniss; eine episode aus Nizamis Jskendername, ubersetz, commentirt und besonders seinem mystischen inhalt nach genauer beleuchtet. Akademie der wissenschaften,* Munich. Philosophisch-philologische und historische classe. Sitzungsberichte. Munchen, 1871.

———. *Chosrou und Schirin.* Trans. and ed. J. Christoph Bürgel. Zürich: Manesse, 1980.

———. *Das Alexanderbuch/Iskandername.* Trans. J. Christoph Bürgel. Zürich: Manesse Verlag, 1991.

———. *Die Geschichte von den Heimsuchungen der Liebenden* (*The Story of the Lovers' Afflictions*). Trans. Rudolf Gelpke. Basel: Birkhäuser, 1977.

———. *Die Geschichte von der unerfüllten Liebe* (*The Story of Unfulfilled Love*). Trans. Rudolf Gelpke. Zürich: Arcade-Presse, 1975.

———. *Die sieben Geschichten der sieben Prinzessinnen* (*The Seven Stories of the Seven Princesses*). Trans. and ed. Rudolf Gelpke. Zürich: Manesse, 1959.

———. *Die sieben Prinzessinnen* (*The Seven Princesses*). Berlin: Rutten und Loening, 1982.

———. *Ferhad und Schirin.* Trans. Herbert Wilhelm Duda. Prague, Orientalni ustav, 1933.

———. *Haft paykar. Die sieben geschichten der sieben prinzessinnen; aus dem Persischen verdeutscht und herausgegeben von Rudolf Gelpke.* Zurich: Manesse Verlag, 1959.

————. *Heft peiker, ein romantisches Epos des Nizami* Genge'i (*Haft Peykar, A Romanic Epic of Nizami Ganjavi*). Eds. H. Ritter and J. Rypka. Prague: Orientalni ustav, 1934.

————. *Heft Peyker, ein romatisches Epos.* Eds. H. Ritter and J. Rypka. Prague: Orientalni ustav, 1934.

————. *Leila und Madschun: Der berühmteste Liebesroman des Morgenlandes* (*Leila and Majnun: The Most Celebrated Love Story of the Orient*). Trans. Rudolf Gelpke. Zürich: Manesse, 1963.

————. *Nizami: Das Alexanderbuch.* Übertragung aus dem Persischen, Nachwort und Anmerkungen J. C. Bürgel. Persian Heritage Series 37. Zürich: 1991.

Oren, Aras. *Leyla und Medjnun: Märchen für Musik* (*Leila and Majnun: Fairytales for Music*). Berlin: Babel Verlag, 1992.

Ritter, Hellmut. *Über die Bildersprache Nizami* (*On Nizami's Figurative Language*). Berlin and Leipzig: W. de Gruyter & Co., 1927.

Rypka, Jan. "Der bose Blick bei Nizami" *Ural-Altaische Jahrbucher/Ural-Altaic Internationale Zeitschrift fur Nord-Eurasien* 36, (1965): pp. 397-401.

————. "Einiges zum Sprichworterschatz in Nizamis Haft Pakjar" Hoenerbach, Wilhelm(ed.); Der Orient in der Forschung: Festschrift fur Otto Spies zum 5. April 1966; Harrassowitz, Wiesbaden Pagination: 557-68. Wiesbaden: Harrassowitz, 1967.

————. "Textkritisch Bemerkungen zu Nizamis Haft Paikar, II. Gesang." *Mitteilungen des Institut fur Orientforschung der Deutschen Akadamie der Wissenschaften zu Berlin* 11, (1965): pp. 17-25.

Wursch, Renate. "König Nosirwan und die Kauzentochter: Eine Wanderlegende und ihre Verbreitung" *Asiatische Studien/Etudes Asiatiques: Zeitschrift der Schweizerischen Asiengesellschaft* 48, no. 3 (1994): pp. 973-86.

————. "Nizamis Reise ins eigene Herz als Erfahrung mystischer Wirklichkeit" *Asiatische Studien/Etudes Asiatiques: Zeitschrift der Schweizerischen Asiengesellschaft* 50, no. 2 (1996): pp. 547-61.

English

Afsaruddin, Asma and A. H. Mathias Zahniser. Eds. *Humanism, Culture, and Language in the Near East: Studies in Honor of Georg Krotkoff.* Winona Lake, Ind.: Eisenbrauns, 1997.

Aliev, R. M. *Nizami Giandzhevi: perevod.* [English] Baku: Iazychy, 1991.

Becka, Jiri. "Nezami Ganjavi in Czechoslovakia and Jan Rypka" *Archiv Orientalni: Quarterly Journal of African, Asian, and Latin-American Studies* Amsterdam, Netherlands 61, no. 4 (1993): p. 433-40.

Browne, E. G. *Literary History of Persia.* Vol. II. Cambridge: The University Press, 1964.

Bürgel, J. Christoph. "The Contest of the Two Philosophers in Nizamis First and Last Epics." *Yad-Nama in memoria di Alessandro Bausani.* Eds.

Biancamaria Scarcia Amoretti and Lucia Rostagno. Vol. 1. Rome: XXX, 1991. 109-17.

———. "The Idea of Non-Violence in the Epic Poetry of Nizami." *Edebiyat: The Journal of Middle Eastern Literatures NS.* 9.1 (1998): 61-84.

———. *The Feather of Simurgh: The "Licit Magic" of the Arts in Medieval Islam.* New York, 1988.

———. "The Romance." *Persian Literature.* Ed. E. Yarshater. New York: Bibliotheca Persica, 1987, 161-79.

Chelkowski, Peter J. *Mirror of the Invisible World: Tales from the Khamesh of Nizami.* New York: Metropolitan Museum of Art, 1975.

———. "Nizami: Master Dramatist." *Persian Literature.* Ed. E. Yarshater. New York: Bibliotheca Persica, 1987, 190-213.

Christensen, A. "Some Notes on Persian Melody-names of the Sassanian Period." *The Dastur Hoshang Memorial Volume.* Bombay: 1918, 368-77.

Dankoff, Robert. "The Lyric in the Romance: The Use of Gazels in Persian and Turkish Maônavīs." *JNES* 43.1 (1984): 9-25.

de Blois, François. "Nizami." *Persian literature: A Bio-bibliographical Survey Begun by the Late C. A. Storey.* Vol. 2: Poetry ca. A.D. 1100 to 1225 and Vol. 3: Appendixes II-IV, Addenda and Corrigenda, Indexes. London: Royal Asiatic Society of Great Britain and Ireland, 1994 and 1997.

de Bruijn, J. T. P. *Of Piety and Poetry.* Leiden: 1983.

Field, Claud. *Persian literature.* London: Herbert & Daniel, 1912.

Gelpke, Rudolf, ed. *The Story of Layla and Majnun.* Oxford: Cassimer, 1966.

Gh. H. D. *Darab Makhzanasrar.* London: n.p., 1945.

Hanaway, William L. "The King, the Poet and the Past" *Iranshenasi: A Journal of Iranian Studies* 3, no. 3 (1991): pp. 49-56.

Krotkoff, George. "Colour and Number in the Haft Paykar." *Logos Islamikos: Studia Islamica.* Eds. Roger M. Savory and Dionisius A. Agius. Toronto: Pontifical Institute of Mediaeval Studies, 1984.

Mason, Herbert. *Legend of Alexander: A Legend of Alexander* and *The Merchant and the Parrot: Dramatic Poems.* Notre Dame: University of Notre Dame Press, 1986.

Meisami, Julie Scott. "Allegorical Gardens in the Persian Poetic Tradition: Nezami, Rumi, Hafez" *International Journal of Middle East Studies* 17, no. 2 (1985): p. 229-60.

———. "Fitnah or Azadah? Nizami's Ethical Poetic" *Edebiyat: The Journal of Middle Eastern Literatures* 1, no. 2 (1989): pp. 41-75.

———. "Kings and Lovers: Ethical Dimensions of Medieval Persian Romance." 1.1 (1987): 1-19.

———. *Medieval Persian Court Poetry.* Princeton: Princeton University Press, 1987.

———. *Persian Historiography to the End of the Twelfth Century.* Edinburgh: Edinburgh University Press, forthcoming.

———. "The Theme of the Journey in Nizami's *Haft Paykar*" *Edebiyat: The Journal of Middle Eastern Literatures* 4, no. 2 (1993): pp. 155-72.

Meletinsky, Elizar M.; Walker, R. Scott (tr.). "The Typology of the Medieval Romance in the West and in the East" *Diogenes* 127, (Fall 1984): pp. 1-22.

Nizami Ganjavi, A. *The Haft Paykar: A Medieval Persian Romance.* Translated with an introduction and notes by Julie Scott Meisami. Oxford and New York: Oxford University Press, 1995.

———. *The Haft Paikar (The seven beauties)* Trans. with a commentary by C. E. Wilson. London: A. Probsthain, 1924.

———. *Haft paikar.* Ed. James Atkinson. Novosibirsk: Nauka, 1987.

———. *The Haft Paykar (The Seven Beauties).* Trans. G. E. Wilson. London: Late Probsthain and Company, 1924.

———. *Haft paykar (The story of the seven princesses).* Trans. and ed. Rudolf Gelpke. Oxford: Cassirer; London: Distributed by Luzac, 1976.

———. *Laili and Majnun; a poem. From the original Persian of Nazami.* Trans. James Atkinson. London: A. J. Valpy, 1836.

———. *Makhzanol Asrar; The Treasury of Mysteries of Nezami of Ganjeh;* translated for the first time from the Persian, with an introductory essay on the life and times of Nizami, by Gholam Hosein Darab. London: A. Probsthain, 1945.

Rubanovich, Julia. "The Reconstruction of a Storytelling Event in Medieval Persian Prose Romance: The Case of the Iskandarnama" *Edebiyat: The Journal of Middle Eastern Literatures* 9, no. 2 (1998): pp. 215-47.

Rypka, Jan. *History of Iranian Literature.* Dordrecht, Holland: D. Reidel Publishing Company, 1968.

Soucek, Priscilla Parsons. *Illustrated Manuscripts of Nizami's Khamseh, 1386-1482.* Ann Arbor: University Microfilms, 1973.

Titley, Norah M. "A Khamsa of Nizami Dated Herat, 1421." *The British Library Journal* 4, no. 2 (Autumn 1978): pp. 161-86.

Persian

Ahmadnizhad, Kamil. *Tahlil-i asar-i Nizami Ganjavi: Nigahi bih Asar-i Nizami ba Mulahazat-i Ttatbiqi dar Barah-i Maakhiz-i Islami va Bastani-i Iskandarnamah.* Tehran: Mu'assasah-i Farhangi va Intisharati-i Paya, 1996

Alaqih, Fatamah. "Sima-yi Zan az Didgah-i Nizami." *Farhang* 10 (Fall 1992): 317-30.

Ayati, Abd al-Majid. *Dastan-i Khusraw va Shirin; Surudah-i Nizami.* Tehran: Shirkat Kitabhay-i Jibi, 1974.

Bigdili, Ghulam Husayn. *Chirah-'i Iskandar dar Shahnamah-'i Firdawsi va Iskandarnamah-'i Nizami.* Tehran: Afarinish, 1990.

———. "Dastan-e Khosrow va Shirin-e Nezami va Adabiyyat-e Tork" *Nashriyyeh-ye Daneshkadeh-ye Adabiyyat va Olum-e Ensani-ye Tabriz* 21, (1969): pp. 25-40, 121-45.

Chelkowski, Peter J. "Aya upra-yi turandut-i Puchini bar asas-i kushk-i surkh-i *Haft Paykar*-i Nizami ast?" *Iran-Shinasi* 3.4 (Winter 1991): 714-22.

Dabashi, Hamid. "Harf-i nakhostin: mafhum-i sokhan dar nazd-i hakim Nizami Ganjavi, A." Iranshenasi III. 4, (Winter 1992): 723-40.

Daliri Malvani, Ibrahim. *Sukhansalar-i Ganjah va Muqallidan-i*. Rasht: Ta'ati, 1996.

Dastgirdi, Vahid. *Kulliyat-i Divan-i Hakim Nizami Ganjah-i*. Tehran: Amir Kabir, 1956.

———, ed. *Namah-i Layli [Layla] va Majnun Nizami Ganjavi, A*. Tehran: Muassasah-i Matbuat-i Ilmi, 1972.

Erdmann, Franz. *Jangha-yi Iskandar ba Rusiyan: az Sharaf'namah-'i Iskandar*. Qazan: s.n., 1826.

Haqiqi-Rad, Gholam-Reza. "Maqni-ye yek Beyt-e Hakim Nezami" *Gowhar* 4, (1977): p. 884-86.

Heshmat Moayyad. "Dar Midar-i Nizami." *Iran-Shinasi* 5, 1 (Spring 1993), 72-89.

Ja'fari, Muhammad Taqi. *Hikmat, 'Irfan, va Akhlaq dar Shi'r-i Nizami Ganjavi, A*. Tehran: Kayhan, 1991.

Ja'fari Langarudi, Muhammad Ja'far. *Raz-i Baqa-yi Iran dar Sukhan-i Nizami*. Tehran: Kitabkhanah-i Ganj-i Danish, 1991.

Maddi, Arjang. "Bar rasi-i Suvar-i Khiyal dar Haft Paykar." *Farhang* 10 (Fall 1992): 331-408.

Matini, Jalal. "Azadigi va Tasahul-i Nizami Ganjavi, A." *Iran-Shinasi* 4.1 (Spring 1992): 1-20.

Muallim, Mina. "Guftigu ba Bihruz Sarvatiyan" ("A Conversation with Bihruz Savatiyan"). *Dunya-i Sukhan* 41 (1991): 26-31.

Mu'in, Muhammad. *An Analysis of Nizami's Haft-paykar (Seven images)*. Tehran, Government Press, 1960.

———. *Tahlil-i haft paikar-i nizami. Bakhsh-i avval*. Tehran: Intisharat-i Danishgah-i Tihran, 1960.

Muna, Khaz'al. *Kushishi bar Manzumah-'i Layli va Majnun*. Tehran: M. Khaz'al, 1990.

Nawruzi, 'Ali. *Pir-i Ganjah: Nigahi bih Zindagi va 'Ishq'namah-i Nizami Ganjavi*. Tehran: Nashr-i Farhang-i Zand, 1994.

Nizami Ganjavi, A. *Bunyad-i Kayan va Sal-i Nizami Ganjah'i*. Los Angeles; Washington, D.C.: Keyan Foundation Publications, 1991.

———. *Daftar-i Haftum az Saba'ah-i Hakim Nizami Ganjavi Musamma bih Ganjinah-i Nizami*, bitashih-i Vahid Dastgirdi. Tehran: Ibn Sina, 1956.

———. *Divan-i Qasa'id va ghazaliyat-i Nizami Ganjavi. Shamil-i sharh va ahval va asar-i Nizami, ba Muqadamah va Tashih va Fihrist-i A'lam va Tashih va Muqabilih bih Kushish-i Sa'id Nafisi*. Tehran: Furughi, 1960.

———. *Khusraw u Shirin*. Ed. Vahid Dastgirdi. 2d ed. Tehran: Ibn Sina, 1954.

———. *Kuliyat-i Khamseh-i Hakim Nizami Ganjah-i*. Ed. Dastgirdi. 4th ed. Tehran: Amir Kabir, 1987.

———. *Layla va Majnun*. Ed. Bihruz Sarvatian. Tehran: Intisharat-i Tus, 1986.

Nizami Ganjavi, A. *Layli va Majnun. Guzidah-'i Layli va Majnun: az Panj ganj-i Nizami Ganjavi; talkhis, muqaddamah, tawzihat-i 'Abd al-Muhammad Ayati.* Tehran: Intisharat va Amuzish-i Inqilab-i Islami, 1991.

———. *Layli va Majnun: nigarish-i dibachah, Manuchihr Adamiyat.* Ed. Hamid Sasani. Tehran: Atuliyah-i Hunar-i Muhammad Salahshur, 1992.

———. *Layli va Majnun. Selections: Khulasah-'i Layli va Majnun.* Ed. Jalal Matini. Tehran: Tus, 1977.

———. *Makhzan al-Asrar-i Nizami (The Treasury of Mysteries).* Ed. Pizhman Bakhtiyar. Tehran: Peygah, 1988.

———. *Makhzanol Asrar (The Treasury of Mysteries).* Trans. with intro. Gholam Nizami and Hosein Darab. London: A. Probsthain, 1945.

Oren, Aras. *Leyla und Medjnun: Marchen fur Musik.* Berlin: Babel Verlag, 1992.

R. Rashid, Muhammad. "Ishq va Itiqad dar Makhzan al-Asrar." *Majjalah-i Danishkadih-i Adabiyat-i Firdawsi* nos. 88-89 (Spring 1990): 87.

Sa'idi Sirjani, A. A. *Sima-yi Du Zan.* Tehran: Nashr-i Naw, 1989.

Sarvatyian, Bihruz. *A'inah-i Ghayb, Nizami Ganjah-'i dar Masnavi Makhzan al-Asrar.* Tehran: Nashr-i Kalamih, 1990.

———. "Barrasi-ye Havashi-ye Marhum-e Vahid-e Dastgerdi bar Makhzan-ol-Asrar-e Nezami" *Nashriyeh-ye Daneshkadeh-ye Adabiyyat va Olum-e Ensani-ye Tabriz* 24, (1972): p. 362-86.

———. *Bayan dar Shi'r-i Farsi.* Tihran: Intisharat-i Barg, 1990.

———. *Sharafnamah-i Ganjah'i.* Tehran: Tus, 1989.

Sarvatian, Mansur, ed. *Majmu'ah-i Maqalat-i Kungrih-i Bayn al-Milali-i Buzurgdasht-i Nuhumin Sadah-i Tavallud-i Hakim Nizami Ganjavi, A.* Tabriz: n. p., 1993.

Sattari, Jalal. *Halat-i 'Ishq-i Majnun.* Tehran: Tus, 1988.

Shafici, Mohammad. "Sokhan-e Nezami-ye Ganjavi" *Gowhar* 4, (1976): p. 674-79.

Shakiba, Parvin. *Nigahi Guzara bar Vizhagiha va Digarguniha-yi shi'r-i Farsi.* Piedmont, CA: Shirikat-i Kitab-i Jahan and Iran Zamin, 1987.

———. *Shi'r-i Farsi az Aghaz ta Imruz.* Tehran: Hirmand, 1992.

Tajlil, Jalil. *Muqayasah-i Layli va Majnun-i Fuzuli va Nizami.* Tehran: Vizarat-i Farhang va Irshad-i Islami, Dabirkhanah-i Kungrih-i Buzurgdasht-i Hakim Muhammad Fuzuli, 1995.

Ushidari, Gita. *Kashf al-abyat-i Khamsah-'i Nizami Ganjavi: Makhzan al-asrar, Layli va Majnun, Khusraw va Shirin, Haft Paykar, Iskandarnamah.* Tehran: Daftar-i Majami' va Fa'aliyatha-yi Farhangi: Mu'assasah-'i Mutala'at va Tahqiqat-i Farhangi, 1991.

Vizhah'namah-'i Furugh-i Azadi bi-munasabat-i buzurgdasht-i Hashtsad va Panjahumin Sal-i Tavallud-i Hakim Nizami Ganjavi. Tabriz: Furugh-i Azadi, 1991.

Zanjani, Barat. *Ahval va Asar va Sharh-i Makhzan al-Asrar-i Nizami Ganjavi.* Tehran: Mu'assasah-'i Intisharat va chap-i Danishgah-i Tehran, 1991.

———. *Layla va Majnun-i Nizami Ganjavi, A.* Tehran: Tehran University, 1990.

Zarrinkub, 'Abd al-Husayn. *Pir-i Ganjah, dar Justaju-yi Nakuja'abad: Darbarah-'i Zindagi, Asar va Andishah-i Nizami.* Tehran: Intisharat-i Sukhan, 1993.

French

Bürgel, J. Christoph. "Conquérant, philosophe et prophète. L'image d'Alexandre le Grand dans l'épopée de Nezami." *Pand-o Sokhan. Mélanges offerts à Charles-Henri de Fouchécour.* eds. C. Balaÿ, C. Kappler, and Z. Vesel, Tehran: Institut francais de recherche en Iran, 1995. 65-78.

Fouchécour, C.-H. de. *La description de la nature dans la poésie lyrique persane du XIè siècle: Inventaire et analyse des thèmes.* Paris: C. Klincksieck, 1969. 60-61.

———. "Les récits d'ascension (me'raj) dans l'oeuvre de Nezami" dans Ètudes Irano-Aryennes Offertes À Gilbert Lazard, Réunies par C.-H. Fouchécour et Ph. Gignoux, Cahier de Studia Iranica, 7. 99-108, Paris: Association Pour L'AÈvancement des Etudes Iraniennes, 1989.

——— *Moralia: les notions morales dans la litterature persane du 3e/9e au 7e/13e siecle.* Paris: Editions Recherche sur les civilisations, 1986.

Corbin, H. *L'homme de lumiere dans le soufisme iranien.* Chambery, Editions Presence, 1971.

Nezamiye Gangavi, A. *Le tresor des Secrets.* Paris: Desclee de Brouwer, 1987.

Nizami Giandzhavi. La guirlande de l'Iran: poems de Firdousi, Nizami, Omar Kheyyam, Saadi, Hafiz. Trans. Rene Patris. Paris: Flammarion, 1948.

Nizami Giandzhavi. *Le Roman de Chosroès et Chîrîn.* trans. Henri Massé. Paris: G.-P. Maisonneuve & Larose, 1970.

———. *Magerramov, T. A. La guirlande de l'Iran: poems de Firdousi, Nizami, Omar Kheyyam, Saadi, Hafiz.* Adapted by Rene Patris. Paris: Flammarion, 1948.

———. *Nizami: Les cinz poemes de Nezami: chef-d'oeuvre persan du XVIIe siecle.* Trans. Francis Richard. Paris: Biblioteque nationale de France, 1995.

Richard, Francis. *Les cinq poemes de Nezami: chef-d'oeuvre persan du XVIIe siecle.* [Paris]: Bibliotheque Nationale de France, 1995.

Stchoukine, Ivan. *Les peintures des manuscrits de la "Khamseh" de Nizami au Topkapi Sarayi M uzesi d'Istanbul.* Paris: P. Geuthner, 1977.

Vesel, Ziva. "Reminiscences de la magie astrale dans les Haft Paykar de Nezami" *Studia Iranica* 24, no. 1 (1995): pp. 7-18.

Wisniewska-Pisowiczowa, Jadwiga. "Quelques remarques sur l'art de Nizami dans son poeme Haft paikar" *Folia Orientalia* 14, (1972-73): pp. 189-206, 31-016 Krakow, Poland.

Other Languages

Chelkowski, Peter. "Nizami's *Iskandarnameh.*" *Colloquio sul poeta persiano Nizami e la leggenda iranica di Alessandro magn.* [Italian] Roma: Accademia nazionale dei Lincei, 1977.

Hasanayn, 'Abd al-Na'im Muhammad. *Nizami al-Ganjawi: sha'ir al-fadilah; 'asrahu wa-bi'athu wa-sha'rhu.* [Arabic] Misr: Maktabat al-Khanji, 1954.

Hasan, Raziyah Akbar. *Nizami Ganjavi. Haidarabad: Maktabah-yi Saba,* 1968.

Fahmi, 'Abd al-Salam 'Abd al-'Aziz. *Manzumat Farhad wa-Shirin lil-Amir 'Ali Shirnawa'i wa-muqaranattuha bi-manzumat "Khisru wa-Shirin" li-Nizami al-Ganjawi.* [Arabic] al-Qahirah: Dar al-Ma'arif, 1981.

Nizami, Abu Muhammad Ilyas ibn Yusuf. *Mahzen-i esrar. M. Nuri Gencosman tarafindan dilimize cevrilmistir.* [Turkish] Ankara: Milli egitim basimevi, 1960.

Nizami Ganjavi, A. *Le Sette principesse: Nezami di Ganje.* A cura di Alessandro Bausani. Bari: Leonardo da Vinci, 1967.

————. *Leyla ile Mecnun (Layla and Majnun).* [Turkish] Trans. Ali Nihat Tarlan Istanbul: Maarif Matbaasi, 1943.

Mallaev, N. M. *Nizomii Ganzhavii merosi va uning ma"rifii-tarbiiavii ahamiiati.* Toshkent: Uqituvchi, 1985.

Okado, Emiko. "Genealogy of Persian Romance Poems" *Area and Culture Studies* 35, (1985): p. 189-202 [in Japanese].

Qubadi, Khana. *Shirin u-Khusra.* Mhmmd-i Mala Krym sagh-i krdwatawa u-farhang-i bo rykkhstwa u-pyshaki-i bo nusiwa. [Kurdish] Arumya, Iran: Nawand-i Blawkrdnawa-y Farhang u-'Adab-i Kurdi, 1989.

Index